iPhone® Application Development

FOR

DUMMIES®

4TH EDITION

by Neal Goldstein

WILEY

John Wiley & Sons, Inc.

iPhone® Application Development For Dummies®, 4th Edition

Published by
John Wiley & Sons, Inc.
111 River Street
Hoboken, NJ 07030-5774

www.wiley.com

Copyright © 2012 by John Wiley & Sons, Inc., Hoboken, New Jersey

Published by John Wiley & Sons, Inc., Hoboken, New Jersey

Published simultaneously in Canada

For general information on our other products and services, please contact our Customer Care Department within the U.S. at 877-762-2974, outside the U.S. at 317-572-3993, or fax 317-572-4002.

For technical support, please visit www.wiley.com/techsupport.

Wiley publishes in a variety of print and electronic formats and by print-on-demand. Some material included with standard print versions of this book may not be included in e-books or in print-on-demand. If this book refers to media such as a CD or DVD that is not included in the version you purchased, you may download this material at http://booksupport.wiley.com. For more information about Wiley products, visit www.wiley.com.

Library of Congress Control Number: 2011946310

ISBN 978-1-118-09134-0 (pbk); ISBN 978-1-118-22333-8 (ebk); ISBN 978-1-118-23680-2 (ebk); ISBN 978-1-118-26173-6 (ebk)

Manufactured in the United States of America

10 9 8 7 6 5 4 3 2 1

WILEY

About the Author

Neal Goldstein is a recognized leader in making state-of-the-art and cutting-edge technologies practical for commercial and enterprise development. He was one of the first technologists to work with commercial developers at firms such as Apple Computer, Lucasfilm, and Microsoft to develop commercial applications using object-based programming technologies. He was a pioneer in moving that approach into the corporate world for developers at Liberty Mutual Insurance, USWest (now Verizon), National Car Rental, EDS, and Continental Airlines, showing them how object-oriented programming could solve enterprise-wide problems. His book (with Jeff Alger) on object-oriented development, *Developing Object-Oriented Software for the Macintosh* (Addison Wesley, 1992), introduced the idea of scenarios and patterns to developers. He was an early advocate of the Microsoft .NET framework, and he successfully introduced it into many enterprises, including Charles Schwab. He was one of the earliest developers of Service Oriented Architecture (SOA), and as Senior Vice President of Advanced Technology and the Chief Architect at Charles Schwab, he built an integrated SOA solution that spanned the enterprise, from desktop PCs to servers to complex network mainframes. (He holds four patents as a result.) As one of IBM's largest customers, he introduced the folks at IBM to SOA at the enterprise level and encouraged them to head in that direction.

Since the release of the iPhone SDK in March 2008, he has been focusing on mobile application. He has eight applications in the App Store. These include a series of Travel Photo Guides (`http://travelphotoguides.com`), developed with his partners at mobilefortytwo, and a Digital Field Guides series (`http://lp.wileypub.com/DestinationDFGiPhoneApp`), developed in partnership with John Wiley & Sons. He also has a free app called Expense Diary that allows you to keep track of things like expenses, mileage, and time by adding them to your calendar.

He has developed mobile strategies for a number of businesses ranging from National Cinemedia to the American Automobile Association (AAA). His strategies focus on Mobile 2.0 — integrating mobile across the enterprise, creating a consistent user experience across devices and applications in an application ecosystem, and developing a user experience architecture that both leverages, and is constrained by, the device. He has spent the last three years working with mobile device users and developers to determine what makes mobile devices so appealing, what users want from an application on a phone or tablet, and what makes an app compelling. These efforts have resulted in the Application Ecosystem model for mobile applications and an underlying Model Application Controller Architecture based on web services that has become a key element in his client work and his books.

Along with those apps and his consulting, he has written several books on iPhone programming, *iPhone Application Development For Dummies* (multiple editions) (Wiley), *Objective-C For Dummies* (Wiley), and he co-authored (with Tony Bove) *iPad Application Development For Dummies* (including multiple editions) (Wiley) and *iPhone Application Development All-in-One For Dummies* (Wiley). He's also the primary author (with Jon Manning and Paris Buttfield-Addison) of *iPhone & iPad Game Development For Dummies*.

Dedication

To my wife, Linda. Without her, I never would have been able to write 11 books in the last three years. She deserves special recognition for her support and patience and for maintaining her (and my) sense of humor. I've got to be the luckiest guy in the world. Thank you.

Author's Acknowledgments

Thanks to my friend Jeff Elias for the San Francisco and Yosemite photographs used in the RoadTrip application.

There is no better Acquisitions Editor than Katie Feltman, who does a superb job of keeping me on track and doing whatever she needs to do to allow me to stay focused on the writing. Thanks also to Project Editor Susan Christophersen and Tech Editor Dave Diamond.

Thanks again to my agent Carole Jelen for her continued work and support in putting and keeping these projects together.

Publisher's Acknowledgments

We're proud of this book; please send us your comments at http://dummies.custhelp.com. For other comments, please contact our Customer Care Department within the U.S. at 877-762-2974, outside the U.S. at 317-572-3993, or fax 317-572-4002.

Some of the people who helped bring this book to market include the following:

Acquisitions, Editorial, and Vertical Websites

Project and Copy Editor: Susan Christophersen

Acquisitions Editor: Katie Feltman

Technical Editor: Dave Diamond

Editorial Manager: Jodi Jensen

Vertical Websites: Rich Graves

Editorial Assistant: Amanda Graham

Sr. Editorial Assistant: Cherie Case

Cover Photo: © iStockphoto.com / Alwyn Cooper

Cartoons: Rich Tennant (www.the5thwave.com)

Composition Services

Project Coordinator: Sheree Montgomery

Layout and Graphics: Joyce Haughey, Sennett V. Johnson

Proofreaders: Susan Hobbs, Lauren Mandelbaum

Indexer: BIM Indexing & Proofreading Services

Publishing and Editorial for Technology Dummies

Richard Swadley, Vice President and Executive Group Publisher

Andy Cummings, Vice President and Publisher

Mary Bednarek, Executive Acquisitions Director

Mary C. Corder, Editorial Director

Publishing for Consumer Dummies

Kathleen Nebenhaus, Vice President and Executive Publisher

Composition Services

Debbie Stailey, Director of Composition Services

Table of Contents

Introduction

*A*lot has changed since I put pen to paper (okay, finger to keyboard) and started writing the first edition of this book back in 2008. The newest iPhone — with its Retina display, 8.0 megapixel front-facing still camera with LED flash, HD video recording, and gyroscope — is truly an amazing piece of hardware, light years ahead of the original iPhone, which was pretty cool to begin with. iOS 5 is a game-changing advancement over iPhone OS 2, becoming both *broader* and *deeper* — broader in the amount of functionality offered and deeper in the control you have over that functionality. And then, of course, it is multitasking.

But one thing hasn't changed. In the first edition of *iPhone Application Development For Dummies,* I said that when Apple opened up the iPhone to developers, I got as excited about developing software as I did when I first discovered the power of the Mac. And you know what? I'm still excited.

As I continue to explore the iPhone as a new platform, I keep finding more possibilities for applications that never existed before. The iPhone is a mobile computer, but it's not simply a mobile desktop. Its hardware and software make it possible to wander the world, or your own neighborhood, and stay connected to whomever and whatever you want. It enables a new class of here-and-now applications that allow you to do what you need to do, based on what's going on around you and where you are.

The first edition of *iPhone Application Development For Dummies* was based on iPhone OS 2.2.1. When iPhone OS 3.0 was released, and then quickly followed by OS 3.1, I knew that I had to do a second edition. The third edition, with iOS 4, added bunch of important new features that I wanted to show readers how to use. Multitasking, to take just one example, allows applications to continue to process events in the background and deliver local notifications to the user.

The new OS also brought with it changes to the nuts and bolts of how to develop iPhone applications that required rewriting several chapters as well as rethinking the examples.

With iOS 5, and more important with Xcode 4.2, application development for the iPhone has changed even more dramatically. Xcode 4.2 has added much more functionality to the integrated development environment (IDE) with which you develop iOS applications, especially when it comes to writing syntactically correct and bug-free, code that manages memory. Storyboards, one of my all-time favorite features, allow you develop applications in a new way, with much less code and a better idea of what the flow of the application (and subsequent user experience) will be. Of course, for all this new functionality, you pay a price — more complexity. But after you get the hang of working with Xcode 4.2, writing applications become much easier than it has ever been. Of course, the rub is getting the hang of Xcode 4.2.

That's where I come in. I carefully take you through Xcode 4.2, pointing out its features and how to use them, and when you are done, you'll have a great understanding of how to take advantage of all those features that will make your life easier.

I have also rethought and rewritten the applications I use to explain the SDK. I've changed from two rather simple ones to a single application that includes features that readers and students have been asking me to add, including more animation and sound, as well as an infrastructure that people can use to develop robust application. The resulting example is an app called RoadTrip, which can send you on your way to developing apps that you can be proud of and that other people will want to have.

This new edition is based on iOS 5 *and* Xcode 4.2. If you want to find out how to develop applications, the tools discussed in this book are the tools you absolutely need to use to do it the right way.

All the new features (and extensions of old features) bundled into iOS 4 are great and exciting and visionary, but all that greatness/excitement/visionary-ness, just as with Xcode 4.2, comes at a cost. Back in 2008, when I first started writing about iPhone application development, it was really difficult to get my head around the whole thing, conceptually speaking; sometimes I found it difficult to figure out exactly how to adapt my vision of how I thought my application should work with the way Apple thought my application should work. iOS 5 brought a whole new set of expectations into the mix.

Back in 2008, lots of resources were out there, quite willing to walk me through the Apple mindset, but to be honest, that was precisely the problem: There were *lots* of resources! As in, *thousands* of pages of documentation and tons sample code to look at. I could get through only a fraction of the documentation before I just couldn't stand the suspense anymore and had to start coding. Naturally enough, I experienced some false starts and blind alleys until I found my way, but it has been (pretty much) smooth sailing ever since.

That's why, when the *For Dummies* folks first asked me to write a book on developing software for the iPhone, I jumped at the chance. Here was an opportunity for me to write the book I wish I'd had when I started developing iPhone software.

But now the iPhone application documentation is even more abundant — and therefore even more overwhelming. As I said, iOS 5 is both broader and deeper, producing many more pages of documentation and sample code. That's why, when the *For Dummies* folks came around again and asked me to write a fourth edition of *iPhone Software Development For Dummies,* I dusted off my typewriter (just kidding) and got to work.

About This Book

iPhone Application Development For Dummies is a beginner's guide to developing iPhone applications. And not only do you *not* need any iPhone development experience to get started, you don't need any Macintosh development experience, either. I've written this book as though you are coming to iPhone application development as a blank slate, ready to be filled with useful information and new ways to do things.

Because of the nature of the iPhone, you can create small, bite-sized applications that can be quite powerful. Also, because you can start small and create real applications that do something important for a user, it's relatively easy to transform yourself from "I know nothing" into a developer who, though not (yet) a superstar, can still crank out quite a respectable application.

But the iPhone can be home to some pretty fancy software as well — so I take you on a journey through building an industrial-strength application and show you the ropes for developing one on your own.

This book distills the hundreds (or even thousands) of pages of Apple documentation, not to mention my own development experience, into only what's necessary to start you developing real applications. But this is no recipe book that leaves it up to you to put it all together; rather, it takes you through the frameworks (the code supplied in the SDK) and iPhone architecture in a way that gives you a solid foundation in how applications really work on the iPhone and also acts as a road map to expand your knowledge as you need to.

I assume that you're in this for the long haul and you want to master the whole application-development ball of wax. I use real-world applications to show the concepts and give you the background on how things actually work on the iPhone — the in-depth knowledge you need to go beyond the simple "Hello World" apps and create those killer iPhone applications. So be prepared! There may be some places where you might want to say, "Get on with it," but — based on my experience (including eight apps in the App Store, nine books (and counting), and untold hours expended on in-person classes and technical talks — I'm giving you what you need to move from following recipes in a cookbook by rote to modifying and even creating your own recipes.

It's a multicourse banquet, intended to make you feel satisfied (and really full) at the end.

Conventions Used in This Book

This book guides you through the process of building iPhone applications. Throughout, you use the provided iPhone framework classes (and create new ones, of course) and code them by using the Objective-C programming language.

Code examples in this book appear in a monospaced font so that they stand out a bit better. That means the code you see will look like this:

```
#import <UIKit/ UIKit.h>
```

Objective-C is based on C, which (I want to remind you) *is* case-sensitive, so please enter the code that appears in this book *exactly* as it appears in the text. I also use the standard Objective-C naming conventions — for example, class names always start with a capital letter, and the names of methods and instance variables always start with a lowercase letter.

Let me throw out that all URLs in this book appear in a monospaced font as well:

```
www.nealgoldstein.com
```

If you're ever uncertain about anything in the code, you can always look at the source code at the Web site associated with this book or on my website at `www.nealgoldstein.com`. From time to time, I provide updates for the code there, and post other things you might find useful. (You can grab the same material from the *For Dummies* website at `www.dummies.com/go/iphoneappdevfd4e`).

Although the code itself will all appear in black, when I ask you to add something, I use color, distinguishing the following elements:

- ✔ *Added* method (by you):
  ```
  - (void)playCarSound {
  ```
- ✔ *Delegate* method implementation:
  ```
  - (BOOL)textFieldShouldReturn:(UITextField *)textField {
  ```
- ✔ Overridden method:
  ```
  -(void) viewDidAppear:(BOOL)animated {
  ```

After the method has been added, the declaration appears in black.

In addition, code you are adding to a method appears in dark green, and code you need to delete will be commented out and in light green:

```
- (BOOL)shouldAutorotateToInterfaceOrientation:
  (UIInterfaceOrientation)interfaceOrientation
{

// return (interfaceOrientation ==
                        UIInterfaceOrientationPortrait);
  return (interfaceOrientation !=
            UIInterfaceOrientationPortraitUpsideDown);
}
```

Foolish Assumptions

To begin programming your iPhone applications, you need an Intel-based Macintosh computer with the latest version of the Mac OS on it. (No, you can't program iPhone applications on the iPhone.) You also need to download the iPhone Software Development Kit (SDK) — which is free — but you do have to become a registered iPhone developer before you can do that. (Don't worry; I show you how to do both.) And, oh yeah, you need an iPhone. You won't start running your application on it right away — you'll use the Simulator that Apple provides with the iPhone SDK during the initial stages of development — but at some point, you'll want to test your application on a real, live iPhone.

This book assumes that you have some programming knowledge and that you have at least a passing acquaintance with object-oriented program-ming, using some variant of the C language (such as C++, C#, or maybe even Objective-C). In case you don't, I point out some resources that can help you get up to speed. The application example in this book is based on the frameworks that come with the SDK; the code is pretty simple (usually) and straightforward. (I don't use this book as a platform to dazzle you with fancy coding techniques.)

I also assume that you're familiar with the iPhone itself and that you've at least explored Apple's included applications to get a good working sense of the iPhone's look and feel. It might also help to browse the App Store to see the kinds of applications available there and maybe even download a few free ones (as if I could stop you).

How This Book Is Organized

iPhone Application Development For Dummies, 4th Edition, has six main parts.

Part I: Getting Started

Part I introduces you to the iPhone world. You find out what makes a great iPhone application and how an iPhone application is structured. In Chapter 2, I give an overview of how Xcode 4.2 works that gets you up to speed on all its features; you can use this chapter as a reference and to return to it as needed. You also create your Xcode project in this chapter, and I take you on a guided tour of what makes up the Xcode project that will become your home away from home.

Part II: Working with the Storyboard and User Interface

In this part of the book, you learn to create the kind of user interface that will capture someone's imagination. I explain Interface Builder editor — much more than your run-of-the-mill program for building graphical user interfaces. You also discover storyboards, which is the icing on the Interface Builder cake — and lets you layout the entire user experience and application flow and save you a lot of coding, to boot.

I also take you on a brief tour of the RoadTrip app, the one you build along with me in this book. I show you not only what the app will do but also how it uses the frameworks and SDK to do that.

Part III: Understanding the Wiring and Plumbing

In Part III, I explain how the main components of an iPhone application go together. I describe how the iPhone applications work from a viewpoint of classes and design patterns, as well as how the app works at runtime. I spend some time on three very important ideas: How to extend the framework classes to do what you want them to, how to manage memory, and how to take advantage of declared properties. I also explain how everything works together at runtime, which should give you a real feel for how an iPhone application works.

Parts I, II, and III give you the fundamental background that you need to develop iPhone applications.

Part IV: Finishing the Basic Application Structure

Now that you have the foundation in place, Part IV starts you on the process of having your application actually do something. You start off by adding animation and sound just to get going, and then I explain how to get down to the real work. You also add navigation to the application — including a screen that shows the features and functions available. You learn how to customize the appearance of the controls provided by the framework to make your application a thing of beauty. You also add the application model, which will connect your interface to the data, and the logic you need to create an application that delivers real value to the user.

Part V: Adding the Application Content

Now that you have the application foundation and the user experience architecture in place, Part V takes you into the world of applications that contain major functionality. I show you how to display the weather using a web page right off the Internet, allow the user to page through local events as if he were reading a book, display a map of where the user is going and where he is right now, and (described in the Bonus Chapter at `www.dummies.com/go/iphoneappdevfd4e`) even find a location that he has always wanted to visit and display it on a map. I don't go slogging through every detail of every detail, but I demonstrate almost all the technology you need to master if you intend to create a compelling application like this on your own.

Part VI: The Part of Tens

Part V consists of some tips to help you avoid having to discover everything the hard way. It talks about approaching application development in an "adult" way right from the beginning (without taking the fun out of it, I assure you). I also revisit the app and explain what else you would need to do to make this app a commercial and critical success.

Icons Used in This Book

This icon indicates a useful pointer that you shouldn't skip.

This icon represents a friendly reminder. It describes a vital point that you should keep in mind while proceeding through a particular section of the chapter.

This icon signifies that the accompanying explanation may be informative (dare I say interesting?), but it isn't essential to understanding iPhone application development. Feel free to skip past these tidbits if you like (though skipping while learning may be tricky).

This icon alerts you to potential problems that you may encounter along the way. Read and obey these blurbs to avoid trouble.

This icon indicates how to use an important part of Xcode functionality. This helps you wade through Xcode's complexity and focus on how to get specific things done.

Where to Go from Here

It's time to explore the iPhone! If you're nervous, take heart: I've received lots of e-mails (and an occasional card or letter) from readers ranging in age from 12 to 67 who tell me how they're doing fine (and yes, I do respond to them all).

Also, be sure to visit the companion website for this book at www.dummies. com/go/iphoneappdevfd4e for source code and other information.

Go have some fun!

Part I
Getting Started

The 5th Wave — By Rich Tennant

"What I'm doing should clear your sinuses, take away your headache, and charge your iPhone."

So you've decided you want to develop some software for the iPhone. You have a good idea for a utility — one that lets you know where and when the next piece of space junk will crash into earth, or one that acts as a data-driven application (say, one that knows where to find the best pizza in Silicon Valley). Now what?

This part of the book lays out what you need to know to get started on the development journey. First, what makes a great iPhone application? Knowing that, you can evaluate your idea, see how it ranks, and maybe figure out what you have to do to transform it into something that knocks your users' socks off.

This part shows you how to use the iPhone Software Development Kit (SDK), which includes Xcode — your home away from home when you are developing your app. You also find out how to create an Xcode project, within which you code and then build and run your app.

Chapter 1

Creating Compelling Mobile Applications

In This Chapter

▷ Knowing what makes mobile devices so appealing

▷ Understanding the strengths and weaknesses of mobile devices

▷ Assessing the right application for the right device — the "Application Ecosystem"

*T*he last time I looked, it seemed as though every developer with an iPhone and a Macintosh had developed an application and put it in the store.

Okay, I exaggerate a bit, but not by much.

But creating a successful mobile app today is a lot different from how it was when Apple first opened the iPhone to third-party developers in March 2008. And being late to this party (as opposed to being an underdressed Californian racing to catch the last flight out of New York on a bitterly cold night) may actually be a good thing. A fairly clear picture is emerging of where things are heading based on what users want and need, and having that picture is a great position to be in when you're developing applications.

In this chapter, I explain what you need to understand about iPhone applications (and mobile applications in general) and what you need to think about before you go out and develop a new app.

Welcome to Mobile 2.0

As is its cousin the World Wide Web, mobile applications are evolving at breakneck speeds. Users are demanding, and developers are creating new kinds of applications all the time. These Mobile 2.0 applications are optimized for the mobile experience and integrated with web and desktop applications to create a seamless and consistent user experience across devices.

This user experience applies not only to externally facing applications developed for the general public or customers (or even other businesses, such as vendors) but also internally facing applications developed for use inside an organization.

That's all fine and good, but what developing apps is about is not what you *can* do, it's about what you *actually* do to create compelling Mobile 2.0 applications. And although this is not a book on application design, it would be a shame to have you go off and create mediocre apps (which most apps are). In fact, Flurry (a mobile analytics developer) reports that after six months, 95 percent of all users are no longer using apps they downloaded.

So before I get started on how to develop iPhone apps, I want to explain what compelling Mobile 2.0 apps are about — but first, I want to be sure that you understand what makes mobile devices so compelling to start with.

What Makes Mobile Devices So Compelling?

Although I had been somewhat involved with mobile for a number of years, it became my number one passion when the iPhone SDK was released in June of 2007.

It became obvious at that point that the iPhone was a real game changer, right up there with the release of the Macintosh. I realized that the iPhone was not simply a smaller personal computer. It was, in fact, an entirely new way of using technology, and one that could create an entirely new user experience. Why?

First, because it is always on, it gives you *immediate* access to everything that is important to you — your personal contacts, calendar, music and videos, and even your games. And if what you want isn't on the iPhone, you can immediately access it through the Internet using its always-there connection. The iPhone also gives you immediate access to everyone who is important to you — whether through a phone call or via text messaging or (recently) notifications and Voice over IP (VoIP).

But to be honest, that is already possible on your personal computer.

What differentiates the iPhone from your personal computer is that it comes with you, you don't have to go to it, and you are always connected through the cell network rather than an Ethernet cable or Wi-Fi. What's more, not only does it come with you, *it knows where it is*, letting you know where you are. It even knows its orientation and heading and movement as you move it from place to place.

And not only does it come with you, but certain applications can run in background and update you with information you might be interested in as you move from place to place.

Okay, to continue being honest, all these abilities are also possible on your laptop using a cell modem.

True enough, but what *really* makes the iPhone different from a small portable personal computer is the way you interact with it. The Multi-Touch user experience makes the user more naturally connected to the device. You can cup it in your hand and interact with the iPhone directly, with no mouse or keyboard acting as an intermediary; also, you use gestures rather than controls whenever possible. These features create a degree of intimacy with your device, making the technology disappear as the device becomes a personal extension of the user. An app may have an infrastructure the size of Texas behind it, but to the user, it always appears to be "just me and my app."

Of course, the mobile phone is more than just a small, mobile personal computer for another reason. Although its features make it possible to be something beyond a personal computer, and do things that either can't be done, or done easily on a personal computer, this is a double-edged sword. There are some things that a laptop does far better than an iPhone, and it's critical to understand that it is not a replacement for a laptop computer.

And along comes the iPad, and things change again, albeit not so dramatically.

Although this is a book that is focused on iPhone development, in this chapter I also talk about the iPad a bit because it's helpful to understand what works best on each of the devices before you go and develop an app for one or the other, or both.

Zero degrees of separation

The iPhone and iPad create what I call zero degrees of separation between the user and his or her personal ecosystem, which is made up of

- The user and her personal stuff
- Other people
- Events, information, data, institutions, tools, and entertainment
- The device

The iPhone and iPad provide the user with a sense of freedom within this ecosystem. The user is not tethered to her desktop but instead has everything she needs with her, or if not, can get it, and can instantaneously communicate to anyone anywhere.

Enhancing mobility

In addition to enabling the user to achieve zero degrees of separation with his personal ecosystem, the iPhone and iPad also offer applications and features that enhance the mobility of the user. For example, the iOS and hardware allow an application to determine the device's current location, or even to be notified when that location changes.

There are already plenty of iPhone and iPad applications that use location information to tell you where the nearest coffeehouse is, or where your friends are. They can even tell you where the nearest subway is and give you directions to where you are going. They also can take that information and put it on a map along with other places you may be interested in.

Increasing the quality of life

At the end of the day, mobile devices and applications further enable a personal ecosystem, as illustrated in Figure 1-1. More important, people use mobile devices to improve the quality of their everyday (nontechnical) life.

Whereas engineers think in terms of applications, what makes a mobile device truly compelling is its ability to enhance the experience of doing what flesh-and-blood people do in the real world.

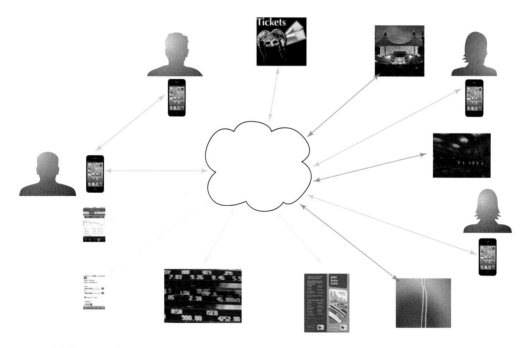

Figure 1-1: A personal ecosystem.

The Device Itself Engages the User

In this section, I explore in more detail some aspects of mobile devices that I mention in the previous section but that developers often tend to ignore: How the mobile device itself engages the user.

Although people normally speak about user experience in using applications, the device itself also creates unique user experience.

The sense of freedom that comes with mobility

The first thing that comes to mind when you think of an iPhone or iPad is mobility — and with mobility comes a sense of freedom, because you are no longer tethered to your desktop or even your laptop. This mobility really has several distinct aspects:

- The iPhone is small and unobtrusive enough to have it with you wherever you go, and you can carry all your personal stuff with you. You can carry your contacts and calendars, your music and videos, and even your games. Add in the camera (the iPhone is the most popular camera on Flickr), and you have everything you need.

  Although the iPad may not be as mobile if you don't have 3G, and you may not be able to fit it in your pocket, it's still small enough to feel like it's something you can take with you, and you can sit on your couch, or lie in bed, and feel connected to everything.

- The device is easily connected to the Internet. This fact leads to an interesting corollary: You don't need to have everything stored on the device. All you really need to know how to do is how to jump on the Internet and grab what you need from there (or have an application that does it for you). You can perform tasks and access information from anywhere.

- The device knows where it is, its orientation, and can even show you on a map.

- Between the phone, Voice over IP, e-mail, and SMS, you can instantaneously communicate with anyone anywhere.

The technology disappears

The Multi-Touch user experience makes the user feel more naturally connected to the device — no mouse or keyboard acts as an intermediary — and what's more, Apple promotes the use of gestures rather than controls as much as possible. If you want to move a map annotation, let the user drag it to where she wants it to be, and provide feedback along the way — don't show arrow or direction controls or force the user to type in a new address (although sometimes that may be the way to go; doing what is best for the user experience is the fundamental principle here). Immediate feedback keeps people engaged, and well-written applications keep on-screen objects visible while the user manipulates them. Standard interface components also give cues to the users.

The iPhone allows an immediacy and intimacy as it blends mobility and the power of the desktop to create a new kind of freedom. I like to use the term *user experience* because it implies more than a pretty user interface and nice graphics. A *compelling* user experience enables users to do what they need to do with a minimum of fuss and bother. But more than that, thinking about creating a compelling user experience forces you, the developer, to think past a clean interface and even beyond basic convenience (such as not having to scroll through menus to do something simple).

Here are several more aspects of a compelling application:

- **Direct manipulation:** This feature makes people feel more in control. On the desktop, having control meant using a keyboard and mouse; on the iPhone and iPad, the Multi-Touch interface serves the same purpose, but more directly. People use their fingers rather than a mouse to select and manipulate objects on screen. In fact, using fingers gives a user a more immediate sense of control; as mentioned previously, there's no intermediary (such as a mouse) between the user and the object onscreen.

    The moves that do the work, called *gestures,* give the user a heightened sense of control and intimacy with the device. There is a set of standard gestures — taps, pinch-close and pinch-open, swipe, pan or drag, rotate, and touch and hold — that are used in the applications supplied with the iPhone.

- **Consistency among applications within the device:** Another aspect that makes the iPhone device so appealing is the consistency of the use of gestures as well as standard user interface components across applications.

- **Immediate feedback:** This keeps the users engaged. Great applications respond to every user action with some visible feedback — such as highlighting list items briefly when users tap them. Users have come to expect onscreen objects to be visible while they manipulate them,

    In addition, the iPhone and iPad use animation to provide feedback. (I especially like the flipping transitions in the Weather application when I touch the Info button.)

The aesthetics

Design, controls, and quality are all something the IPhone and iPad are known for. One of the more striking of these, although most users are used to it now, is the quality of the screen. The media playback is actually quite extraordinary. It is tempting to think of the iPad here, but the iPhone with its retina display delivers that playback experience as well, albeit in a smaller format.

Never underestimate the importance of style and panache of these devices and their applications. And never forget the "cool" factor.

One thing I want to make clear is that I don't say all this because I'm an Apple fan boy. As a developer of applications, you need to recognize how these characteristics of the Apple devices appeal to ordinary (not technical) people and make them special and appealing in their eyes.

It's extensible

You can also add new hardware accessories to the iPhone and iPad and communicate with them either by a physical connection or Bluetooth. For example, there's a dongle that contains a transmitter that you can use to broadcast audio from an iPhone to an FM radio. You can use a Bluetooth keyboard with an iPad. You can even turn your iPhone into a projector.

Exploiting the Device Features to Create a Great Application

I've been talking a lot about mobility and what it means for developing iPhone apps, but a number of other hardware and software features built in to the device also enable a rich and compelling experience for the user. Clearly, one of the keys to creating a great application involves taking advantage of precisely these features. In the following sections, I offer a brief survey of the various device features you may want to use. I hope this survey begins to pique your imagination.

Personal stuff

One of the things people like about their phones is the ability to have all their personal "stuff" all in one place, and always with them. As a developer, you can take advantage of desire in your applications.

Address Book, Contacts, and Calendar

Your application can access the user's contacts on the phone and display that information in any way you would like, or use those contacts as information in your application. As a user of a travel application, for example, you could enter the name and address of your hotel, and the application would file it in your Contacts database. That way, you have ready access to the hotel address — not only from the application, but also from your phone and other applications. Then when you arrive at your destination, the application can retrieve the address from Contacts and display directions for you. What's more, you can also present the standard system interface for picking and creating contacts in the Address Book.

If you can leverage the information stored in the Address Book and Contacts databases, it stands to reason that you can do the same thing with the

Calendar application. You can remind a user when she needs to get her car ready for her trip, for example, or create Calendar events based on what's happening this week at places along the way. These events show up in the Calendar application and in other applications that support that framework.

Camera and Photo Library

Your application can also access the pictures stored on the user's phone — and by "access," I mean not only display them but also use or even modify them. The Photos application, for example, lets you add a photo to a contact, and several applications enable you to edit your photos on the iPhone itself. You can also incorporate the standard system interface to actually use the camera in your application as well.

Even more advanced use of the camera is supported. One of the most interesting is *augmented reality,* where you're looking through the iPhone camera at the real world that has computer-generated graphics superimposed. (Making use of augmented reality is much easier — and cooler — than it may sound.)

Media and games

The iPhone OS makes it easy to play and include audio and video in your application. You now can even record and edit HD videos. The multichannel audio and mixing capabilities enable you to play sound effects, and you can also create your own music player that has access to all the audio contents of the user's iPod Library.

In playing back movies, the iPhone and iPad support many standard movie file formats. You can configure the aspect ratio and specify whether or not controls are displayed. This means that your application can not only use the iPhone and iPad as media players but also use and control prerendered content. Keep in mind that if iMovie can do it, you probably can add those features to your app, too.

The graphics capabilities of the hardware and the animation support in iOS make both the iPad and iPhone a great game platform. And while the iPhone's portability makes it great for casual games, the iPad gives game consoles a run for their money.

Accessing the Internet

If you don't have some information that you need with you, you can always get it.

The ability to access websites and servers on the Internet allows you to create applications that can provide real-time information to the user. It can tell me, for example, that the next tour at the Whitney is at 3 p.m. This kind of access also allows you, as the developer, to go beyond the limited memory and processing power of the device and access large amounts of data stored on servers, or even offload the processing. I don't need all the information for every city in the world stored on my iPhone or have to strain the poor CPU to compute the best way to get someplace on the Bart in San Francisco. I can send the request to a server and have it do all that work.

What I'm talking about here is *client-server computing* — a well-established software architecture in which the client provides a way to make requests to a server on a network that's just waiting for the opportunity to do something. A web browser is an example of a client accessing information from other websites that act as servers.

Maps and location and orientation and movement

iOS and iPhone and iPad hardware allow a developer to determine the device's current location, or even to be notified when that location changes. As people move about from place to place, it may make sense for your application to tailor itself to where the user is moment by moment.

Plenty of applications already use location information to tell users where the nearest coffeehouse is, or even where their friends are. When you know the user's location, you can put it on a map, along with other places that user may be interested in.

An application that provides these kinds of services can also run in the background, and what's more, because using the GPS chip can be a significant drain on the battery, as a developer you can use services that consume less battery power — including a location-monitoring service that tracks significant changes by using only cell tower information and the ability to define arbitrary regions and detect boundary crossings into or out of those regions.

Tracking orientation and motion

The iPhone and iPad contain three *accelerometers* — devices that detect changes in movement. Each device measures change along one of the primary axes in three-dimensional space. An app can, for example, know when the user has turned the device from vertical to horizontal, and it can change the view from Portrait to Landscape if doing so makes for a better user experience.

Through an accelerometer, the device can also determine other types of motion such as a sudden start or stop in movement (think of a car accident or a fall) or the user shaking the device back and forth. The accelerometer makes some way-cool features easy for a developer to implement — for example, the Etch-A-Sketch metaphor of shaking the iPad or iPhone to undo an operation. You can even control a game by moving the iPhone or iPad like a controller; in the game Chopper2, for example, you can even control the actions of a helicopter on your iPad by using your iPhone.

it more easily. With fewer items in a small display, users can find what they want more quickly. A small screen forces you to ruthlessly eliminate clutter and keep your text concise and maintaining a laser-like focus.

Designing for fingers

Although the Multi-Touch interface is an iPhone asset, it has some limitations as well. First, fingers aren't as precise as a mouse pointer, which makes some operations even more difficult on an iPhone or iPod touch than on an iPad (text selection, for example). User interface elements need to be large enough (Apple recommends that anything a user has to select or manipulate with a finger be a minimum of 44 x 44 pixels in size), and spaced far enough apart so that users' fingers can find their way around the interface comfortably.

You also can do only so much by using fingers. You definitely have many fewer possibilities when using fingers than the combination of multi-button mouse and keyboard.

Because making a mistake when using just fingers is likelier, you also need to ensure that you implement a robust — yet unobtrusive — undo mechanism. You don't want to have your users confirm every action (thereby making the application tedious), but on the other hand, you don't want your application to let anybody mistakenly delete a page without asking, "Are you *sure* this is what you *really* want to do?" Lost work is worse than tedium.

Another issue with fingers is that the keyboard is not that finger friendly. I admit that using the iPhone keyboard is not up there on the list of things I really like about my iPhone. Remember: Although the iPhone is at the top of the class, no one likes to type on *any* smartphone. So rather than require the user to type some information, Apple suggests that you have a user select an item from a list. But on the other hand, the items in the list must be large enough to be easily selectable, which gets back to the first problem (the small screen).

But again, this limitation can inspire (okay, maybe force) you to create a better application. To create a complete list of choices, for example, the application developer is forced to completely understand the context of (and be creative about) what the user is trying to accomplish. Having that depth of understanding then makes focusing the application on the essential possible, eliminating what is unnecessary or distracting. It also serves to focus the user on the task at hand.

Limited computer power, memory, and battery life

As an application designer for the iPhone, you have several balancing acts to keep in mind:

- ✔ Although significant by the original Macintosh's standards, the computer power and amount of memory on the iPhone are limited.

- ✔ Although access to the Internet can mitigate the power and memory limitations by storing data and (sometimes) offloading processing to a server, those operations eat up the battery faster.

- ✔ Although the power-management system in the iPhone OS conserves power by shutting down any hardware features that aren't currently being used, a developer must manage the trade-off between all those busy features and shorter battery life. Any application that takes advantage of Internet access by using Wi-Fi or the 3G network, core location, and the accelerometer will eat up the battery.

The iPhone is particularly unforgiving when it comes to memory usage. If you run out of memory, in order to prevent corruption of other apps and memory, the system will simply *shut down* your app (unfortunately, not to the tune of "Shut Down" by the Beach Boys).

This just goes to show that not *all* limitations can be exploited as "assets."

Where it shines

Where the iPhone truly shines is its small size and the fact that you can always take it with you. It really enhances the quality of users' everyday life by making it easy for them to access the information they need and communicate with others.

iPad strengths and weaknesses

When the iPad was first released, some critics dismissed it as just a big iPhone (even though it doesn't, as my editor pointed out to me, have a phone). After some time in the field, as user and developer response has shown, the iPad is really a different kind of device than the iPhone, with its very own set of features that you can leverage for use in your own application, as well as with its limitations that you need to take into account:

- ✔ It's hard on users with "fat fingers" (me again).

- ✔ It has limited computer power, memory, and battery life.

- ✔ It has no phone.

- ✔ It's not pocket sized.

Designing for fingers

Although its limitations are not as pronounced as the iPhone/iPod touch with their smaller displays, (for example, its bigger screen size allows more margin for error, especially when using the keyboard) the Multi-Touch interface on the iPad does have similar limitations.

Limited computer power, memory, and battery life

Although the iPad's battery life is certainly better than that of the iPhone, it has its issues as well — and this is especially true if you have a 3G-enabled iPad.

It has no phone

I once read that the phone was the least used application on the iPhone. Although that may or may not be true, the lack of a phone is an iPad limitation, although it is somewhat mitigated by the Voice over IP applications available.

It's not pocket sized

The iPad does offer much of the same intimacy as the iPhone (many people like to use it lying on the coach or even in bed), it is bigger, and most people won't find it as convenient to carry it around with them all of the time. Also, users probably are not going to pull it out of their pockets to use it as a camera on a trip (although surprisingly some people do).

Where it shines

Although the iPad can display more information or content because of its screen size, that is only the beginning. Because of its mobility, and the use of gestures and direct manipulation rather than the mouse and keyboard as an intermediary, the iPad is about *immersion*. And although I am not going to talk much about that here, this being an iPhone book, I will be devoting an entire book to the iPad (*iPad Application Development For Dummies,* Third Edition).

Creating Your Own Applications

What I have been talking about so far has generally been describing the characteristics and features of the device, what this book is about, after all, is building your own apps.

But before I get to *building* an app, you really need to understand what *kinds* of apps to build. I want to emphasis that this book is about developing applications, not games or media — both topics for another book. Also, I am talking about *new kinds* of applications, not just variations on those that already come on the iPhone.

Although it goes without saying, any iPhone or iPad application needs an intuitive, well-designed user interface. The purpose and function of what you are doing with the app needs to be obvious and consistent with the device's look and feel. The user interface should be a natural extension of the user's world, which means making the experience of using the device seamless and transparent, and having the application's objects and actions modeled on objects and actions in the real world.

The more true to life your application looks and behaves, the easier it is for people to understand how it works and the more they enjoy using it.

Of course, this idea applies to any user facing application on any platform, but the intimacy of the device enables the developer to take this idea much further on the iPhone and iPad.

When the iPad first came out, as I said, many of its detractors called it a bigger iPhone. Nothing could be further from the truth. Although they do share much of the same functionality, iPhone and iPad applications provide value in different ways. The following sections tell you how.

iPhone applications

Applications on the iPhone, with its small screen size and extreme portability, work best when they are focused on improving the quality of a user's day-to-day experiences. iPhone applications need to be embedded in whatever the user is doing so that the technology in effect disappears from the user's immediate awareness.

Because the user is doing something else at the time, the point is not to be doing something *on the iPhone*, it is to be doing something *using the iPhone* that adds to what they are currently doing. Its functionality, to a large extent, needs to be driven by the context.

Allowing for this type of use requires a laser-like focus in the application, and the developer must ensure that every piece of an iPhone application is important to the task and also to what point the user is at concerning that task. Every action has to be 100 percent relevant, and seconds count. The app should have no learning curve and zero start-up time.

Otherwise, the competition wins: other apps, the phone, texting, or even paper.

In that same light, some tasks just aren't easy to do well on the iPhone. I wouldn't want to write a book on the iPhone (and in fact, I want to have to type on it as little as possible), or read one on it, for that matter. I also would not want to do lots of research and planning, because the amount of information you can see at one time, and the possibilities for manipulating that information, are limited by the screen size.

For those kinds of tasks, you want to turn to the iPad.

iPad applications

If the iPhone is about embedding the device in the context, the iPad is about immersing yourself in the content.

If you're familiar with iPhone apps and Mac OS X applications, think somewhere in between. With the iPad touch-sensitive display, you no longer have to create different screens of menus (as you might for an iPhone app) or deploy drop-down menus and toolbars (as you might for an Mac OS X app) to offer many functions. The iPad is a device with much of the desktop functionality but that is more intimate than the desktop, and more likely to immerse you in the content.

In Landscape mode, the iPad offers a Split view to display more than one view onscreen at a time — the kind you see in the Mail and iPod applications. In Portrait mode, the Mail application, for example, displays a Main view, and rather than display two views side by side, you can display a popover view to give users access to information or choices without requiring them to leave the context of the Main view.

The large iPad screen also gives you a lot more room for multifinger gestures, including gestures made by more than one person. With a display the size of a netbook, you have much more screen real estate to allow dragging and two-finger gestures with graphics and images, and depending on what you're doing, a tap or gesture on a particular part of the screen can have a particular function.

You can put up pages that look like web pages or book pages if you want, and you can easily mix content for an immersive experience. Even "utility" apps can be rethought to provide a better experience. On the iPhone, the Contacts app is a list, but on the iPad, Contacts is an address book that looks almost real.

An iPad app can also make accessing information a more immersive experience compared with an iPhone app by embedding fully functional videos (not just videos that appear in a separate window) and slideshows with music and so on. You can play sound effects or take advantage of the multichannel audio and mixing capabilities available to you. People can enjoy this content while away from their desks — meaning, on living room couches, in coffee shops, on the train, or even in bed, and more easily show it to others than they can with an iPhone.

To create this kind of immersive experience, an iPad application's functionality needs to be driven by the content.

Immersive applications are about exploration, discovery, activity — and they must be continually interesting, which means being regularly updated with fresh content. And, depending on the application, a feeling of accomplishment as the user progresses through the app. As with the iPhone, you have to keep in mind that other ways of performing an activity are competing with your app: other apps, the phone, texting, paper, the PC/laptop, and more.

An Application Ecosystem

In one corner, you have a light, small, mobile device that you can take with you — one that almost disappears as it become part of a user's daily life. In the other corner, you have a device that shines at presentation and can immerse the user in content — a device you can think of as somewhere in-between an iPhone and a Mac.

But often, it's not one or the other. I would, for example want to use an iPad to research and plan a road trip, but while I'm traveling, I'd like to be able to access all that information on my iPhone, which is a lot easier to take along as I explore. What I don't want is one app for planning and a different app for traveling. Instead I want a seamless integration between the two, and although I may prefer to do one task on one device versus the other, I also want to be able to do either on both. It is a function of user interface design and primary versus secondary functionality based on what the device does best.

What's more, you should keep the laptop/desktop in the picture as well (yes, personal computers do still have a place in this brave new world). Although the PC is not a subject I cover in this book, don't ignore the laptop or even the desktop. If a user has to engage in a lot of manipulation or data entry, the PC is far better to work with than the iPad.

All these devices combine to serve the user in what I call an *Application Ecosystem.* The idea of an Application Ecosystem, which I depict in Figure 1-2, is to distribute functionality to the device that does it best. To do that, it helps to understand what application functionality is best suited for which device.

For example, imagine an application aimed at photographers. The app could show you the best sites to photograph, the best time of day to photograph them, and the best setting to use on your camera. The app could even map the locations to take them from. On an iPad, the user could take advantage of the large display to go through the photographs and decide which ones she wanted to take. She could select those photographs to create a shot list that she could order by time of day and location. Then when she was done, she could access that shot list from her iPhone. She could carry just the iPhone with her, and as she took the photographs, she could update the ones she had taken with the actual settings and time of day, and then be able to access that information from her iPad.

Or imagine a road trip. A user would plan it on his iPad and access directions, maps, hotel reservations, and places to eat from his phone. He could even take notes on his phone about his experience, and add his own photographs from his phone to document his trip. He could then use his iPad to create his own trip album.

The possibilities are endless.

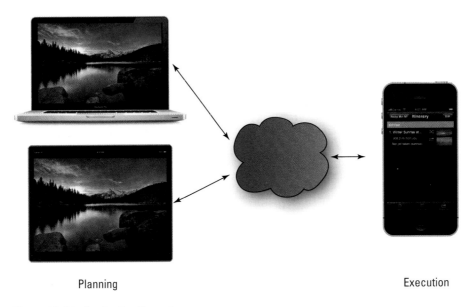

Planning   Execution

Figure 1-2: The Application Ecosystem.

If you want to provide applications for the right device and the right function, and you want seamlessness and consistency across all platforms, does that mean one universal app, or two or three apps with lots of duplicate functionality? Fortunately, you won't need lots of apps — that's where the cloud comes in.

Enter the Cloud

Apple, of course, created a great deal of excitement when it announced iCloud. However, iCloud is more than just an integral part of the built-in applications; it can also be used by developers to implement at least part of the Application Ecosystem I discuss in the previous section.

iCloud lets you create applications that share data between two devices. For example you could create a RoadTrip application that allowed the user to plan a trip on an iPad, and then access and even update that data on an iPhone.

But although iCloud does let you share *data* between the same application running on different devices (which in itself is great), it does not allow you to share business logic, nor, at this point, allow you to access that data from a web application, an Android, or a Windows Mobile device. What's more, it does not allow multiple users to access shared data (something you would want in a social networking or calendar application, for example).

At this point, the easiest and best way to implement an Application Ecosystem is by using web services and an architecture that supports them. These services can be hosted on a third-party cloud-hosting solution, or they can be hosted on enterprise-based servers with an infrastructure bus that can access other services or data (as some of my clients are doing).

That, of course, needs to be in another book, and as it happens, I'm writing that one as this one goes to press.

Developing an App the Right Way Using the Example App in this Book

Although iCloud, web services, and the Application Ecosystem is where certain kinds of apps are going, it is certainly not the place for most developers of iPhone applications to start. Also, I don't want to imply that an app necessarily needs to be cloud based. There are lots of opportunities for apps that live only on the device. But if you are thinking about an app that can take advantage of an Application Ecosystem, I want to pique your curiosity and give you a frame of reference to start thinking in those terms.

So this book is about apps that live on the device, and that is the place to start. And after you've mastered that, you can think about the cloud.

As I mention in the introduction of this book, the point of this book is not to learn how to program in Objective-C using the iOS frameworks; instead, the point is to learn how to build applications, and that is what you'll be doing — learning the *right way* to develop applications for the iPhone.

The best way I could think of to show you how to build an app was to build one, and I take you through doing that throughout this book. The app you build is called RoadTrip, and it's based on an application I started to develop many years ago, and still think is a good idea. Think of it as a travel guide that you can keep in your back pocket. Although the original version that I envisioned had more features, this one is not too shabby. It allows you to check the weather, see the events happening at your destination, see the destination, sights, and your current location on a map, as well as display any location by entering the address or the name of a point of interest. You can find this information in the Bonus Chapter at www.dummies.com/go/iphone appdevfd4e. You can also choose between destinations.

As simple as it is, RoadTrip shows you how to do many of the tasks that are common to iPhone apps. You add animation and sound, display views and navigate through them, use controls such as buttons, as well as use the navigation controllers like the kind you find in the Music app and many "industrial strength" applications on the phone.

As you build the RoadTrip app, you even learn to display a web page, and navigate its links (and return). You also download and display data from the Internet.

Let's get started!

Chapter 2

Getting to Know the SDK

Up until now, I never really considered Xcode a true partner in the development process. Using it was like having to include your little brother when you went out to play with your friends because your parents made you.

With Xcode 4.2, that has changed. Xcode, if you work with it, can make your development much easier with fewer errors. In this chapter I take you on a guided tour of the features you'll find in Xcode — giving you the view for 30,000 feet. If you have never used Xcode before, some of its features may not make all that much sense.— but not to worry, I'll be going through it all in detail as you use it. The point of this chapter is to provide a frame of reference as you move forward, and a complete reference for you to look back on.

Developing Using the SDK

The iOS Software Development Kit (SDK) provides support for developing iOS applications and includes the complete set of Xcode tools, compilers, and frameworks for creating applications for iOS and Mac OS X. These tools include the Xcode IDE and the Instruments analysis tool, among many others.

You can download Xcode from the (Mac) App Store, or better yet, become a registered developer. (Go to `developer.applc.com/devcenter/ios`, where you will find a link to become a registered developer as well as documentation sample code and a lot of other useful information). But if you want to actually run your application on your phone and submit it to the store, you need to join the iOS Developer Program, which you can do after you become a registered developer.

These links do change from time to time, so if a link I provide in this book doesn't work, you can always start at `developer.apple.com/` and navigate to the iOS Dev Center from there.

Xcode 4 is the latest iteration of Apple's integrated development environment (IDE), a complete toolset for building Mac OS X and iOS applications. With Xcode 4, you can develop applications that run on iPhone, iPad, or iPod touch running iOS. You can also test your applications using the included iOS Simulator, which supports iOS 5.

The Xcode IDE includes a powerful Source editor, a sophisticated graphical User Interface editor , and many other features, including source code repository management. As you code, Xcode can identify mistakes in syntax and even suggest fixes.

Xcode includes everything you need to create your app — which is both the good news and the bad news. The good news is that it has everything you need. The bad news is that because it has everything you need, it can be pretty complex. But again, not to worry: I guide you through everything involved in creating an app step by step.

To start with, I give you an overview of Xcode and how you'll use it to develop your app. As you move from step to step, I provide more detail on how to use Xcode to specifically do what you need to in a given step.

Using XCode to Develop an App

To develop an iPhone, iPod touch, or iPad app, you have to work within the context of an *Xcode project*. Although I don't explain any development methodologies in this book, I can tell you that Xcode supports the following activities that are parts of developing your application:

- Creating an Xcode project
- Developing the application (designing the user interface using a storyboard; coding; running and debugging the code)
- Tuning application performance
- Distributing the application

The following sections tell you more about each of these tasks.

Creating an Xcode project

To develop an iOS application, you start by creating an Xcode project. A project contains all the elements needed to create an application, including the source files, a graphical representation of the user interface, and build settings needed to build your application. You work on your project in the *Workspace window*, which allows you to create all of these elements as well as build, run, debug, and submit your application to the App store.

Developing the application

You have a lot to do to develop an application. You need to design the user experience and then implement it as a user interface. You need to write code to implement the features of the app. You also need to test and debug the app.

Designing the user interface using a storyboard

Interface Builder is the editor you use to assemble your application's user interface using preconfigured objects found in the Library. The objects include windows, controls (such as switches, text fields, and buttons), and views you'll use, such as Image, Web, and Table views. The Interface Builder editor allows you to add objects, configure their properties, and create connections between user interface objects, and between user interface object and your code.

When you use a storyboard (which you do in this book), most if not all of your screens are displayed in the storyboard, and Interface Builder saves your storyboard in a storyboard file. When you don't use a storyboard, each screen is saved separately as a nib file. Either way, these files contain all the information iOS needs to reconstitute the user interface objects in your application at runtime.

Interface Builder saves you time and effort when it comes to creating your application's user interface. You don't have to code each object (thereby saving you a lot of work), and what's more, because Interface Builder is a visual editor, you get to see exactly what your application's user interface will look like at runtime.

Coding

To code, you use the Source Code editor, which supports features such as code completion, syntax-aware indentation, and code folding (to hide code blocks temporarily). You can get context-based help to assist you, and if you need information about a particular symbol, you can get a summary of a symbol's documentation directly in the editor, or more extensive documentation in the Organizer.

Xcode's Live Issues and Fix-it work together to point out mistakes as you enter your code and offers to fix those mistakes for you.

Running and debugging

When you run your application to debug or test it, you can run it in the iOS Simulator on your Mac and then on an iOS-based device (if you are in the developer program). Using the simulator, you can make sure your application behaves the way you want. You can also get debugging information, as you run, in the Debugger area. And you can run your app on a device connected to your Mac (and even use the debugger) to observe the actual user experience and how the app will perform.

Tuning application performance

The Instruments application enables you to analyze the performance of your application as it runs in the simulator or on a device. The Instruments application gathers data from your running application and presents that data in a graphical timeline.

Among other measurements, you can gather data about your application's memory usage, disk activity, network activity, and graphics performance. This data enables you to analyze your application's performance and identify performance and resource usage problems.

In-depth coverage of Instruments is beyond the scope of this book.

Distributing the application

Xcode provides two kinds of distribution. The first is to application testers before release; the second is to the App Store. You create an archive of your application that contains debugging information, making it easier to track down bugs reported by users of your application. You can even run the some of the same software-validation procedures on your applications that iTunes Connect performs when you submit them for review, and passing these tests makes your application's approval process as fast as possible.

The Workspace Window

Command central for Xcode is the Workspace window, and here's where you'll do all the things you need to do to develop your app.

In this section, I present only an overview — more or less the map of what's in the Workspace window and what each bar and button is and does. I developed this as quick reference to the Workspace window to help you see all its elements, including the various bars and buttons and what they do.

Figure 2-1 shows a "map" of the window. Although at first glance it may seem overwhelming, don't worry: I explain each part. You can use Figure 2-1 as a reference throughout the book. As I take you through using Xcode to develop your app, I go into more detail as needed. So for now, take a quick read through the upcoming sections just to familiarize yourself with the lay of the land and then return to Figure 2-1 as needed for quick reference.

Although I have color coded the Workspace window components in this chapter here for easy reference, figures in the remainder of the book show the components as they appear on your screen.

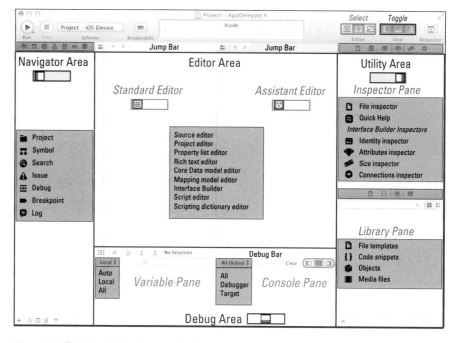

Figure 2-1: The Xcode Workspace window.

The Workspace window consists of:

- ✔ The toolbar
- ✔ An optional tab bar
- ✔ Areas

The following sections describe each these areas — which make up the heart of Xcode.

Workspace areas

The Workspace is divided into four *areas.* These areas are outlined in blue, with blue text, in Figure 2-1, shown previously.

- ✔ Editor area (always shown)
- ✔ Navigator area
- ✔ Utility area
- ✔ Debug area

Workspace area configuration

You can configure the Workspace area in a number of ways. You can hide and show the *areas*. The Editor area is always present and can also be configured. The Debug and Utility areas are already configured with panes. In the Debug area, you can select the pane configuration.

Editor area (always present)

The Editor area is always present. If you want, you can show or hide various "editors" contained within the Editor area; you do so using the Editor selector, which is a group of buttons in the toolbar, as you can see in Figure 2-2.

The term *editor* here is really a misnomer, even though that is the term used in the documentation. The "editors" you can select in the Editor area are really editor area *configurations,* within which you use the *content* editors available to you (see the "Editor area content editors" section, later in this chapter).

The editors (configurations) you have available are as follows:

Figure 2-2: The Editor selector

   ✓ **Standard editor:** The button for this Editor area configuration is on the left of side of the Editor selector. It displays a single pane for editing and is always shown.

   ✓ **Assistant editor:** Select this Editor area (configuration) using the center button. This adds an additional pane to the Editor area, with a content editor in each. The additional Assistant pane has some navigation features that I explain in Chapters 6 and 8. You can further split this pane into two panes.

   ✓ **Version editor:** Open this editor using the right button on Editor selector. This enables you to compare two different versions of files you have saved in repositories. Repositories and the Version editor are beyond the scope of this book.

I explain the tasks you can perform within in these areas later.

Additional areas to view as needed

You use the View selector, which is outlined in blue in the toolbar (see Figure 2-3), to toggle between showing and hiding any of the optional areas. By *optional,* I mean that you can open and close these areas as needed. These areas are as follows:

Figure 2-3: The View selector.

✔ **Navigator area** (left button): No further configuration possible (you don't divide this area into other views).

✔ **Debug area** (center button): Displays various panes depending on what you need to see; you change panes using the Debug area scope bar, shown in Figure 2-4 (it's also outlined in orange and shown with orange text in the Debug bar in Figure 2-1)

Figure 2-4: The Debug area Scope bar.

The Debug area Scope bar toggles from one to another of the following:

- Variables pane only (left button)
- Both Variables and Console panes (center button)
- Console pane only (right button)

✔ **Utility area** (right button): Is further configured with two panes in light-blue text (either can be expanded to hide the other):

- Inspector pane
- Library pane

When you hover your mouse pointer over a toolbar button, a tool tip describes its function.

Displaying an area's content

Each area displays certain content, and each area has its own way to display its content:

✔ **The Navigator area** has navigators

✔ **The Editor area** has content editors

✔ **The Utility area** has

- *Quick help* or *Inspectors* in the Inspector and Quick Help pane
- *Libraries* in the Library pane

✔ The Debug area has

- *Debugger variables* in the Variables pane
- *Debugger output* in the Console pane

The following sections tell you about these areas in more detail.

Navigator area navigators

The Navigator area contains a host of navigators that organize the tasks and components you use within your Xcode project. You use a Navigator selector to select the navigator you need. Figure 2-5 shows the Navigator selector. The navigators are as follows:

Figure 2-5: The Navigator selector.

 ✔ **Project navigator:** Here's where you manage all the files in your project. You can add, delete, and place files in Groups. Selecting a file in the Project navigator launches the appropriate editor in the Editor area.

 ✔ **Symbol navigator:** Displays the symbols in your project. Symbols are elements such as variable, method, and function name. Selecting a symbol highlights it in the editor.

 ✔ **Search navigator:** Finds any string within your projects and frameworks.

 ✔ **Issue navigator:** Displays issues such as diagnostics, warnings, and errors that arise when you're coding and building your project.

 ✔ **Debug navigator:** Displays the call stack (what method has called what method) information during program execution.

 ✔ **Breakpoint navigator:** Manages and edits the breakpoints in your project or Workspace.

 ✔ **Log navigator:** Examines the logs that Xcode generates when you run and debug your application.

Editor area content editors

The Editor area has a number of editors you use to edit specific content. Content editors are context based, meaning that the selection you make in a Navigator or Editor Jump bar (a Jump bar appears at the top of each Editor area pane and is a way to navigate through the files and symbols in your project) determines the Content editor. Here are the Content editors and the tasks you perform with each (not all of them are applicable to iOS application development):

✔ **Source editor:** Write and edit your source code; set and enable or disable breakpoints; control program execution.

✔ **Project editor:** View and edit settings such as build options, target architectures, and code signing.

- **Interface Builder:** Graphically create and edit user interface files in storyboards and xib files.

- **Property list editor:** View and edit various types of small, highly structured property lists (plists).

- **Rich text editor:** View and edit rich text (.rtf) files, much as you would with Text Edit.

- **Core Data model editor:** Implement or modify a Core Data model.

- **Mapping model editor:** Graphically create and edit a mapping between an old Core Data store and a new one.

- **Script editor:** Create and edit AppleScript script files.

- **Scripting dictionary editor:** Create and edit the scripting definition (.sdef) file for your application.

- **Viewer:** Display files for which there is no editor (some audio, video, and graphics files, for example) using the same Quick Look facility used by the Finder.

Utility area

The Utility area has two panes: the Inspector and Quick Help pane; and the Library pane. You can expand either pane to hide the other. Keep reading for more details about each of these panes.

The Inspector and Quick Help pane

You click a button in the Inspector selector (shown in Figure 2-6) to select an Inspector. A navigator or a Content editor selection will determine which Inspectors are available, which include:

Figure 2-6: The Inspector selector.

- **File inspector (first button):** View and manage file metadata such as its name, type, and path.

- **Quick Help (second button):** View (applicable) details about what has been selected in an editor such as an abstract or concise description, where and how it is declared, and selection-based information such as its scope, the parameters it takes, its platform and architecture availability, references, sample code, and so on. The following selections are supported:

  Symbols, in the Source editor

  Interface objects, in Interface Builder

  Build settings, in the Project editor

Additional inspectors are available in some editors; for example, Interface Builder offers these:

- ✔ **Identity inspector:** View and manage object metadata such as its class, runtime attributes, label, and so forth.

- ✔ **Attributes inspector:** Configure the attributes specific to the selected interface object. For example, some text field attributes include text alignment and color, border type, and editability.

- ✔ **Size inspector:** Specify characteristics such as the initial size and position, minimum and maximum sizes, and autosizing rules for an interface object.

- ✔ **Connections inspector:** View the outlets and actions for an interface object, make new connections, and delete existing connections.

Library pane

You click a button in the Library selector (shown in pink in Figure 2-7) to select a library of resources you can use in your project. The following libraries are available:

Figure 2-7: The Library selector.

- ✔ **File templates:** Templates for the common types of files you find using the New File menu. To add a file of that type to your project, drag it from the library to the Project navigator.

- ✔ **Code snippets:** These are short pieces of source code for use in your application. To use one, drag it directly into your source code file.

- ✔ **Objects:** Interface objects that make up your user interface. To add one to a view, drag it directly into your storyboard or nib file in the Interface Builder editor.

- ✔ **Media files:** These are graphics, icons, and sound files. To use one, drag it directly to your storyboard or nib file in the Interface Builder editor.

Debug area

A selection in the *Debug area Scope bar, shown* in Figure 2-8, determines the information the debugger displays.

Figure 2-8: The Debug area Scope bar.

Local ⬍ The pop-up menu in the *Variables pane Scope bar* lets you display:

> ↙ **Auto:** Display recently accessed variables

> ↙ **Local:** Display local variables

> ↙ **All:** Displays all variables and registers

All Output ⬍ The pop-up menu in the *Console pane Scope bar* lets you display:

> ↙ **All Output:** Target and debugger output

> ↙ **Debugger Output:** Debugger output only

> ↙ **Target Output:** Target output only

There are also other controls and filters for what gets displayed that you will have to explore on your own.

Xcode has extensive contextual help articles that you can view by Control-clicking in the Workspace window in the context you need help on.

The toolbar and Tab bar

The *toolbar* (see Figure 2-9) includes Workspace-level tools for managing and running schemes (instructions on how to build your application), viewing the progress of executing tasks, and configuring the Workspace window. In reality, the toolbar has three parts: Flow control, Activity viewer, and Workspace configuration.

The *Flow controls* are for defining, choosing, running, and stopping projects. A *scheme* defines characteristics such as build targets, build configurations, and the executable environment for the product to be built in. The Flow controls are as follows:

> ↙ **Run button:** Clicking the Run button builds and runs the targets. (A *target* is a product to build as well as the instructions for building that product from a set of files in a project or Workspace for the currently selected scheme). Pressing and holding the mouse button opens a menu (which is also available in the Product menu) that allows you to Run, Test, Profile, or Analyze your application.

> ↙ **Stop button:** Terminates your executing application in the Simulator or the device.

> ↙ **Scheme menu:** Lets you select the scheme and build destination to use.

> ↙ **Breakpoints button:** Activates or deactivates all breakpoints.

Also on the toolbar is the Activity viewer, which shows the progress of tasks currently executing. This viewer displays status messages, build progress, and other information about your project. Click the Issues icon in the Activity viewer to open the Issue navigator (explained earlier in this chapter).

You use the final part of the toolbar, the Workspace configuration controls, to configuring the Xcode workspace window to suit your needs. As I explain in the previous section, "Displaying an area's content," you use these controls to select an editor type, show or hide optional view areas, and open the Organizer window.

Showing the *Tab bar* is optional. Choose View⇨Show Tab Bar to show the Tab bar. You can reorder tabs, close them individually, or drag them out of the bar to create a new window.

If you lose the toolbar (or Tab bar), you can add it to any window by selecting View⇨Show Toolbar (or View⇨Show Tab Bar). The View menu also allows you to configure the Workspace window.

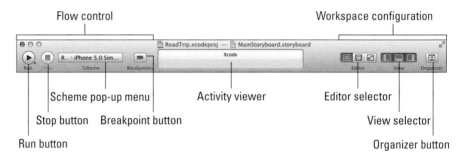

Figure 2-9: The toolbar with Tab bar.

The Organizer window

The Organizer window (see Figure 2-10) enables you to do the supplemental tasks associated with development such as accessing documentation and managing devices, archives, and project-related metadata.

To display the Organizer window, click the Organizer button in the Workspace window toolbar or choose Window⇨Organizer. The Organizer window includes five individual organizers, which enable you to do the following:

✏ **Devices organizer:** Provision a device, manage your developer profile, install iOS on the device, and work with your application and its data.

✏ **Repositories organizer:** Create, view, and manage Git and Subversion repositories for your Workspace.

✏ **Projects organizer:** Manage the derived data and the snapshots of your projects.

✏ **Archives organizer:** Submit your application to the App Store or testers and manage your product archives.

✏ **Documentation organizer:** Access documentation and sample code from within Xcode.

Each of these organizers includes task-oriented contextual help that you get by Control-clicking an organizer's content pane.

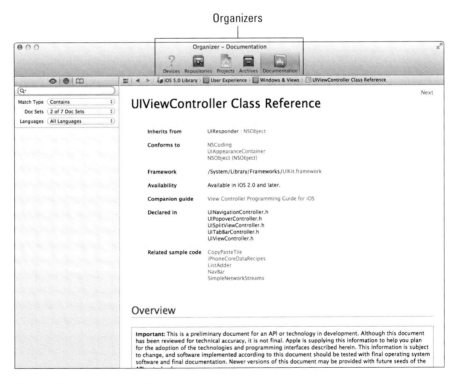

Figure 2-10: The Organizer window.

Chapter 3

The Nuts and Bolts of an Xcode Project

*A*s I explain in Chapter 2, to use Xcode to create an app, you need to create an Xcode project. An Xcode project includes all the files, resources, and information required to build your application. It is your partner in creating your application, and the sooner you make friends with it, the easier your life will become.

In this chapter, I show you how to create an Xcode project and then build and run your app in the Simulator.

Creating Your Project

Because developing an iPhone app requires you to work in an *Xcode project,* it's time to create one. The app you'll be building is called RoadTrip (and will also be the name of the project). The app, as I mention in the introduction, is like a travel guide on your iPhone. Here's how it's done:

1. **Launch Xcode.**

   After you've downloaded the SDK, launching Xcode is easy. By default, it's downloaded to *computer*/Developer/Applications (where *computer* stands for whatever you computer's name is). Find it and double-click to launch it.

   Here are a couple of hints to make Xcode handier and more efficient right from the start:

   • Drag the icon for the Xcode application to the Dock so that you can launch it from there; or after you have launched it, right-click the Xcode icon in the Dock and then choose Options⟳Keep in Dock.

You'll be using Xcode a lot, so it wouldn't hurt to be able to launch it from the Dock.

• When you first launch Xcode, you see the Welcome screen with several links. (After you use Xcode to create projects, your Welcome screen lists all your most recent projects in the right column.) (If you don't want to be bothered with the Welcome screen in the future, deselect the Show This Window when Xcode Launches check box. You can also just click Cancel to close the Welcome screen.) If you want to see it again, you can access it through the Window menu or by pressing Shift+CMD+1.

2. **Click the Create a New Xcode Project link on the Welcome screen, or choose File⇨New⇨New Project to create a new project.**

   You can also just press Shift+CMD+N.

   No matter how you decide to start a new project, you're greeted by the Choose a Template for Your New Project dialog, as shown in Figure 3-1.

   The Choose a Template for Your New Project dialog does exactly what its name says. Note that the leftmost pane has two sections: one for iOS and the other for Mac OS X.

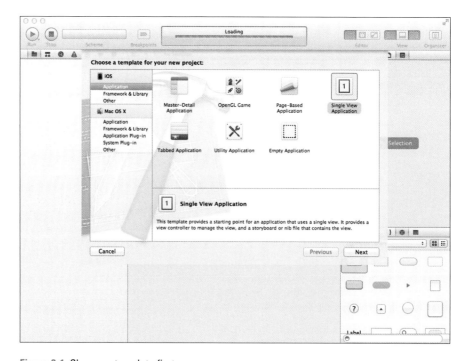

Figure 3-1: Choose a template first.

3. **In the upper-left corner of the Choose a Template dialog, click Application under the iOS heading (if it isn't already selected).**

   After clicking Application, the main pane of the Choose a Template dialog refreshes, revealing several choices. (Refer to Figure 3-1.) Each choice is actually a template that, when chosen, generates code to get you started.

4. **Select Single View Application from the template choices displayed (as I have in Figure 3-1) and then click Next.**

   After you click Next, the Choose Options for Your New Project dialog appears.

   Note that when you select a template, a brief description of the template is displayed underneath the main pane. (Again, refer to Figure 3-1 to see a description of the Single View Application template.) In fact, go ahead and click some of the other template choices just to see how they're described as well. Just be sure to click the Single View Application template again, and then click Next, to follow along with developing the RoadTrip app.

   These template names do change from time to time, so don't be surprised if yours are a little different from the ones I refer to in this book. For the most part, the kinds of application they build tend to stay the same.

5. **In the Choose Options dialog (see Figure 3-2), enter a name for your new project in the Product Name field, and add a company name (or your name) in the Company field.**

   I named this project RoadTrip. (You should do the same if you're following along with developing RoadTrip.)

   Class prefix is something that will prepended to the classes the template will generate, so enter **RT** (for RoadTrip) in the Class Prefix field. (If you don't enter a prefix here, the template will create generically named classes that seem to have no connection to your project.)

6. **In the Device Family pop-up menu in the Options dialog there are choices for iPhone, iPad, or Universal (which runs on both iPhone and iPad). Select iPhone from the pop-up menu (if it is not already selected).** Doing so creates a skeleton app that will configured to run on the iPhone or iPod touch.

   Other options to select or deselect in this dialog are the following:

   - *Use Storyboard:* Select this check box. This enables you create the entire application flow graphically.

   - *Use Automatic Reference Counting:* Select this check box. As I explain in Chapter 7, this option makes memory management much easier.

- *Include Unit Tests:* Deselect this check box. Although unit testing is a valuable feature, covering it is beyond the scope of this book. Unit tests are part of a style of programming that involves writing test cases before writing the code to be tested. You can set requirements in concrete before writing any code. I don't use unit testing for RoadTrip because it would make the process of explaining Xcode more complicated. The feature is worth examining on your own, however.

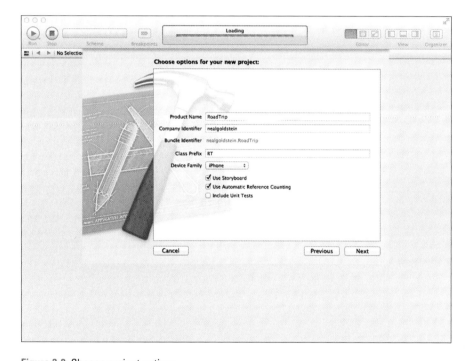

Figure 3-2: Choose project options.

In some of the templates, you can also choose to add Core Data resources to use Core Data for storage. The Core Data framework supports object persistence and is beyond the scope of this book. You can find quite a bit of sample code in the iOS Dev Center that does a good job of illustrating how to use it.

7. **Click Next choose a location to save the project (the Desktop or any folder works just fine), deselect the Source Control: Create Local git Repository for This Project check box, and then click Create.**

You can create a local Git repository when you save the new project. Git is a software control management (SCM) system that keeps track of changes in the code and saves multiple versions of each file on your hard drive. Git can be used as a local repository, or you can install a Git server on a remote machine to share files among team members. Git is beyond the scope of this book — but if you want to learn more about it, check out the Xcode 4 User Guide (choose Help⇨Xcode User Guide).

After you click Create, Xcode creates the project and opens the Workspace window for the project — which should look like what you see in Figure 3-3.

Xcode will remember your choices for your next project.

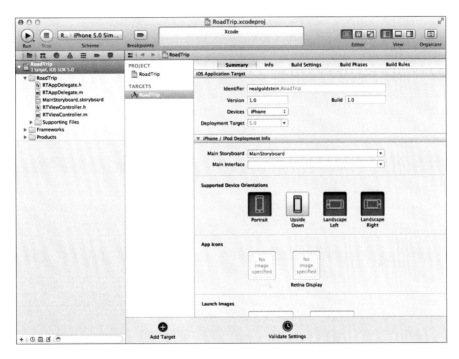

Figure 3-3: The Xcode Workspace window.

Exploring Your Project

As I said, to develop an iPhone app, you have to work within the context of an Xcode project, very much like the one shown in Figure 3-3. This is, in effect, Command Central for developing your iPhone app; it displays and organizes your projects, source files, and the other resources needed to build your apps.

The Project

If the project is not open, open it in Xcode. As I explain in Chapter 2, the Navigator area appears on the left side of the Workspace window. To display what you see in Figure 3-3 the Single View Application template you just used results in these selections for you when the project is created:

- ✔ Hide the Utility and Debug areas
- ✔ Show the Navigator area
- ✔ Select the Project navigator
- ✔ Show the Standard editor
- ✔ Select the RoadTrip project in the navigator area

As a result, what you see in the editor is the Project editor displaying the RoadTrip project.

The Project Editor

Select the Road Trip project in the Navigator area as shown in Figure 3-4. In the first column of the Project editor, you see the project (a Workspace can actually have more than one project but you won't be doing that in this book). Below that you see the target (there can also be more than one). A project defines default build settings for all the targets in the project (each target can also specify its own build settings, which override the project build settings).

The Project editor shows tabs across the top; clicking these tabs open panes that enable you to examine and change project settings. Most of the default settings will work for your needs, but as you develop the example project in this book, you will be examining some of them. The tabs are as follows:

- ✔ **Summary:** Each setting in the Summary pane is also found in one of the other panes. When you edit a setting, Xcode updates the other pane automatically, and you probably won't have to go into the other tabs.

  The iOS Application Target and iPhone/iPad Deployment Info sections of this pane display settings based on the choices you made when you created the RoadTrip project. (Notice that one of the settings is Deployment Target. Although you must compile your project using the current SDK, you can target it to run on earlier iOS versions. I cover that in more detail in a document on my website — Running Backwards.)

  In the summary tab, you can also add an icon for the RoadTrip app (you do that in "Adding an Application Icon," later in this chapter) as well as a launch image for your app. The launch image is what you'll see displayed while your app is launching until it is completely launched and ready to use.

Project is selected   Project editor

Figure 3-4: The template-generated Workspace window configuration.

You will also be able to add a framework (I cover adding a new framework in Chapter 9) and set Entitlements. (Entitlements are used when you are developing apps that use iCloud and are beyond the scope of this book.)

✔ **Summary:** The Summary pane enables you to edit the basic settings. The Summary pane contains the basic settings that you need to inspect and edit when working on an iOS target.

✔ **Info:** If you created the RoadTrip project earlier in this chapter, when you open the disclosure triangle next to supporting files in the project navigator, you'll see a file called `RoadTrip-Info.plist`. The Info tab contains more or less the same information as that file. An information property list file contains essential configuration information for a bundled executable. The system uses these keys and values to obtain information about your application and how it is configured. As a result, all bundled executables (plug-ins, frameworks, and applications) are expected to have an information property list file.

✔ **Build Settings:** Most developers can get by with the default build settings. But if you have special needs — ones that require anything from tweaking a setting or two to creating an entirely new build configuration — you'll take care of them in this tab.

✓ **Build Phases:** There are a number of panes in this tab which control how Xcode builds your products. For example, Xcode detects when one of your products is dependent on another and automatically builds those products in the correct order. However, if you need to control the order in which Xcode builds your products, this you can create explicit target dependencies by using the Build Phases pane in this tab.

✓ **Build Rules:** Xcode processes your source files according to the file type using a set of built-in rules. For example, property list (plist) files are copied into the product using the CopyPlistFile script located in the Xcode directory. You won't need this for a long time, and if you're lucky, never.

The Project navigator

The template you select for a project displays the Project navigator for you. I introduce the Project navigator in Chapter 2 but give you the full tour of this navigator here.

(By the way, Xcode has a lot of context-based help. Whenever you are curious about something, try right-clicking in an area and you'll likely find a menu with a help selection. In Figure 3-5, for example, I Control+clicked in the Project navigator area to bring up a help menu.)

The Navigator area is an optional area on the left side of the Workspace window. To hide or show it, click the left View selector button in the Workspace toolbar (see Figure 3-6).

This area includes the Navigator selector bar, the content area, and a filter bar. It can also include other features specific to the selected navigator.

The Project navigator enables you to do things like add, delete, group, and otherwise manage files in your project or choose a file to view or edit in the Editor area. (Depending on which file you choose, you'll see the appropriate editor, as I explain in Chapter 2.) In Figure 3-7, for example, I have all the disclosure triangles open and the Project navigator displays all of the files in the project.

The *filter bar* lets you restrict the content that is displayed — such as recently edited files, unsaved files, or filenames.

The Project navigator shows an outline view of the contents of the RoadTrip project files. You can move files and folders around and add new folders. If you select an item in the navigator, the contents of the item are displayed in the Editor area.

Figure 3-5: Project navigator help.

Figure 3-6: The View selector in the Workspace toolbar.

The first item in the Project navigator, as you can see in Figure 3-7, is labeled RoadTrip. This item contains all the source elements for the project, including source code, resource files, graphics, and a number of other pieces that will remain unmentioned for now (but I get into those in due course). Although each template organizes these source elements in different ways, the Single View Application template organizes the interface header and implementation code files along with the Storyboard file and a Supporting Files folder inside the RoadTrip folder. It also includes a Frameworks folder and a Products folder. Here's what gets tossed into each folder for the RoadTrip project:

Navigator selector bar

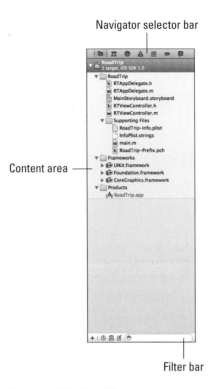

Content area

Filter bar

Figure 3-7: The RoadTrip Project navigator.

✏ **Application Delegate:** The `RTAppDelegate.h` and `RTAppDelegate.m` files contain the code for app-specific behavior that customizes the behavior of a framework object (so that you don't have to subclass it — as I describe in Chapter 7). A behavior-rich framework object (used as is) delegates the task of implementing one of its responsibilities to an application delegate for a very specific behavior. The *delegation* pattern of adding behaviors to objects is described in more detail in Chapter 7.

✏ **Storyboard:** The `MainStoryboard.storyboard` file. The storyboard is a way to create and implement an overall view of the flow of your application and the user interface elements. I go into great detail on storyboards in Chapter 4. Soon you'll like the `.storyboard` files as much as I do.

✏ **View controllers:** The `RTViewController.h`, and `RTView Controller.m`, contain the code to control the Main view of the RoadTrip (based on the Single View Application template). You start working with the `RTViewController` in Chapter 9.

✏ **Supporting Files:** In this folder, you typically find the precompiled headers of the frameworks you will be using — such as `RoadTrip_Prefix. pch` — as well as the property list (`RoadTrip-Info.plist`) and `main.m`, your application's main function. You may even find images and other media files, and some data files. The `InfoPlist.strings` file is used for localization.

- **Frameworks:** This folder holds the code libraries that act a lot like prefab building blocks for your app. (I talk about frameworks in Chapter 4.) By choosing the Single View Application template, you let Xcode know that it should add the `UIKit`, `Foundation`, and CoreGraphics frameworks to your project, because it expects that you'll need them in this kind of application.

    You'll be adding more frameworks yourself to just these three frameworks in developing RoadTrip. You find out how to add more frameworks in Chapter 8.

- **Products:** The Products folder is a bit different from the others. In it you find the final `RoadTrip.app` — not the source code of the app, but rather the *built* version of the app, which means that it has been translated from the source code into the object code for the iPhone's processor to execute. At the moment, this file is listed in red because the file can't be found.

 When a filename appears in red, this means that Xcode can't find the underlying physical file. And because you have never compiled the RoadTrip app, it makes sense that the `RoadTrip.app` file (the app itself) is missing.

 These templates are tweaked for time to time, so what you see may not be exactly what I describe here.

 You may notice that some items in the Project navigator look like folders, although often they may not be. If you happen to open the `RoadTrip` folder on your Mac, you won't see all the "folders" that appear in the Xcode window. That's because those folders are simply groupings that help organize and find what you're looking for; this list of files can grow pretty large, even in a moderate-size project. Most have a little triangle (the disclosure triangle) next to them. Clicking the little triangle to the left of a folder expands the folder to show what's in it. Click the triangle again to hide what it contains.

Preferences Galore! Setting Your Xcode Preferences

Xcode gives you options galore. I'm guessing that you won't change any of them until you have a bit more programming experience under your belt, but a few options are actually worth thinking about now, so in this section, I show you how to set some of the preferences you might be interested in.

Follow these steps to set some of the preferences you'll find useful:

1. **With Xcode open, choose Xcode⇔Preferences from the main menu.**

2. **Click the Behaviors tab at the top of the Preferences window to show the Behaviors pane.**

   The Xcode Preferences window refreshes to show the Behaviors pane.

   The right side of the pane shows the Events pane, and on the left side shows the possible actions for an event.

3. **Select Run Generates Output in the left column and then choose the Show, Hide, or If No Output Hide option from the Debug Area pop-up menu in the right pane.**

   This step controls what appears while you run your app. By default, you'll find a check box selected that will show the debugger in the Debug area (see Chapter 9 for more about debugging). You can also change options, such as playing a sound (something I like to do) or bouncing the Xcode icon in the Dock, for Build Starts, Build Generates New Issues, Build Succeeds, and Build Fails. You can change many options in the Behaviors pane — too many to cover in this chapter! But take a look through them and experiment — they can make your life much easier.

   Figure 3-8 shows the behaviors I have chosen if the run pauses. (By *pause,* I mean hit a breakpoint, for example; I cover breakpoints in Chapter 8.) I like to have a sound inform me in case I'm busy daydreaming (submarine seems appropriate here).

   Figure 3-9 shows the behaviors I have chosen if a build fails. I like to use a sound for this occurrence as well. I also want to have the Issue navigator display (see Chapter 8 for more about the value and use of the Issue navigator).

4. **Click the Documentation tab at the top of the Preferences window.**

5. **Select the Check for and Install Updates Automatically check box, and then click the Check and Install Now button.**

   This step ensures that the documentation remains up-to-date and allows you to load and access other documentation.

6. **Click the red button in the top-left corner of the window to close the Xcode Preferences window.**

You can also change the Xcode Workspace theme by selecting the Fonts & Colors tab. When I get bored, I sometimes change the Theme to Midnight to get a black background.

You also can set your editing and indentation options in the Text Editing pane of the Preferences window. I set the Indent width to 2 in the Indentation settings to get as much code on a line as possible.

Figure 3-8: Behaviors.

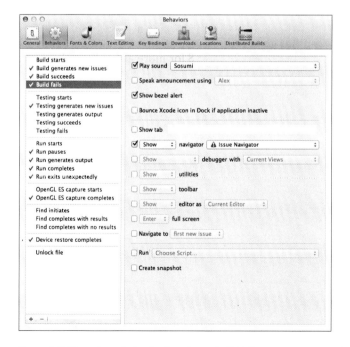

Figure 3-9: Choosing a behavior for when a build fails.

Building and Running Your Application

As I mention in Chapter 2, the toolbar (Figure 3-10) is where you do things like run your application. I spell the process out a bit more here.

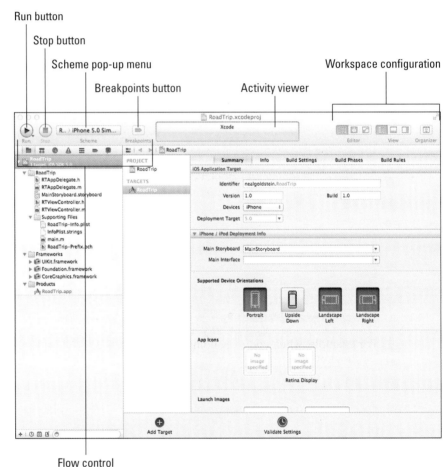

Figure 3-10: The Xcode toolbar.

The Flow controls are for defining, choosing, running, and stopping projects. A *scheme* defines characteristics such as build targets, build configurations, and the executable environment for the product to be built. They consist of:

> ✔ **Run button:** Pressing the run button builds and runs the targets (a product to build and the instructions for building the product from a set of files in a project or Workspace for the currently selected scheme).

Pressing and holding the mouse button opens a menu (which are also available in the Product menu) that allows you to Run, Test, Profile, or Analyze your application

Holding various modifier keys while clicking this button allows you to select other run options:

- Control key: Run without building

- Shift key: Build without running

- Option key: Edit the scheme and run

✔ **Stop button:** Terminates your executing application in the simulator or the device.

✔ **Scheme menu:** Lets you select the scheme and build destination to use. The Scheme pop-up menu lets you specify the active SDK and active configuration, which is called a *Scheme*. I describe schemes in the next section of this chapter, and I describe how to set up a scheme for final app submission in a document you can download from www.dummies. com/go/iphoneappdevfd4e.

✔ **Breakpoints button:** Activates or deactivates all breakpoints The Breakpoints button turns breakpoints on and off. (A breakpoint tells Xcode to stop execution at a point in the code. I explain breakpoints in Chapter 9.)

The *Activity viewer* shows the progress of tasks currently executing, displaying status messages, build progress, and other information about your project. Click the issues icon in the Activity viewer to open the Issues navigator. Look here for messages about your project. (None exist yet in Figure 3-10.) For example, when you're building your project, Xcode updates the status bar to show where you are in the process — and whether or not the process completed successfully.

Building an app

Building an app in Xcode means compiling all the source code files in the project. It's really exciting (well, I exaggerate a bit) to see what you get when you build and run a project that you created from a template. Building and running is relatively simple; just follow these steps:

1. **Choose a scheme.**

   A *scheme* tells Xcode the purpose of the built product. The schemes in the Scheme pop-up menu specify which targets (actual products) to build, what build configuration to use when building them, which debugger to use when testing them, and which executable to launch when running them on the device or Simulator. Xcode automatically creates several schemes with configurations for you, and you can create more schemes and edit any of the schemes.

To work with the example app we develop in this book (the RoadTrip app), you just want to make sure that the scheme is set to the Simulator and the proper SDK. If it isn't already chosen, choose iPhone 5.0 Simulator in the by clicking in the right section of the Scheme pop-up menu in the upper-left corner of the Workspace window (refer to Figure 3-11) to set the active SDK and active build configuration to use the Simulator. If you click in the left section, you have to choose RoadTrip⇨ iPhone 5.0 Simulator. Here's what all that means:

- When you download an SDK, you actually download *multiple* SDKs — a Simulator SDK and a device SDK for each of the current iOS releases.

- You should use the Simulator SDK for iOS 5.0 as of this writing for apps that you want to submit to the App Store (until a newer version of iOS is released). In a document on my website, I show you how to switch to the device SDK and transfer your app to a real-world iPhone. But before you do that, there's just one catch.

- You have to be in the iOS Developer Program to run your app on a device, even on your very own iPhone. Go to `www.developer.apple.com/devcenter/ios` to learn about enrolling in the program if you haven't done so already.

2. **Choose Product⇨Run from the main menu to build and run the application.**

You can also click the Tasks button (set to Run) in the top-left corner of the Workspace window. The Activity viewer (shown in Figure 3-11) tells you all about build progress, build errors such as compiler errors, or warnings — and (oh, yeah) whether the build was successful.

Figure 3-11 shows you what you'll see in the Simulator. I know it's not much, but it is a start, and it is a functioning iPhone app.

If you want to look at how the build works, now is a good time to explain the Log navigator.

The Log navigator

You can select the Log navigator using the Navigator selector or you can Choose View⇨Navigators⇨Log to view the logs that Xcode generates during the build process; these logs list the actions performed. (Figure 3-12 shows all my recent builds.

Figure 3-11: Not much of an app, but it *is* yours.

The Log navigator lists two types of actions:

- **Tasks:** The task log lists the operations Xcode performed to carry out the task, such as building tasks, archiving tasks, and source control tasks.

- **Sessions:** A session log is the transcript of the events that occurred during a session (a period during which an activity is performed), such as the output of the debugger while you debug your application. Running or debugging an application generates a session log.

The Log navigator contains the task and session list. When you select an item in this list, the corresponding log appears in the Log viewer, in the editor area. You can filter this list with the filter bar.

You won't need to use the Log navigator for the example app in this book. You examine the debug activity in the Debug area instead, and any task related issues in the Issue navigator.

The success (or failure) of your build is also displayed in the Activity viewer.

Debug session

Build task

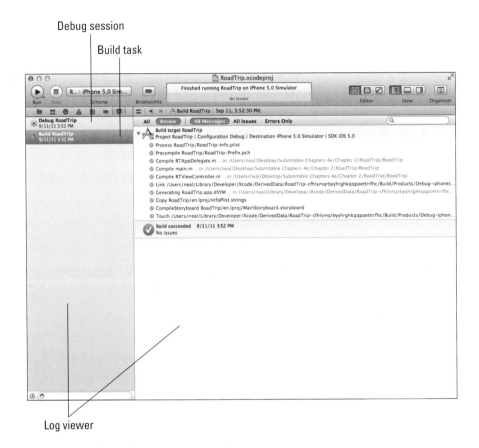

Log viewer

Figure 3-12: Build results.

Running in the Simulator

When you run your app, Xcode installs it on the Simulator (or on a real device if you specified a device as the active SDK) and launches it. Using the Hardware menu and your keyboard and mouse, the Simulator mimics most of what a user can do on a real device, albeit with some limitations that I point out shortly.

The Simulator first first appears to be like any iPhone model, and your first app looks a lot like what you see in Figure 3-11, in the previous section.

To see what your app looks like on an iPhone 4, choose Hardware⇨Device⇨ iPhone (Retina).

Click the Home button at the bottom center of the Simulator window once to quit your app. The app appears with a standard blank icon. Click the blank icon once to launch the app again.

Interacting with simulated hardware

You also use the Simulator Hardware menu when you want your device to do the following:

- **Device:** Switch the simulated device to an iPad, any model iPhone, or an iPhone (Retina) for current iPhone 4 and fourth-generation iPod touch models.

- **Version:** Switch to a different version of iOS.

- **Rotate left:** Choosing Hardware⇨Rotate Left rotates the Simulator to the left. If the Simulator is in Portrait view, it changes to Landscape view; if the Simulator is already in Landscape view, it changes to Portrait view.

- **Rotate right:** Choosing Hardware⇨Rotate Right rotates the Simulator to the right, with the same effect as choosing Hardware⇨Rotate Left.

- **Use a shake gesture:** Choosing Hardware⇨Shake Gesture simulates shaking the device.

- **Go to the Home screen:** Choosing Hardware⇨Home does the expected — you go to the home screen.

- **Lock the Simulator (device):** Choosing Hardware⇨Lock locks the Simulator, which then displays the lock screen.

- **Send the running app low-memory warnings:** Choosing Hardware⇨ Simulate Memory Warning fakes out your app by sending it a (fake) low-memory warning.

- **Toggle the status bar between its Normal state and its In-Call state:** Choose Hardware⇨Toggle In-Call Status Bar to check out how your app functions when the iPhone is not answering a call (Normal state) and when it supposedly *is* answering a call (In-Call state).

   The status bar becomes taller when you're on a call than when you're not. Choosing the In-Call state here shows you how things look when your application is launched while the user is on the phone.

- **Simulate the hardware keyboard:** Choose Hardware⇨Simulate Hardware Keyboard to check out how your app functions when the device is connected to an optional physical keyboard dock or paired with a Bluetooth keyboard.

- **TV Out:** To bring up another window that acts like an external display attached to the device, choose Hardware⇨TV Out and then choose 640x480, 1024x768, or 1280x720 for the window's display resolution. Choose Hardware⇨TV Out⇨Disabled to close the external display window.

Making gestures

On the real device, a gesture is something you do with your fingers to make something happen in the device, such as a tap, a drag, and so on. Table 3-1 shows you how to simulate gestures using your mouse and keyboard.

Table 3-1	Gestures in the Simulator
Gesture	iPhone Action
Tap	Click the mouse.
Touch and hold	Hold down the mouse button.
Double tap	Double-click the mouse button.
Two-finger tap	1. Move the mouse pointer over the place where you want to start.
	2. Hold down the Option key, which makes two circles appear that stand in for your fingers.
	3. Click the mouse button.
Swipe	1. Click where you want to start and hold the mouse button down.
	2. Move the mouse slowly in the direction of the swipe and then release the mouse button.
Flick	1. Click where you want to start and hold the mouse button down.
	2. Move the mouse quickly in the direction of the flick and then release the mouse button.
Drag	1. Click where you want to start and hold down the mouse button.
	2. Move the mouse slowly in the drag direction.
Pinch	1. Move the mouse pointer over the place where you want to start.
	2. Hold down the Option key, which makes two circles appear that stand in for your fingers.
	3. Hold down the mouse button and move the circles in (to pinch) or out (to unpinch).

Uninstalling apps and resetting your device

You uninstall applications on the Simulator the same way you do it on the iPhone, except you use your mouse instead of your finger. Follow these steps:

1. **On the Home screen, place the pointer over the icon of the app you want to uninstall and hold down the mouse button until all the app icons start to wiggle.**

2. **Click the app icon's Close button — the little *x* that appears in the upper-left corner of the icon — to make the app disappear.**

3. **Click the Home button — the one with a little square in it, centered below the screen — to stop the other app icons from wiggling and finish the uninstallation.**

You can also move an app's icon around by clicking and dragging with the mouse.

You can remove an application from the background the same way you'd do it on the iPhone, except you use your mouse instead of your finger. Follow these steps:

1. **Double-click the Home button to display the applications running in the background.**

2. **Place the pointer over the icon of the application you want to remove, and hold down the mouse button until the icon starts to wiggle.**

3. **Click the icon's Remove button — the red circle with the "x" — that appears in the upper-left corner of the application's icon.**

4. **Click the Home button to stop the icons from wiggling and then once again to return to the Home screen.**

To reset the Simulator to the original factory settings — which also removes all the apps you've installed — choose iOS Simulator⬠Reset Content and Settings, and then click Reset in the warning dialog.

Living with Simulator's limitations

Keep in mind that running apps in the Simulator is not the same thing as running them on the iPhone. Here's why:

✓ **Different frameworks:** The Simulator uses Mac OS X versions of the low-level system frameworks, instead of the actual frameworks that run on the device. That means that occasionally some code may run fine in the Simulator but not on the iPhone. Although the Simulator is useful for testing functionality, there is no substitute for debugging the app on the device itself to know how it will actually run.

✔ **Different hardware and memory:** The Simulator uses the Mac hardware and memory. To accurately determine how your app will perform on an honest-to-goodness iPhone, you have to run it on a real iPhone.

✔ **Different installation procedure:** Xcode installs *your* app in the Simulator automatically when you build the app using the iOS SDK. That's all fine and dandy, but you don't have a way to get Xcode to install *other* apps from the App Store in the Simulator.

✔ **Lack of GPS:** You can't fake the Simulator into thinking that it's lying on the beach at Waikiki.

You can, however, choose to simulate a location in the Debug area. I tell you more about simulating a location in Chapter 16.

✔ **Two-finger limit:** You can simulate a maximum of two fingers. If your application's user interface can respond to touch events involving more than two fingers, you need to test that on an actual device. The motion of the two fingers is limited in the Simulator — you can't do two-figure swipes or drags.

✔ **Accelerometer differences:** You can access your computer's accelerometer (if it has one) through the UIKit framework. Its reading, however, will differ from the accelerometer readings on an iPhone (for some technical reasons that I don't go into).

✔ **Differences in rendering:** OpenGL ES (OpenGL for Embedded Systems), one of the 3D graphics libraries that works with the iOS SDK, uses renderers on devices that are slightly different from those it uses in iPhone Simulator. As a result, a scene on the Simulator and the same scene on a device may not be identical at the pixel level.

Adding an Application Icon

If you select the Home button on the simulator (or the iPhone), you can't help noticing the rather undistinguished looking application icon.

Even though your app doesn't do anything yet, though, you can have a nice, shiny app icon by following these steps:

1. **Download the RoadTrip Resources folder from my website** neal goldstein.com/support/downloads.

2. **Right-click the RoadTrip project in the Project navigator, choose Add Files to "RoadTrip" and then use the dialog that appears to navigate to and select the folder (or individual files) you want. Or choose File⇨ Add Files to "RoadTrip" as shown in Figure 3-13.**

Xcode asks you whether you want to make a copy of the file. Otherwise, it simply creates a pointer to the file. The advantage of using a pointer is that if you modify the file later, Xcode will use that modified version. The disadvantage is that Xcode won't be able to find the file if you move it.

3. Select the Copy Items into destination group's folder (if needed) check box and then click Add to copy the files.

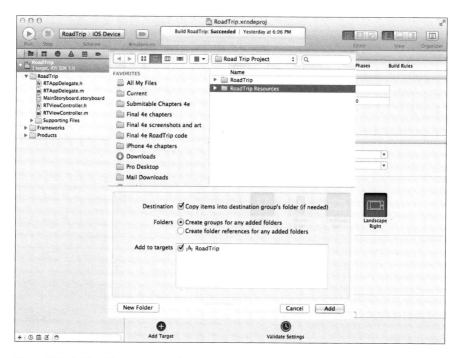

Figure 3-13: Adding files to your project.

You can also drag files into the Project navigator.

Standard and retina display images

Starting with iOS 4, you can include two separate files for each image resource (you use just a single file in this book, however). One file provides a standard-resolution version of a given image, and the second provides a high-resolution version of the same image. The naming conventions for each pair of image files is as follows:

- **Standard:** <ImageName><device_modifier>.<filename_extension>
- **High resolution:** <ImageName>@2x<device_modifier>.<filename_extension>

The <ImageName> and <filename_extension> portions of each name specify the usual name and extension for the file. The <device_modifier> portion is optional and contains either the string ~ipad or ~iphone. You include one of these modifiers when you want to specify different versions of an image for iPhone and iPad. The inclusion of the @2x modifier for the high-resolution image lets the system know that the image is the high-resolution variant of the standard image.

When creating high-resolution versions of your images, place the new versions in the same location in your application bundle as the original.

If you click one of the resources, you see it displayed in the Editor area. Because Xcode does not have a graphics editor, as I explain in Chapter 2, Xcode uses the same quick-look functionality as that used by the Finder.

Adding the icon

An application icon is simply a 57-by-57-pixel .png file. I created an icon matching those measurements in a graphics program, and you can find it in the Resources folder (the one you download in Steps 1–3 in "Adding an Application Icon").

1. **Select the Project navigator by clicking the first icon in the Navigator selector bar — it looks like a folder.**

   The Project navigator displays the RoadTrip project container and the files and resources in your project.

2. **Select the Road trip project container (the first item in the Project navigator).**

   The Project editor launches.

3. **Right-click the first selection box in the App Icon section and choose Select File.**

4. **Navigate back to the Resources folder you downloaded, select AppIcon, and click Choose.**

   The message shown in Figure 3-14 appears because you added this icon to the project as part of the Resources folder (see Steps 1–3 in "Adding an Application Icon," earlier in this chapter). Just click Yes.

You could have deleted this image from the Resources folder when you added it instead, since you were going to add it again.

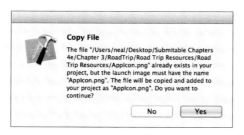

Figure 3-14: Click Yes.

Great, now you have two AppIcon files. This makes it a good time to show you how to delete files from your project.

Delete the duplicate file by selecting it and pressing Delete.

Figure 3-15 shows you the dialog that appears, asking whether you want to permanently delete the file or just remove the reference. If you copied the file (that is, if the Copy items check box was selected; refer to in Figure 3-13), you can safely choose Delete. If you choose Remove Reference Only and you copied the file into your project, it will just be removed from the Project navigator but will remain in your (real) project folder, and you will not be able to add another file with that name.

If you didn't copy the file, and you choose Delete, it will be deleted it from its orginating folder — so be careful.

If you need to delete a framework file, you should always choose Remove Reference Only.

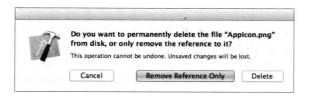

Figure 3-15: Delete permanently (or not).

You could (although I won't) have a high-resolution version of the app icon as well. But since I'm obviously not a graphic artist, I leave that up to you.

Run your project

To run your project, just select Run in the Xcode toolbar. Then click the
Home button, and you should see your application icon (Figure 3-16).

Figure 3-16: The app icon in all its glory.

Part II
Working with the Storyboard and User Interface

*K*iller iPhone apps start with the user experience. This goes beyond a pretty interface and includes how people use your app to accomplish want they want.

Of course, the boys and girls at Apple really understand that and have included the Interface Builder editor — which is much more than your run-of-the-mill program for building graphical user interfaces — in Xcode to enable you to build a real interface. In this part, you also discover the storyboard, which is the icing on the Interface Builder cake. The storyboard lets you lay out the entire application flow and save you a lot of coding, to boot.

In this part, you find out how to use Xcode to lay out the first screen of your application. You add background images and controls that will be new user's first experience with your application.

Of course, you need code to make your application do something beyond just sitting there and looking nice. The iOS frameworks provide what you need to make your application an application. You use frameworks to display your windows and views on the screen, navigate, add animation and sound and mostly anything else you might need. Next, before you can actually build that sucker, you look under the hood at how iPhone applications work — what goes on behind the screen that ends up with a user seeing something in a window and interacting with controls.

In this part, I also take you on a brief tour of the RoadTrip app, the one you'll be building along with me in this book. I show you not only what the app will do but also how it uses the frameworks and SDK to do it.

Chapter 4

Storyboards and the
User Experience

*A*s I mention in the Introduction, my goal for this book is for you to learn the *right way* to develop applications for the iPhone. Since you will be developing the RoadTrip application, now is a good time to explain the application — what it does, it's architecture.

One thing that makes iPhone software development so appealing is the richness of the tools and frameworks provided in the iOS Software Development Kit (SDK). The frameworks are especially important. Each one is a distinct body of code that actually implements your application's generic functionality — in other words, frameworks give the application its basic way of working. This is especially true of one framework in particular: the UIKit framework, which is the heart of the user interface.

In this chapter, you find out about most of the iPhone's user interface architecture, which is a mostly static view that explains what the various pieces are, what each does, and how they interact with each other. This chapter lays the groundwork for developing the RoadTrip app's user interface.

I also go through the what's available in the SDK (classes and frameworks) that you should know about. These are both the classes and frameworks you'll be using in the RoadTrip app and other classes and frameworks you should know about so that you can use them in your own apps. I also talk about something Apple calls *design patterns,* or programming paradigms that the frameworks are based on.

But the place I want to start is a new feature in Xcode 4.2 — the storyboard, which allows you to lay out the user interface and the application flow, or the relationships between various screens, in a "white board" sort of way.

Introducing the Storyboard

I really like storyboards. When I saw them for the first time it was a dream come true (well, okay, not quite). Here was what I needed — not only for building my own apps but also for teaching other people how to build an app.

As I say in Chapter 1, using a storyboard is analogous to sketching the user interface and app flow on a white board, and then having that sketch turn into something your app can use without any coding on your part.

Working with a storyboard saves you time and effort and reduces the code you have to write. It also helps you to fully understand the app flow. If you haven't developed before, you'll find that using a storyboard makes it easier to get up and running in a more complex app.

You use a storyboard to lay out the entire flow of you application. Figure 4-1 shows what the storyboard for a finished application looks like. You'll find that when you lay out an app in a storyboard, you can actually run your program, before you even add any content, and get a sense of how the user experience will unfold.

To get to the storyboard to edit it, you use the Project navigator and select the storyboard file you are interested in. Doing so brings up the Interface Builder editor. You will also use the Utility area as well to add user interface elements, use the inspectors to set attributes, and so on.

As you develop your application, you use Interface Builder to graphically add user interface elements to each one of your *views* in the storyboard. (I tell you more about views in the "Working with Windows and Views" section, later in this chapter; for now just think of them as displaying what you see on the iPhone screen.) User interface elements are things like controls, images, and placeholders for content you'll displaying. After you've added those elements, all you have to do is fill in code where it's needed. If you have used Xcode to program in the past, you'll find that you have to write a lot less "plumbing" code and, in some cases, none at all.

Typically, I lay out the entire flow of my application early on in the development process, but for the example app developed in this book, I'm not doing that because I want to first show you all the basics of developing an app with Xcode. In Chapter 11, you'll lay out the rest of the RoadTrip app using the storyboard. I promise, though, that when you do an app of your own, you'll be ready to start with the storyboard and design your application flow in the way I just described.

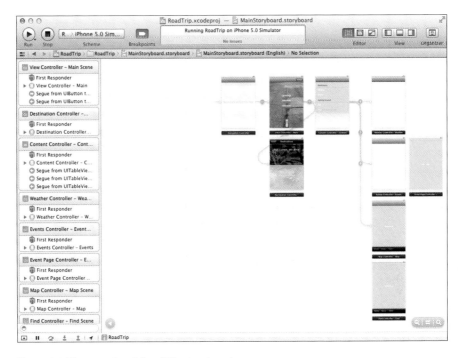

Figure 4-1: The completed RoadTrip storyboard.

The previous section gives you a general idea of what a storyboard is. In this section, I go into a bit more detail of the components you use while working within the storyboard. To follow along with me, go back to Xcode and select the `MainStoryboard.storyboard` file in the Project navigator. This is the file that Xcode created for you when you used the Single View Application template and selected the Use Storyboard check box (see Chapter 3). The name *Main* implies that, of course, there can be others. (In fact, there can even be more than one storyboard, but you won't be using multiple ones in this book.)

As you can see in Figure 4-2. selecting `the MainStoryboard.storyboard` file in the Project navigator opens that file in the Interface Builder editor.

Storyboards are the new way to define your application's user interface. In the olden days (pre iOS 5 and Xcode 4.2), you used *nib* files to define your user interface one view controller at a time. View controllers manage what you see on the iPhone screen (more on these controllers later in this chapter, in "The View Controller — the Main Storyboard Player").

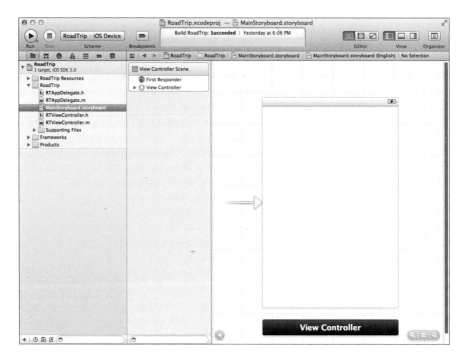

Figure 4-2: RoadTrip `MainStoryboard.storyboard` file.

The term *nib* (with its corresponding file extension `.xib`) is an acronym for NeXT Interface Builder. The Interface Builder application was originally developed at NeXT Computer, whose OPENSTEP operating system was used as the basis for creating Mac OS X.

A nib file is a special type of resource file that you use to store the IOS user interface you create with the Interface Builder editor. Storyboards are actually just a series of connected nib files.

As you create your storyboard, you create an *object graph* that is then archived when you save the file. When you load the file, the object graph is unarchived.

So, what's an object graph?

Object-oriented programs are made up of complex webs of interrelated objects. They are linked to one another in a variety of ways. One object can contain another object, for example, or own or reference it as well. All the items that you see in your storyboard (and some items that you don't see) are all objects and are part of that web of objects. The Interface Builder editor allows you to create this network graphically and then, at runtime, it makes the connections for you.

A storyboard file captures your entire user interface in one place and lets you define both the individual view controllers and the transitions between those view controllers. As a result, storyboards capture the flow of your overall user interface in addition to the content you present.

If you are creating new applications, the Xcode templates come preconfigured to use storyboards. For other applications, you can add storyboards, but you won't need to do that in this book

In the application you build in this book, you use a single storyboard file to store all the view controllers and views, but then the Interface Builder takes the contents of the storyboard file and divides it into discrete pieces that can be loaded individually for better performance.

So far in this chapter, I provided a look at the storyboard and its purpose. For you to truly get a feel for the essence of the storyboard, however , you need to understand how an iOS application is structured — that is, the iOS application architecture. The best way to do that is within the context of a real application. So before I get into even more detail about working in the storyboard, I want to give you a sense of basic functions and purpose of the application developed throughout this book — RoadTrip.

Defining What You Want an Application to Do: The RoadTrip Application

Necessity is the mother of invention, and the RoadTrip project was inspired by a necessity of a sort. My evil twin, Skippy, was about to leave on a 7,000-mile road trip around the United States in the family's pink 1959 Cadillac Eldorado convertible (at 8 mpg that's (only) one of the reasons we call him evil).

I walked in one day and found his him on his living room with maps and tour books spread out all over the floor. "Okay, brother," he said, "since you're so smart, can't you figure out a way so that when I am traveling I don't have the maps and paper all over my car and can have what I need on my iPhone?"

Being the good brother I am, I started to give it some thought.

To make RoadTrip a useful application, I had to move from Skippy's problem — all those maps and tour books all over his car — to the app's solution, which is to present information that's relevant to one of the following:

- Where you are
- Where you plan to be

By concentrating on that kind of relevance, you reduce the app to the amount of information you need to deal with at any one time.

Guided by the app's purpose — as well as by what the iPhone does best — I developed a clearer picture of what Skippy would want the app to do.

While Skippy is planning to go to New York, I thought I would give him a choice of other destinations (on the left in Figure 4-3). On the home screen (in the center in Figure 4-3), he can also select Test Drive to drive his car around the screen (with sound effects, no less — he is easily amused). On the right side of Figure 4-3, you can see his choices when he selects New York (San Francisco is identical but with a different background image):

Figure 4-3: Decide what to do and decide on a destination.

- ✔ **Get real-time weather access.** Snow in New York in August? Not likely, but these days you never can tell. You can see real-time weather access at work in Figure 4-4.

- ✔ **Find out what is going on in wherever he is.** Figure 4-5 shows an event that Skippy might be interested in.

- ✔ **Bring up a map based on the destination.** The map shows Skippy's destination, and points of interest (and also allows him to center on his current location). (see Figure 4-6).

Figure 4-4: The weather in New York.

> ✔ **Find some place on a map.** If Skippy has an address that he wants to find it on the map, he should be able to do that, and get its GPS coordinates as well (I threw that in because Skippy is a map freak). Figure 4-7 gives an example of finding a point of interest on a map.

There are of course a lot of other features you'll want to add to this app to make it worth the $.99 you'll be charging, and I talk about some of those in Chapter 20, as well as how this app fits into an Application Ecosystem of the kind I explain in Chapter 1.

Given the user interface described in this section, the big question is, how do you create an application from your knowledge of the problem, and how do you want the app to help solve it?

The answer to that question is found in the application architecture.

Figure 4-5: RoadTrip describes some things for you to do while you are in a city.

Creating the Application Architecture

At a basic level, the RoadTrip application is made up of the following:

- **Models:** Model objects encapsulate the logic and (data) content of the application.

- **Views:** Views present the user experience, so you have to decide what information to display and how to display it. You have several different *kinds* of views — different ways to display both information and navigation choices. You use view classes available on the iPhone to present information and accept user input.

- **View controllers:** View controllers manage the user experience. They connect the views that present the user experience with the models that provide the necessary content. View controllers also manage the way the user navigates the application.

Figure 4-6: Finding your way with literal pinpoint accuracy.

The MVC (Model-View-Controller) model is pretty much the basis for all iPhone application development projects. I explain MVC in more detail in the section "The Model-View-Controller (MVC) pattern," later in this chapter. The trick is to come up with just the right views, view controllers, and model objects to get your project off the ground.

Using Frameworks

A *framework* offers common code that provides generic functionality. The SDK provides a set of frameworks for incorporating technologies, services, and features into your apps. For example, the UIKit framework gives you event-handling support, drawing support, windows, views, and controls that you can use in your app.

Figure 4-7: Where is Radio City Music
Hall anyway?

A framework is designed to easily integrate the code that runs, say an app
or game or that delivers the information that your user wants. A framework
is similar to a software library, but with an added twist: It also implements
a program's *flow of control* (in contrast to a software library, whose components are arranged by the programmer into a flow of control). So, when working within a framework, the programmer doesn't decide the order in which
things should happen — such as which messages are sent to which objects
and in what order when an application launches, or when a user touches a
button on the screen. Instead, the order of those events, or flow of control, is
a part of the framework.

When you use a framework, you provide your app with a ready-made set of
basic functions; you've told it, "Here's how to act." With the framework in
place, all you need to do is add the specific functionality that you want in the
app — the content as well as the controls and views that enable the user to
access and use that content.

The frameworks and iOS provide pretty complex functionality, such as

- Launching the app and displaying a window on the screen

- Displaying controls on the screen and responding to a user action — changing a toggle switch, for example, or scrolling a view, such as the list of your contacts

- Accessing sites on the Internet, not just through a browser but also from within your own program

- Managing user preferences

- Playing sounds and movies

Some developers talk in terms of "using a framework" — but in reality, your code doesn't use the framework so much as the framework uses your code. Your code provides the functions that the framework accesses; the framework needs your code to become an app that does something other than start up, display a blank window, and then end. This perspective makes figuring out how to work with a framework much easier.

If this seems too good to be true, well, okay, it is — all that complexity (and convenience) comes at a cost. It can be really difficult to get your head around the whole thing and know exactly where (and how) to add your app's functionality to the functionality that the framework supplies. That's where design patterns, which I discuss next, come in. Understanding the design patterns behind the frameworks gives you a way of thinking about a framework — especially UIKit because it based on the MVC design pattern— that doesn't make your head explode.

Using Design Patterns

When it comes to iPhone app development, the UIKit framework does a lot of the heavy lifting for you. That's all well and good, but working with that framework is a little more complicated than just letting it do its work. The framework is designed around certain programming paradigms, also known as *design patterns*. The design pattern is a model that your own code must be consistent with.

To understand how to take best advantage of the power of the framework — or (better put) how the framework objects want to use your code best — you need to understand design patterns. If you don't understand them or if you try to work around them because you're sure that you have a "better" way of doing things, your job will actually be much more difficult. (Developing software can be hard enough, so making your job more difficult is definitely something you want to avoid.) Getting a handle on the basic design patterns that the framework uses and expects will help you develop an app that makes the best use of the framework. This means doing the least amount of work in the shortest amount of time.

The design patterns can help you to understand not only how to structure your code but also how the framework itself is structured. They describe relationships and interactions between classes or objects, as well as how responsibilities should be distributed among classes so that the iPhone does what you want it to do. In programming terms, a design pattern is a commonly used template that gives you a consistent way to get a particular task done.

The iOS design patterns

To develop an iPhone app, you need to be comfortable with the following basic design patterns:

- ✓ Model-View-Controller (MVC)
- ✓ Delegation
- ✓ Block Objects
- ✓ Target-Action
- ✓ Managed Memory Model

Of these, the Model-View-Controller design pattern is the key to understanding how an iPhone app works and is the focus of the following section. I explain the remainder of the patterns as they're put to use in this book.

Another basic design pattern exists as well: Threads and Concurrency. This pattern enables you to execute tasks concurrently (including the use of Grand Central Dispatch, that aiding-and-abetting feature introduced in OS X Snow Leopard for ramping up processing speed) and is way beyond the scope of this book.

The Model-View-Controller (MVC) design pattern

The iOS frameworks are object oriented. An easy way to understand what that really means is to think about a team working in an office. The work that needs to get done is divided up and assigned to individual team members (in this case, objects). Each team member has a job and works with other team members to get things done. What's more, a good team member doesn't care how other members do their work, just that they do it according to the agreed upon division of labor. Likewise, an object in object-oriented programming takes care of its own business and doesn't care what the object in the virtual cubicle next door is doing, as long as it will do what it is supposed to do when asked to do it.

Object-oriented programming was originally developed to make code more maintainable, reusable, extensible, and understandable by encapsulating all the functionality behind well-defined interfaces. The actual details of how something works (as well as its data) are hidden, which makes modifying and extending an application much easier.

Great — so far — but a pesky question still plagues programmers:

Exactly how do you decide on the objects and what each one does?

Sometimes the answer to that question is pretty easy — just use the real world as a model. (Eureka!) In the RoadTrip app, for example, some of the classes of model objects are `Trip`, `Events`, `Destination`, and so on. But when it comes to a generic program structure, how *do* you decide what the objects should be? That may not be so obvious.

The MVC pattern is a well-established way to group application functions into objects. Variations of it have been around at least since the early days of Smalltalk, one of the very first object-oriented languages. The MVC is a high-level pattern — it addresses the architecture of an application and classifies objects according to the general roles they play in an application.

The MVC pattern creates, in effect, a miniature universe for the application, populated with three kinds of objects. It also specifies roles and responsibilities for all three types of objects and specifies the way they're supposed to interact with each other. To make things more concrete (that is, to keep your head from exploding), imagine a big, beautiful, 60-inch, flat-screen TV. Here's the gist:

- **Model objects:** These objects together comprise the content "engine" of your app. They contain the app's data and logic — making your app more than just a pretty face. In the RoadTrip application, for example, the model maintains a list of events and sights, as well as the name and location of the destination and a background image to use.

  You can think of the *model* (which may be one object or several that interact) as a particular television program, one that, quite frankly, does not give a hoot about what TV set it is being shown on.

  In fact, the model shouldn't give a hoot. Even though it owns its data, it should have no connection to the user interface and should be blissfully ignorant about what is being done with its data.

- **View objects:** These objects display things on the screen and respond to user actions. Pretty much anything you can see is a kind of view object — the window and all the controls, for example. Your views know how to display information they receive from the model object and how to get any input from the user the model may need. But the view itself should know nothing about the model. It may handle a request to display some events, but it doesn't bother itself with what that request means.

You can think of the *view* as a television screen that doesn't care about what program it is showing or what channel you just selected.

The UIKit framework provides many different kinds of views, as you find out in the section "Working with Windows and Views," later in this chapter.

If the view knows nothing about the model, and the model knows nothing about the view, how do you get data and other notifications to pass from one to the other? To get that conversation started (Model: "I've just updated my data." View: "Hey, give me something to display," for example), you need the third element in the MVC triumvirate, the controller.

✏ **Controller objects:** These objects connect the application's view objects to its model objects. They supply the view objects with what they need to display (getting it from the model) and also provide the model with user input from the view.

You can think of the *controller* as the circuitry that pulls the show off of the cable and then sends it to the screen or requests a particular pay-per-view show.

The basic application architecture the looks like Figure 4-8.

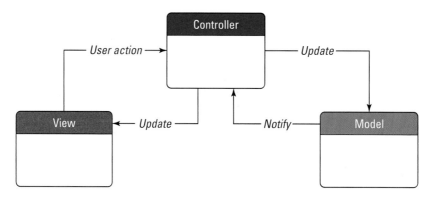

Figure 4-8: The model view controller.

When you think about your application in terms of Model, View, and Controller objects, the UIKit framework starts to make sense. Understanding the framework this way also begins to lift the fog hanging over where to make at least part of your application-specific behavior go. Before you delve into that topic, however, you need to know a little more about the classes that the UIKit provides and that implement the MVC design pattern — windows, views, and view controllers.

Working with Windows and Views

iPhone apps have a single window, so you won't find separate document windows for displaying content. When your application is running — even though other apps may be hibernating or running in the background — your app's interface takes over the entire screen.

Looking out the window

The single window that you see displayed on the iPhone is an instance of the UIWindow class. This window is created at launch time, either programmatically by you or automatically by UIKit when you use a storyboard. In general, after you create the Window object (that is, if you create it instead of having it done for you), you never really have to think about it again.

A user can't directly close or manipulate an iPhone window. It is your app that programmatically manages the window.

Although your application never creates more than one window at a time, iOS can support additional windows on top of your window. The system status bar is one example. You can also display alerts on top of your window by using the supplied Alert views.

Figure 4-9 shows the window layout on the iPhone for the for the Map view in the RoadTrip app.

Admiring the view

In an iPhone app world, view objects are responsible for the view functionality in the Model-View-Controller architecture. A *view* is a rectangular area on the screen (on top of a window). Your custom content appears between the upper and lower bars shown in Figure 4-9.

In the UIKit framework, windows are really a special kind of view, but for the purpose of this discussion, I'm referring to views that sit on top of the window.

What views do

Views are the main way for your app to interact with a user. This interaction happens in two ways:

✔ **Views display content.** This happens, for example, by making drawing and animation happen on-screen. In essence, the view object displays the data from the model object.

✔ **Views handle touch events.** They respond when the user touches a button, for example. Handling touch events is part of a *responder chain* (which I explain in Chapter 7).

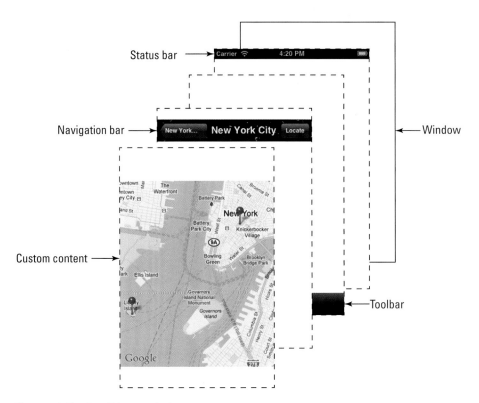

Figure 4-9: The RoadTrip app windows.

The view hierarchy

Views and subviews create a view hierarchy. You have two ways of looking at it (no pun intended this time): visually (how the user perceives it) and pro-grammatically (how you create it). You must be clear about the differences or you'll find yourself in a state of confusion that resembles the subway at rush hour.

Looking at it visually, the window is at the base of this hierarchy with a *Content view* on top of it (a transparent view that fills the window's Content rectangle). The Content view displays information as well as allows the user to interact with the application, using (preferably standard) user-interface items such as text fields, buttons, toolbars, and tables.

In your program, that relationship is different. The Content view is added to the window view as a *subview*.

- Views added to the Content view become *subviews* of it.
- Views added to the Content view become the *superviews* of any views added to them.
- A view can have one (and only one) superview and zero or more subviews.

It seems counterintuitive, but a subview is displayed *on top of* its parent view (that is, on top of its superview). Think about this relationship as containment: A superview *contains* its subviews. Figure 4-10 shows an example of a view hierarchy.

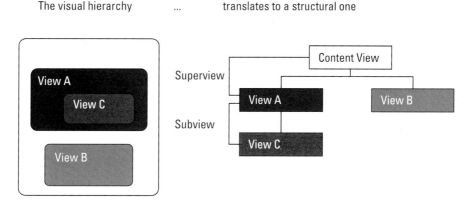

Figure 4-10: The view hierarchy is both visual and structural.

Controls — such as buttons, text fields, and so on — are actually view subclasses that become subviews. So are any other display areas that you may specify. The view must manage its subviews, as well as resize itself with respect to its superviews. Fortunately, much of what the view must do is already coded for you. The UIKit framework supplies the code that defines view behavior.

The view hierarchy also plays a key role in both drawing and event handling. I explain event handling in Chapter 7.

You create or modify a view hierarchy whenever you add a view to another view, either programmatically or with the help of the Interface Builder. The UIKit framework automatically handles all the relationships associated with the view hierarchy.

Developers typically gloss over this visual-versus-programmatic-view-hierarchy stuff when starting out — and without understanding these concepts, it is really difficult to get a handle on what's going on.

The kinds of views you use

The UIView class defines the basic properties of a view, and you may be able to use it as is — as you'll do in the in the main screen of the RoadTrip app — by simply adding some controls.

This screen acts as an "introduction" to the application, as you can see in Figure 4-11. Here you provide a way for the user to decide where he or she wants to going using the Destination button. You also allow the user to take a test drive. (Later in the book, I show you how to animate the car so that it leisurely "drives" to the other side of the screen, turns around, drives back, and then turns around one more time so that it's back to where it started on the screen.) This screen is also where you provide a way for the user to tailor the app's settings to his or her preferences. Although you won't be doing it here, you can also provide something like an Info button that would bring up a modal dialogue to allow the user to set program relevant preferences (such as sound and so on).

Figure 4-11: A view with controls.

The UIKit framework also provides you with a number of other views that are subclassed from `UIView`. These views implement the kinds of things that you as a developer need to do in the user interface.

It's important to think about the view objects that are part of the `UIKit` framework. When you use an object such as a `UISlider` or `UIButton`, your slider or button behaves just like a slider or button in any other iPhone app. This enables the consistency in appearance and behavior across apps that users expect. (For more about why this kind of consistency is one of the characteristics of a great app, see Chapter 1.)

Container views

Container views are a technical (Apple) term for content views that do more than just lie there on the screen and display your controls and other content.

The `UIScrollView` class, for example, adds scrolling without your having to do any work. Most of the time, they just do their thing in the background (as part of other views you use, for example, Table views), and I don't explain any more about them in this book because you won't need to use or manage them explicitly.

`UITableView` inherits this scrolling capability from `UIScrollView` and adds the ability to display lists and respond to the selections of an item in that list. Think of the Contacts application (and a host of others). `UITableView` is one of the primary navigation views on the iPhone.

Table views are used a lot in iPhone applications to do two things:

- **Display hierarchal data:** For an example, think of the iPod application, which gives you a list of albums and, if you select one, a list of songs.

- **Act as a table of contents:** Now, think of the Settings application, which gives you a list of applications that you can set preferences for. When you select one of those applications from the list, it takes you to a view that lists what preferences you're able to set as well as a way to set them.

In the RoadTrip app, the *List* views — such as the ones shown earlier in Figure 4-3 left and right — are Table views.

Another container view, the `UIToolbar` class, contains button-like controls, which you find everywhere on the iPhone. In the Mail app, for example, you tap an icon on the bottom toolbar to respond to an e-mail. In RoadTrip, you find them at the bottom of the Map view (refer to Figure 4-6) to allow you to decide on how you want the map displayed.

Controls

Controls are the fingertip-friendly graphics that are used extensively in a typical application's user interface. Controls are actually subclasses of the

UIControl superclass, a subclass of the UIView class. They include touchable items such as buttons, sliders, and switches, as well as text fields in which you enter data.

Controls make heavy use of the Target-Action design pattern, which you get to use with the three buttons in Figure 4-11.

Display views

Think of display views as controls that look good but don't really do anything except, well, look good. These include the following: UIImageViews used to display images (which you see in the background in Figure 4-11, for example); UILabel, which displays the *Pick a place, any place* text you use in the Destinations view in Figure 4-3; UIProgressView; and UIActivityIndicatorView. I add an activity indicator to the views where I download data (refer to the Events view shown in Figure 4-5, for example).

Text and Web views

Text and *Web views* provide a way to display formatted text in your application. The UITextView class supports the display and editing of multiple lines of text in a scrollable area. The UIWebView class provides a way to display HTML content. These views can be used as the main view, or as a subview of a another view. You encounter UIWebView in the RoadTrip app in as Weather views. UIWebView is also the primary way to include graphics and formatted text in text display views.

The views that display content — such as the views shown previously in Figures 4-4 and 4-5 — are *Web* views, for some good practical reasons.

First and foremost, some of the views must be updated regularly. *Web views*, in that context, are the perfect solution; they make it easy to access data from a central repository on the Internet. (Client/server is alive and well!)

As for other benefits of Web views, keep in mind that real-time access isn't always necessary — sometimes it's perfectly fine to store some data on the iPhone. It turns out that Web views can easily display formatted data that's locally stored, which is very handy.

Finally, I use Web views for the simple reason that they can access websites. If users want more detailed weather information, they can get to the ten-day forecast by simply touching a link.

Alert views and action sheets

Alert views and *action sheets* present a message to the user, along with buttons that allow the user to respond to the message. Alert views and action sheets are similar in function but look and behave differently from one another. For example, the UIAlertView class displays a blue alert box that pops up on the screen, and the `UIActionSheet` class displays a box that slides in from the bottom of the screen (see Figure 4-12).

I have you add an Alert view to inform the user when the Internet is not available in Chapter 9.

Figure 4-12: Users need the Internet alert, so be sure to include it.

Navigation views

Tab bars and Navigation bars which I explain in Chapter 5, work in conjunction with view controllers to provide tools for navigating in your app. Normally, you don't need to create a `UITabBar` or `UINavigationBar` directly — it's easier to use Interface Builder or configure these views through a Tab bar or navigation controller, respectively.

The window

The *window* provides the surface for drawing content and is the root container for all other views.

View Controllers — the Main Storyboard Player

Early in this chapter, I provide an overview of the storyboard (the white board, so to speak, on which you lay out the flow of the elements, or design pattern, of your application. In this book, the example application developed throughout — RoadTrip — uses the Model-View-Controller (MVC) design pattern, and *view controllers* implement the controller component of that design pattern. These controller objects contain the code that connects the app's view objects to its model objects. Whenever the view needs to display something, the view controller goes out and gets what the view needs from the model. Similarly, view controllers respond to controls in your Content view and may do things like tell the model to update its data (when the user adds or changes text in a text field, for example), compute something (the current value of, say, your U.S. dollars in British pounds), or change the view being displayed (like when the user presses the Detail Disclosure button on the iPod application to find out more about a song).

View controllers, as you can see in Figure 4-13, are the objects that control what is displayed and that respond to user actions. They are the heart and soul of the storyboard.

As I explain in more detail in Chapter 6, a view controller is often the (target) object that responds to the on-screen controls. The Target-Action mechanism is what enables the view controller to be aware of any changes in the view, which can then be transmitted to the model. For example, Figure 4-14 shows what happens when the user taps the Events entry in the RoadTrip app to check out what's going on.

Imagine that an iPhone user starts the RoadTrip app. When the user taps the Travel button, a new view slides into place that displays a Table view, which in turn displays New York. (The Table view got that name from the model.) The user may tap a button that requests events. The Events controller is then launched and sends a message to the appropriate method in the model to get the events. The model object returns a list of URLs and so on. The controller then delivers that information to the view, which promptly displays the information to the user.

The sequence of events is as follows:

1. A message is sent to that view's view controller to handle the request.

2. The view controller's method interacts with the `Trip` model object.

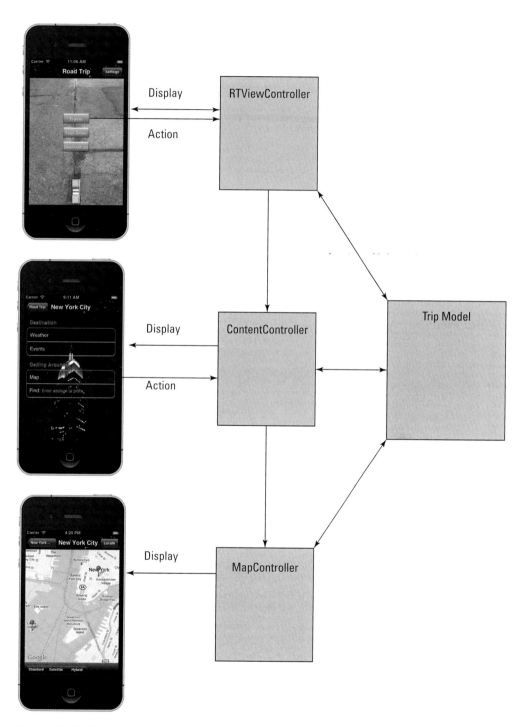

Figure 4-13: It's all about the view controller.

3. The model object processes the request from the user for the current events.

4. The model object sends the data back to the view controller.

5. The view controller creates a new view to present the information.

View controllers have other vital iPhone responsibilities as well, such as the following:

- **Managing a set of views**: This includes creating them or flushing them from memory during low-memory situations.

- **Responding to a change in the device's orientation:** An example is responding to a change from landscape to portrait orientation by resizing the its views to match the new orientation.

- **Creating a Modal (not model) view:** A Modal view is a child window that displays a dialog that requires the user to do something (tap the Yes or Cancel button, for example) before returning to the application.

You use a Modal view to ensure that the user has paid attention to the implications of an action (for example, "Are you *sure* you want to delete all your contacts?"). The Destination view on the left side of Figure 4-8, shown previously, is a Modal view.

View controllers are also typically the objects that serve as delegates and data sources for Table views (more about those in Chapter 18) and other kinds of framework views.

In addition to the base `UIViewController` class, UIKit includes the following: subclasses such as `UITabBarController` (to manage the Tab bar); `UITableViewController` (which you use to manage Table views); `UINavigationController`, which implements navigation back and forth between view controllers); `UIPageViewController` (to allow users to navigate between view controllers using the specified transition); `UIImagePickerController` (to access the camera and Photo library on the iPhone; and `UISpiltViewController` (used on the iPad).

Even if you're developing a graphics-intensive app, you'll want to use a view controller just to manage a single view and auto-rotate it when the device's orientation changes.

As I mention earlier, view controllers are responsible not only for providing the data for a view to display, but also for responding to user input and navigation.

Using naming conventions

When creating your own classes, it's a good idea to follow a couple of standard framework-naming conventions:

- Class names (such as `View`) should start with a capital letter.

- The names of methods (such as `view DidLoad`) should start with a lowercase letter.

- The names of instance variables (such as `frame`) should start with a lowercase letter and additional "words" within the name should start with an uppercase letter (`rootViewController`).

When you follow these conventions, you can tell from the name what something actually is. A few more such conventions are good to know, and I explain them as they arise in the course of the book.

What About the Model?

As this chapter shows (and as you will continue to discover), much of the functionality you need in an application is already in the frameworks.

But when it comes to the model objects, you're on your own for the most part. You need to design and create model objects to hold the data and carry out the logic. In the RoadTrip app, for example, you create a `Trip` object that owns the data and logic and uses other objects to perform some of the actions it needs.

I talk about the model and model classes more in Chapter 12.

You may find classes in the framework that help you get the nuts and bolts of the model working. But the actual content and specific functionality are up to you. As for actually implementing model objects, you find out how to do that in Chapter 12. There are some data-related classes that can help.

To implement the structure that enables me to include several destinations in the RoadTrip app, I need to have the data. I use *property lists* (XML files, in other words) to take care of that because they're well suited for the job, and (more important), support for them is built in to the iPhone frameworks.

I tell you more about property lists in Chapter 12.

iOS now includes a `UIDocument` class for managing the data associated with user documents. If you are implementing a document-based application, you can use this class to reduce the amount of work you must do to manage your document data. If you are implementing an application that supports iCloud storage, the use of document objects makes the job of storing files in iCloud much easier. I don't cover the `UIDocument` class in this book, but I do explain on how to use it to use it with iCloud in a forthcoming book about cloud development.

It's Not That Neat

It would be nice if everything fit neatly into Model, View, or Controller (not to mention amazing), but it doesn't work that way.

There is one other kind of class you really need to know about.

The `UIApplication` class handles routing of incoming user events, dispatches action messages from controls, and numerous other basic plumbing functions that are not the responsibilities of a Model, View, or Controller. It typically works with an *application delegate,* a piece of code that allows you to customize how your application responds to events such as application launch, low-memory warnings, and application termination. The app delegate (as it's often referred to) is also the place you'll create your model. I explain the application delegate in Chapter 7.

Taking a Look at Other Frameworks

So far, all of the things I have talked about are in the UIKit framework Its purpose is to provide all the classes that an application needs to construct and manage its user interface, but quite a few other frameworks are put into play as well.

For example, the template automatically adds the Foundation and Core Graphics frameworks.

The Foundation framework

The Foundation framework is similar to the UIKit framework in that it defines general-purpose classes. The difference is that whereas the UIKit has the classes that implement the user interface, the Foundation framework handles the most of the rest of what you need in your app.

For example, it defines basic object behavior, memory management, notifications, internationalization, and localization.

The Foundation framework also provides object wrappers or equivalents for numeric values, strings, and collections. It also provides utility classes for accessing underlying system entities and services, such as ports, threads, and file systems as well as networking date and time management. This framework deals with just about everything else you need to build an application that is not in the user interface.

The Core Graphics framework

The Core Graphics framework contains the interfaces for the Quartz 2D drawing API and is the same advanced, vector-based drawing engine that is used in Mac OS X. It provides support for path-based drawing, anti-aliased rendering, gradients, images, colors, coordinate-space transformations, and PDF document creation, display, and parsing. Although the API is C based, it uses object-based abstractions to make things easier for you.

Even more frameworks

Beside the UIKit Foundation and Core Graphics frameworks, you use a handful of others in this book's example application as well as in your own application. They are as follows:

- **MapKit:** The Map Kit framework lets you embed a fully functional map interface into your application. The map support provided by this framework includes many of the features normally found in the Maps application.

- **AVFoundation:** The AV Foundation framework provides an Objective-C interface for playing back audio with the control needed by most applications. The AV Foundation framework provides an Objective-C interface for managing and playing audio-visual media in your iOS application.

- **AudioToolbox:** The Audio Toolbox framework contains the APIs that provide application-level services — for playing sounds, for example.

- **Media Player:** The Media Player framework provides basic functionality for playing movie, music, audio podcast, and audio book files, as well as to the iPod Library.

- **SystemConfiguration:** The System Configuration framework contains interfaces for determining the network configuration of a device.

- **CoreLocation:** The Core Location framework provides location data to support functionality such as social networking. It also include classes to do both forward and reverse geocoding (which I explain in Chapter 17).

You can find many, many more frameworks for your apps in iOS Technology Overview Appendix B: iOS Frameworks which you can find in the iOS Developer Library (http://developer.apple.com/library/ios/navigation/index.html). Be advised, if you want to be able to do something, there is probably a framework to support it.

Understanding How the MVC Model Is Expressed in the Project

As one might expect, when you create an Xcode project, classes added to the project by the template correspond to the Model View Controller design pattern.

If you look carefully, you can see how the MVC model is expressed in a project. In the project navigator, you see you see `RTViewController` .h and .m files (this is the what the main view controller is named), and `RTAppDelegate` .h and .m files.

The interface (.h file) contains the class declaration and defines the methods and properties associated with the class. But although it has traditionally also included the instance variables, as you will see, you include them in the implementation file instead to keep them away from prying eyes. (You can find more on hiding the instance variables in Chapter 7.)

The implementation (.m file) contains the actual code for the methods of the class and includes your instance variables.

The `RTViewController`, corresponds to the controllers I explain in "View Controllers — the Main Storyboard Player," earlier in this chapter.

But where are the classes that correspond to the views?

To find out, select the mainStoryboard file in the Project navigator and you see the view controller in the dock. Each view controller in a storyboard file manages a single scene. Select the disclosure triangle to expand the view controller and you see its view in Figure 4-14.

When you click the view controller in the dock you see a blue line around the window to represent the view controller. The cube icon that represents the view controller is highlighted.

If you can't see the dock, you can use the Hide/Show Dock control, shown in Figure 4-14. You can also zoom in and out of a storyboard by double-clicking in the Interface Builder Editor or using the zoom control shown in Figure 4-14.

Now click the view in the Dock, and you'll see the a display of view itself — waiting for you to add all sorts of interesting images and controls (which you do in the next chapter). You can see that in Figure 4-15.

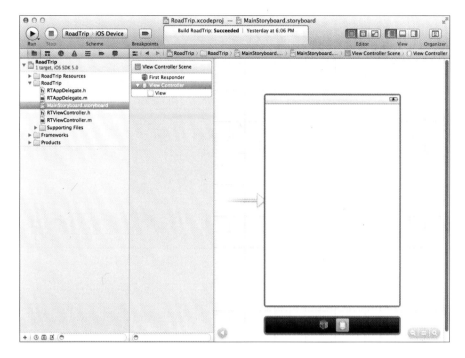

Figure 4-14: The view controller.

So now that you have controllers and views, what about models? Well, they are not there . . . yet. But I explain a great deal about model classes and how to add them in Chapter 12.

You can also see some of the other parts of the application infrastructure I mention earlier in the Project navigator. The `RTAppDelegate` .h and .m files in the Project navigation area correspond to the App Delegate.

The storyboard Dock, it turns out, also gives you a good view of the application infrastructure.

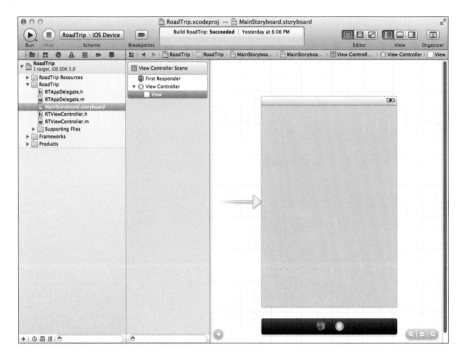

Figure 4-15: The view in the storyboard.

The three icons (the cube, circle, and square) arranged vertically in the Dock act as a table of contents for each scene file.

✏ **First Responder:** This object is the first entry in an app's dynamically constructed responder chain (a term I explain along with more about the application infrastructure at run time in Chapter 7) and is the object with which the user is currently interacting. If, for example, the user taps a text field to enter some data, the First Responder would then become the Text Field object.

Because the responder chain of an application cannot be determined at design time, the First Responder proxy acts as a stand-in target for any action messages that need to be directed at the application's responder chain.

Although you might use the First Responder mechanism quite a bit in your apps, you have to do nothing to manage it. It's automatically set and maintained by the UIKit framework.

You'll also see the view controller and view (which I just explained) in the storyboard Dock.

Chapter 5

Creating the RoadTrip User Interface Using the Storyboard

....

In This Chapter

▷ Understanding how storyboards work

▷ Working in the Utility area

▷ Understanding and adding navigation controllers

▷ Using Interface Builder to add objects to your storyboard

....

*I*f you've read the preceding chapters, you have the foundation for understanding the tools you need to build an app, with particular focus on the example app developed in this book. Now you're ready to find out how to add a user interface to your app via the storyboard.

In this chapter, I show you how to add items to the `RTViewController`'s view using Interface Builder and the user interface objects available to you in the Library pane in the Utility area . I also show you how to embed the `RTViewController` in a navigation controller so that the user can navigate back and forth in your application.

Creating Your User Interface in the Storyboard

In the Project navigator, select the `MainStoryboard,storyboard` file to see the view controller in the Dock. Each view controller in a storyboard file manages a single scene. Select the disclosure triangle to expand the view controller and you see its view.

If you can't see the Dock, you can use the Hide/Show Dock control in Figure 5-1. You can also zoom in and out of a storyboard by double-clicking in the storyboard canvas, or using the zoom control in Figure 5-1. The = sign returns the storyboard to full size, which is the only way it is editable.

To add user interface elements, select the View in the view controller in the Dock.

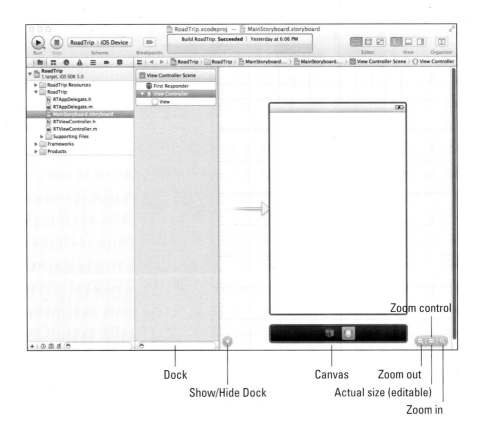

Dock

Show/Hide Dock

Canvas

Zoom control

Zoom out

Actual size (editable)

Zoom in

Figure 5-1: The Initial MainStoryboard.

It's about the view controller

The editor that is launched when you select a storyboard file in the Project navigator is Interface Builder, and you use Interface Builder to create storyboard files for your application. Most applications need only one storyboard file, but you can create multiple storyboard files if you want. Every storyboard file has a view controller known as the *initial view controller*. This view controller represents the entry point into the storyboard. For example, in your application's main storyboard file, the initial view controller would be the first view controller presented by your application.

The view controller is the big kahuna here, and each view controller in a storyboard file manages a single scene. For iPhone applications, a scene manages one screen's worth of content, but for iPad applications, the content from multiple scenes can be onscreen simultaneously. To add new scenes to your storyboard file, all you have to do is drag a view controller from the library to the storyboard canvas. You can then add controls and views to the view controller's view.

Besides the ability to layout your application as a whole, storyboards also reduces the amount of code you have to write.

For example, when you want to create a transition from one view controller to another, all you need to do is Control-click a button or table view cell and drag to the view controller you want displayed. Dragging between view controllers creates a *segue*, which appears in Interface Builder as a configurable object. Segues support all the same types of transitions available in UIKit, such as navigation and modal transitions. A segue also enables you to define custom transitions.

I explain more about segues and view controller transitions in Chapter 11, when you add more scenes and segues to the RoadTrip app.

Using Interface Builder to add the user elements

As an editor, Interface Builder enables you to create a storyboard by enabling you lay out your user interface graphically in each view controller (as well as create the storyboard). You can use it to design your app's user interface and then save what you've done as a resource file, which is then loaded into your app at runtime. This resource file is then used to automatically create the window and your app's view controllers, as well as all your views and controls.

If you don't want to use Interface Builder, you can also create your objects programmatically — creating views and view controllers and even things like buttons and labels using your very own application code. I show you an example of creating objects programmatically in Chapter 14.

So how do you actually get those cute little controls into the view that lives in the view controller scene? For that, you use another area of the workspace — the Utility Area.

As I explain in Chapter 2, you use the View selector in the toolbar to display or hide the Utility area. The Utility area is an optional area in the right side of the Workspace window. To hide or show the Utility area, click the right view selector button in the Workspace toolbar. The view selector allows you to open and close areas of the window. Selecting one of the button toggles between hiding and showing an area. In Figure 5-2, I'm using the view selector to open the Utility area.

Figure 5-2: The view selector.

When you hover your mouse pointer over a toolbar button, a tool tip describes its function.

In Figure 5-3, I showed the Utility area by selecting the Utility area in the toolbar's view selector. I have resized the library window and also selected the icon view in the Library pane's view selector (the right segmented control selection at the top right of the Library pane). Personally, I find that easier to work with.

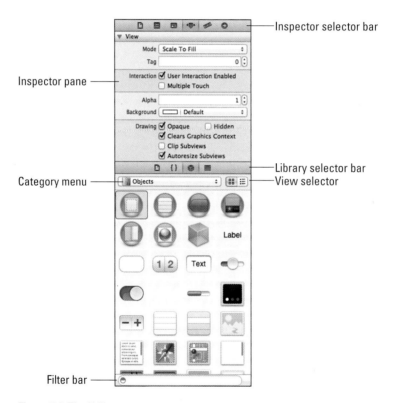

Figure 5-3: The Utility area.

As you can see, this area includes two panes, the top one for Quick Help and other inspectors, and the bottom one for libraries of resources.

Working within the Utility Area

The Utility area consists of the Inspector and Library *panes* and their corresponding Inspector and Library *selector bars*. You use the utility area to view and access Quick Help and other inspectors, and to use ready-made resources in your project. You use both the Inspector and Library panes in this chapter.

Inspector and Quick Help pane

A selection in the *Inspector selector* shown in Figure 5-4 selects an inspector. (A Navigator or a Content editor selection determines the available inspectors.)

Figure 5-4: The Inspector selector.

Utility area inspectors perform a variety of tasks. Following is a list of important inspectors and what you use them for.

- ✔ **File inspector (first button):** View and manage file metadata such as its name, type, and path.

- ✔ **Quick Help (second button):** View (applicable) details about a what has been selected in an Editor such as an abstract or concise description, where and how it is declared, and selection-based information such as its scope, the parameters it takes, its platform and architecture availability, references, sample code and so on. The following selections are supported:

    • **Symbols**, in the Source editor

    • **Interface objects**, in Interface Builder

    • **Build settings**, in the Project editor

Additional inspectors are available in some editors; for example, Interface Builder offers these:

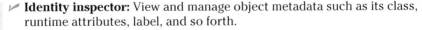

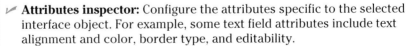

- ✔ **Identity inspector:** View and manage object metadata such as its class, runtime attributes, label, and so forth.

- ✔ **Attributes inspector:** Configure the attributes specific to the selected interface object. For example, some text field attributes include text alignment and color, border type, and editability.

- ✔ **Size inspector:** Specify characteristics such as the initial size and position, minimum and maximum sizes, and autosizing rules for an interface object.

- ✔ **Connections inspector:** View the outlets and actions for an interface object, make new connections, and delete existing connections.

Library pane

A selection in the *Library selector, shown in* Figure 5-5, in the Library pane selects a library of resources that you can use in your project.

Figure 5-5: The Library selector.

- **File templates:** Templates for the common types of files you find using the New file menu. To add a file of that type to your drag it from the library to the Project navigator.

- **Code snippets:** Short pieces of source code for use in your application. To use one, drag it directly into your source code file.

- **Objects:** Interface objects that make up your user interface. To add one to a view drag it directly into your storyboard or nib file in the Interface Builder editor.

- **Media files:** Graphics, icons, and sound files. To use one, drag it directly to your storyboard or nib file in the Interface Builder editor.

You can enter text into the text field in the filter bar (at the bottom of the Library pane) to restrict the items displayed in the selected library.

Understanding the Navigation Controller

Although view controllers are the major participants in a storyboard, a background player that is also of consequence is the navigation controller.

If you look at the views of the RoadTrip application described in Chapter 4, you see that as the user moves from one view to another, a Back button is prominently displayed. Having a Back button is, of course, a requirement for any application if you want the user to be able to navigate through the app's functionality.

Apple has built this ability into the iOS architecture and as an integral part of the view controller architecture as personified in the navigation controller (okay, I know it is not a person, but you get the idea).

A navigation controller is a container view controller that enables the user to navigate back and forth between view controllers. A navigation controller is an instance of the `UINavigationController` class, which is a class you use as is and do not subclass. The methods of this class provide support for managing a stack-based collection of custom view controllers. This stack represents the path taken by the user through the application, with the bottom of the stack reflecting the starting point and the top of the stack reflecting the user's current position in the application.

Although the navigation controller's primary job is to act as a manager of other view controllers, it also manages a few views. Specifically, it manages a *Navigation bar* that displays information about the user's current location in the data hierarchy, a Back button for navigating to previous screens, and any custom controls the current view controller needs.

As you can see in Figure 5-6, when the user taps a button in the RTController's view, or an entry in a table view, the view controller (courtesy of the storyboard) pushes the next view controller on to the stack. The new controller's view slides into place, and the Navigation bar items are updated appropriately. When the user taps events in the Content view, the same thing happens, with the Event controller sliding into view. When the user taps the Back button in the Navigation bar, the current view controller pops off the stack, that view slides off the screen, and the user finds himself back in the previous view.

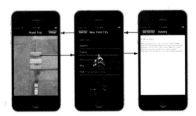

Figure 5-6: An example of RoadTrip application navigation.

The navigation controller maintains a stack of view controllers, one for each of the views displayed, starting with the *root view controller*. The root view controller is the very first view controller that the navigation controller pushes onto its stack when a user launches the application. It remains active until the user selects the next view to look at. When you are done adding the navigation controller, the root view controller will be the RTViewController that is created for you when you choose the Single View application template.

If you had chosen the Master-Detail Application template, the MasterView Controller would have already had the navigation controller set up. But that would have meant that your application would have opened with a Table view. Although that might be what you want in your application, I often get questions from readers and students on how to create an application that opens with a view with controls, from which you can launch a Table view or anything else.

A *stack* is a commonly used data structure that works on the principle of "last in, first out." Imagine an ideal boarding scenario for an airplane: Passengers would be seated in the last seat in the last row, and they'd board the plane in back-to-front order until they got to the first seat in the first row, which would contain the seat for the last person to board. When the plane reached its destination, everyone would deplane (is that really a word?) in the reverse order. That last person on — the person in row one seat one — would be the first person off.

A computer stack works on the same concept. Adding an object is called a *push* — in this case, when you tap the Travel button, the view controller for the that view is pushed onto the stack. Removing an object is called a *pop* — touching the back button pops the view controller for the view being displayed. When you pop an object off the stack, it's always the last one you pushed onto it. The controller that was there before the push is still there and now becomes the active one. In this case, it's the root view controller.

Navigation bars enable a user to navigate the hierarchy. Here's what you need to know to make that work:

- The view below the Navigation bar presents the current level of the application.

- A Navigation bar includes a title for the current view.

- If the current view is lower in the hierarchy than the top level, a Back button appears on the left side of the bar; the user can tap it to return to the previous level. The text in the Back button tells the user what the previous level was.

- A Navigation bar may also have an Edit button on the right side — used to enter editing mode for the current view — or even custom buttons such as the Locate button, which is shown at the right in Chapter 4, Figure 4-6.

The Navigation bar for each level is managed by a navigation controller, as mentioned in the previous section.

Adding the Navigation Controller

To add a navigation controller to the storyboard, you should be in the Interface Builder editor. Make sure that the `MainStoryboard.storyboard` is selected in the Project navigator and that the view controller is selected.

Because I have limited space on a book page, I'm hiding the Navigation area, as you can see in Figure 5-7. (When I work on my large-screen monitor, I usually keep the Navigation area shown.)

Now, just choose Editor⇨Embed In⇨Navigation Controller, as shown in Figure 5-7. (There are a few other choices there, but I don't go into those here).

A navigation controller scene should now have been added, along with something called a *relationship* from UINavigationController to View Controller (in Figure 5-7, I have zoomed out to make this relationship visible). You can also hide the Dock using the Show/Hide Dock button for even more room and also hide the Navigation area, as I have done using the View sector (Figure 5-8) in the toolbar.

If you expand the navigation controller, you can see that it has a Navigation bar as well.

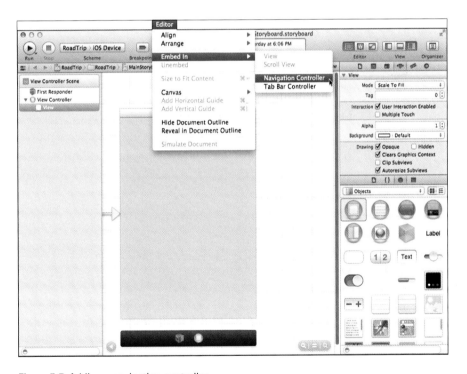

Figure 5-7: Adding a navigation controller.

Figure 5-8: Hiding the Navigation area.

As shown in Figure 5-9, a Navigation bar has also been added to the view controller.

Before I go any further, I want you to look at the navigation controller in the Attributes inspector, which I have selected in the Inspector selector bar in Figure 5-9. As you can see, the controller has properties that you can set using Interface Builder. To see those properties, you need to zoom to full size. Full size is the only time Interface Builder objects are editable.

Although you won't be setting any such properties here, remember that the Attributes inspector is the place where you will be setting properties of the controls and other view objects you add to the view. Also remember that almost all the properties you might set in Interface Builder can be set programmatically.

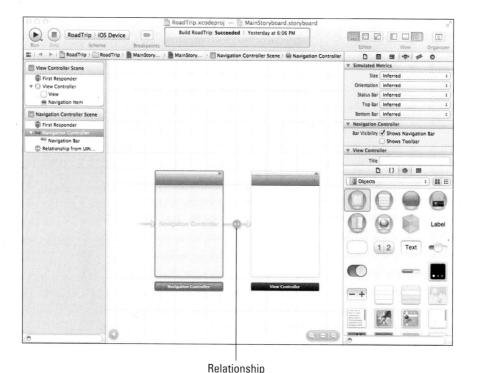

Relationship

Figure 5-9: The navigation controller added.

Adding an identifier to the view controller

In Figure 5-10, I zoomed in the Interface Builder editor view to full size, and then clicked on the view controller and then selected the Attributes inspector in the Inspector selector bar. I have entered Main in the Title and Identifier fields in the View Controller section. I have done that because if you want to do anything special with a view controller in a storyboard you need to be able to find it, and that is done using the Identifier. While you may not need an identifier for every view controller, it's a good idea to get in the habit of doing it just in case you do. The Title enables you to distinguish which view controller is which in the storyboard. You'll notice that in the Dock it now says View Controller – Main Scene.

Remember, though, what you type in a field is not really added until you press Return or click in another field.

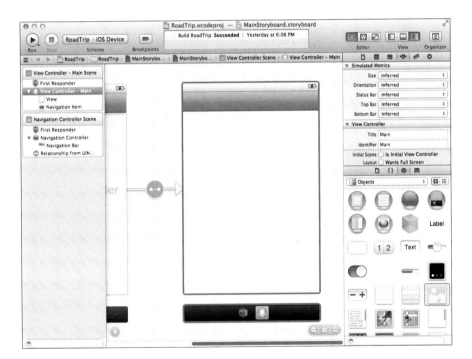

Figure 5-10: Adding a title and identifier.

Adding the User Interface Objects

At this point, I could continue building out my storyboard by adding more elements such as views (and segues, which I explain in Chapter 11). But by now I'm itching to really *do something*, which means get some actual objects into the storyboard. So it's time to add some of those now.

To add an object to the storyboard, select `MainStoryBoard.storyboard` in the Project editor to open Interface Builder. Select the view in the View Controller – Main Scene and then select the Attributes inspector in the Inspector selector bar.

The Attributes inspector enables you to set the object properties. For example, to change the color of the view's background, choose the background color from the Background pop-up menu. As you can see in Figure 5-11, Default is currently selected (a white background). But you can also select anything else in the list.

If you select Other or click in the color displayed in the Background field, you see the Color window (Figure 5-12).

As you can see, the toolbar at the top of the Color window gives you a number of options for selecting a color. These are the standard options available for choosing a color on the Mac, and I'll leave you to explore them on your own.

Although I know you need to know how to change the background color for a view, you aren't going to be doing that here. Instead you are going to add an image view.

The important thing to remember is that the view objects that you'll be using have *properties*, such as color, or a background image, or whether a user can interact with them — that is, respond to touches. These are generally set using the Attributes inspector in Interface Builder, or programmatically.

To add a background image, follow these steps:

1. **Scroll down in the Library window and drag an Image view from the library onto the view, as shown Figure 5-13.**

   An Image view is a view that used to display an image (see Chapter 4 for more on views).

   What you just did is add an Image view as a *subview* of the RoadTrip RTViewController's view, the one created for you by the template.

   If you click an object in the library, it will tell you what it is. It will also tell you what class it is, as you can see in Figure 5-14.

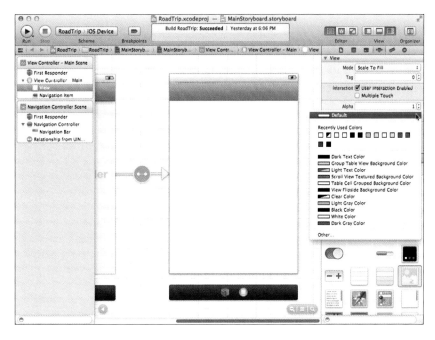

Figure 5-11: Selecting the background color.

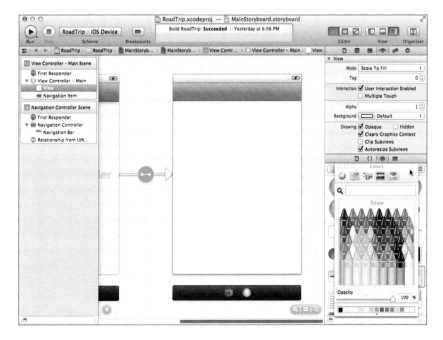

Figure 5-12: Pick a color.

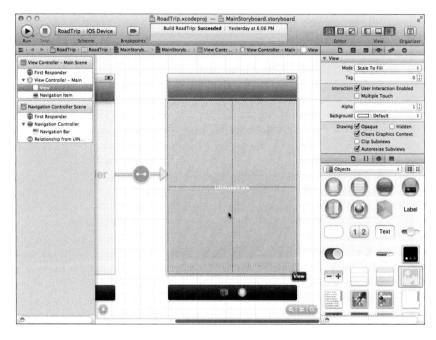

Figure 5-13: Adding an Image view.

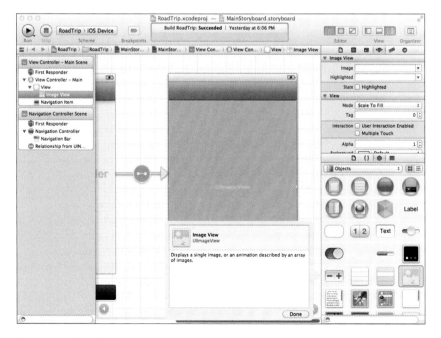

Figure 5-14: More Xcode context-based help.

Notice the blue lines displayed by Interface Builder in Figure 5-13. They're there to make it easy to center the image. Interface Builder also displays blue lines at the borders to help you conform to Apple User Interface Guidelines.

You can also add a horizontal and vertical guide to help you line things up by choosing Editor⇨Add Horizontal Guide or Editor⇨Add Vertical Guide, respectively.

Select the Image view in the view. Doing so changes what you see in the Attributes inspector. It now displays the attributes for the Image view.

2. **Using the Attribute inspector's Image drop-down menu, scroll down to select SeeTheUSA.**

   This adds the image you want to use to the Image view (see Figure 5-15).

   When you're done, you should see what is shown in Figure 5-16.

   The preferred format for the image is `.png`. Although most common image formats display correctly, Xcode automatically optimizes `.png` images at build time to make them the fastest and most efficient image type for use in iPhone applications.

   Drag in another Image view and place it as you see in Figure 5-17.

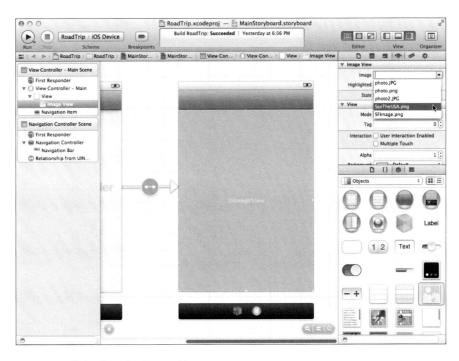

Figure 5-15: Selecting a background image.

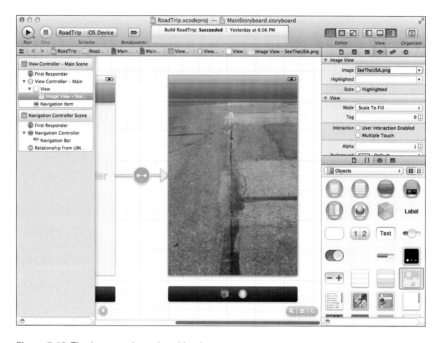

Figure 5-16: The image selected and in place.

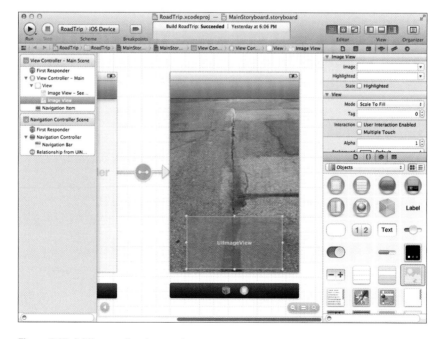

Figure 5-17: Adding another Image view.

3. **This time, select CarImage.png in the drop-down Image menu, choose Editor⇨Size to Fit Content, and place and size it as you see in Figure 5-18.**

   With the Image view selected, I have also chosen Editor ⇨ Add Horizontal Guide and Editor ⇨ Add Vertical Guide to help me position it.

   In Chapter 10, I show you how to animate the car so that it leisurely drives to the top of the screen, turns around, drives back, and then turns around one more time, returning to where it started.

   This is the vintage pink 1959 Cadillac Eldorado convertible my evil twin Skippy plans to drive cross country to New York. (The thought of driving it, much less parking it, in New York staggers the imagination.)

Now you can add the buttons for you need in the view.

1. **Select the Round Rect Button in the library and drag it into the view; then click the Attributes inspector button in the Inspector selector bar.**

   The things you set in the Attributes inspector are Objective-C *properties* that you can also set programmatically, as you do in Chapter 8.

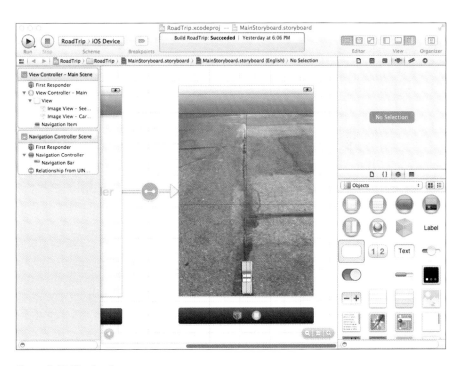

Figure 5-18: The family car.

As you can see in Figure 5-19, this button is set to type Rounded Rect on the Type pop-up menu in the Attributes inspector. In Figure 5-19, you can see what the button looks like in its default state configuration. Click the State Config pop-up menu under the Type pop-up menu to choose other configurations, such as Highlighted or Selected. You can then change the font, text color, shadow, background, and other attributes in the Attributes inspector for those states.

In this case, the attributes are all the same, but when you add your own button image, as I show you how to do next, you can use a different image for each state (you won't here, though).

This button, of course, being generic button, is remarkably unexciting. So I'm having you use an image for the button that I created. You will find the image in the Resources file that you downloaded and added to your project in Chapter 3.

2. **Choose Custom from the Type pop-up menu (Custom appears among the other standard button type choices), as I have in Figure 5-20.**

   You could add an image to the Rounded Rect Button, but doing so would simply place the image within the generic button. You want to replace it the generic button altogether in this case.

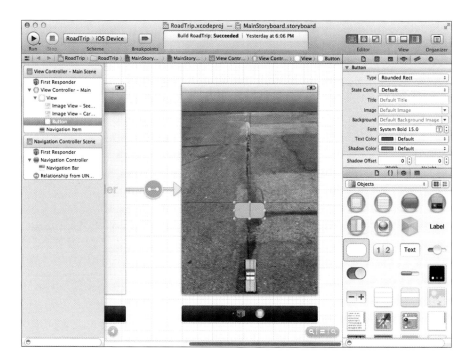

Figure 5-19: Adding a button.

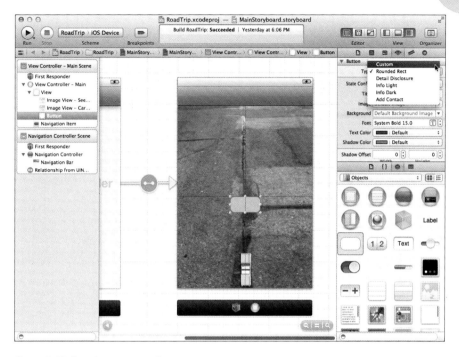

Figure 5-20: Creating a custom button.

TIP

When you choose Custom from the menu, the button disappears. Just keep it selected (it still is selectable if you can find it). If you do lose it, just select Button under the View in the Dock and you'll see the resize handles.

3. **In the Background drop-down menu, choose Button, as I have in Figure 5-21.**

So what is the difference between Background and Image in the Attributes inspector? When you choose Background, you are simply doing that — setting the image for the button. You still add the title and so on using the Attributes inspector. If you were to choose Image, you would have included the title as part of the image, and you would not have been able to add it in the inspector.

XCODE NAVIGATION

4. **Resize the button to 96 by 38 it using the resize handles, or select the Size inspector, as I have in Figure 5-22, and enter the width and height in the fields provided.**

You may have to re-center the button after you resize it.

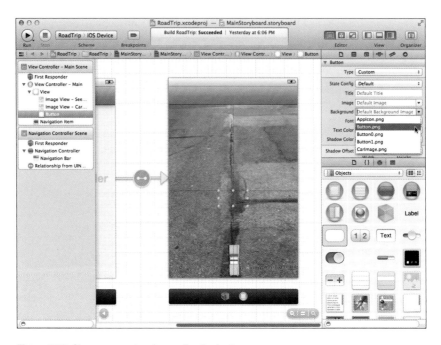

Figure 5-21: Choose a custom image for the button.

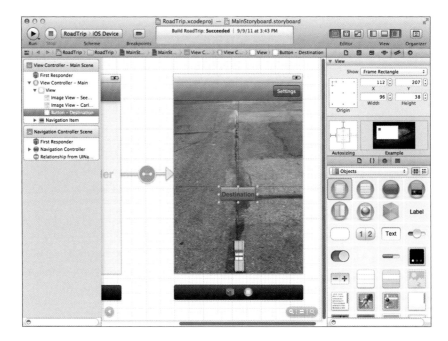

Figure 5-22: Using the Size inspector.

5. Give this button a title (buttons don't have text; they have titles) by going back to the Attributes inspector, entering Destination in the Title field, and pressing Return.

You could double-click the button and enter the Title there and press Return as well. In my experience, though, doing so may cause the button to resize itself.

You could select a different Background image and title for each state by cycling through the State Config choices and repeating Steps 2 through 5. I'll leave that for you to explore on your own.

For the RoadTrip app, you want two more buttons just like the one you just created. You can go through the same exercise in Steps 1 through 5 or use copy and paste. To copy and paste, select the button and press ⌘+C or choose Edit⇨Copy to copy it and then ⌘+V or Edit ⇨ Paste to paste it, or you can (much easier) Option drag the button to duplicate it.

Place the button as I have in Figure 5-23, setting the title of the button in the middle to Test Drive and the button on the top to Travel.

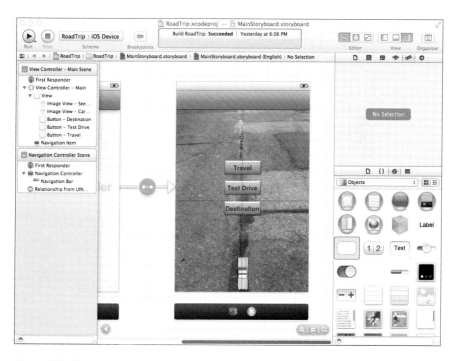

Figure 5-23: Placing the buttons.

Finally, add a Settings button to the Navigation bar by following these steps:

1. **Drag a Bar Button Item onto the Navigation bar, as I have in Figure 5-24.**

   Although it's tempting to use the same kind of button — a Rounded Rect Button — you need to use a Bar Button Item instead. A Bar Button Item is a button specialized for placement on a toolbar or Navigation bar object and for additional initialization methods and properties used on toolbars and Navigation bars.

2. **In the Attribute inspector, replace the default Item title with Settings in the Title field (see Figure 5-24) and press Return.**

   You won't be implementing Settings in this book's example app. In this section, I just wanted to show you how to add a button to a Navigation bar using Interface Builder. In Chapter 19, I do, however, explain what you need to do to implement settings in RoadTrip.

Whenever you enter text, be sure to press Return. Anything you enter will not change the current setting unless you press Return or click in another field.

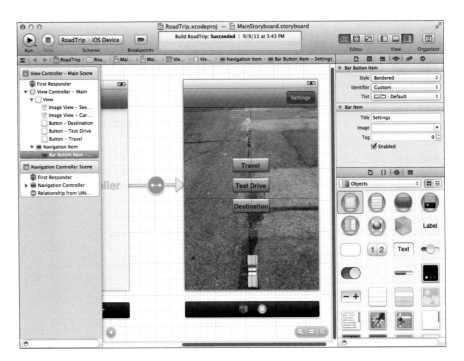

Figure 5-24: The Settings Bar Button Item.

After you've added an object to your storyboard, you can check the results of your efforts at anytime to see how things look. To do so, choose Run in the toolbar and make sure you have the iPhone Simulator scheme selected.

You should now see the results of your work in the simulator Although clicking a button doesn't do anything *yet*, at least you don't have just a blank screen!

Occasionally you might make a change to your app (usually having to do with a resource) and then, when you run your app, nothing seems to have changed. When you select Run, Xcode does only what it needs to do to the parts of your app that have changed , and if it gets "confused" (yes, there are bugs in Xcode), your change won't be linked into the app. If you think that has happened, choose Product⫐Clean, and Xcode will recompile all the pieces of your app.

*A*n application has a bunch of moving parts, and in this section you find out what they are and how to create an application that uses them correctly.

You learn to connect all those views and controls that you've added in Interface Builder to your code to make them do something — such as have a '59 pink Cadillac Eldorado Biarritz convertible drive across the screen.

You can work along with me and then take all that knowledge and start working on your own app. Of course, before you get into the guts of coding your app, you need to know about what goes on during runtime inside those itty-bitty chips — and I take you through that, as well.

Chapter 6

Adding Outlets and Actions to Your RoadTrip Code

In This Chapter

▹ Connecting your user interface to your code

▹ Using the Assistant

▹ Taking advantage of the Connections inspector

▹ Understanding how connections are made at runtime

*W*hen you write your own code, it is pretty obvious how a program works. For example, you create an object, initialize it, and then send it messages.

When you work with storyboards, however, how your program works may not be so obvious. How do you go from the objects you added to your user interface in Interface Builder to code that enables you to access these objects (such as to an Image view to change its image) or receive a message that the user has tapped a button?

The objects in your user interface must communicate with each other and with your source code if your program is to allow the user to interact with it. To access a user interface object and to specify which messages are sent and received, you use Interface Builder to create connections. There are two basic types of connections you can create:

▹ **Outlet** connections, which connect your code to interface builder objects that enables you to get and set properties (change the image in an Image view, for example).

▹ **Action** connections, which specify the message to be sent to your code when the control is interacted with (the user taps a button, for example).

In this chapter, I explain how to create both outlets and actions in your code.

Understanding Outlets

An outlet is a way to connect your code to an object you added to a view in your storyboard that will become part of your user interface at runtime. The connections between your code and its outlets are automatically reestablished every time the object referenced by the outlet is loaded.

The object containing an outlet is usually a custom controller object such as the view controller generated for you by the template. In the class declaration of that custom controller, you declare an outlet as a property with the type qualifier of IBOutlet.

Listing 6-1 shows you what the RTViewController class declaration will look like after you are done with this chapter.

Listing 6-1: Outlets (and Actions) Declared

```
#import <UIKit/UIKit.h>

@interface RTViewController : UIViewController
@property (strong, nonatomic) IBOutlet UIImageView *car;
@property (strong, nonatomic)
                   IBOutlet UIButton *testDriveButton;
@property (strong, nonatomic)
                   IBOutlet UIImageView *backgroundImage;
- (IBAction)testDrive:(id)sender;

@end
```

An *outlet* is a property that points to another object, enabling an object in an application to communicate with another object at runtime. Using an outlet, you have a reference to an object defined in the storyboard (or a nib file) that is then loaded from that storyboard file at runtime. You can make outlet connections between any objects that you add to your storyboard in Interface Builder.

For example, in Figure 6-1, you use an outlet to get the text the user typed in the Find text field.

But before you go setting up outlets for anything and everything, make sure that you really need one. You don't have to use outlets to be able to access all Interface Builder objects. Instead, as you will see in Chapter 8, you can access the Navigation bar to change its background indirectly through other connections established by the nib loader.

```
#import "MapController.h"
@interface FindController : MapController
@property (weak, nonatomic: NSString * findlocation;
@end
```

Figure 6-1: Using an outlet to get the text entered by the user.

Adding Outlets

To recap from the previous section, outlets are the way your code can access (send messages or set properties) the Interface Builder objects in your storyboard. In previous versions of Xcode, you had to declare an outlet in the header file of a class, and make a connection between the outlet and another object using Interface Builder, Now however, you can do all this graphically in Interface Builder, and the required code is generated for you. Read on to find out more about how this works.

Opening the Assistant editor

To create an outlet, you need to connect the interface object in Interface Builder with your code. Although you have a couple of ways to make this connection, the easiest and most clear cut is to use the Assistant editor to automatically display the code file that's most relevant to the interface element you're working with. To make the Assistant editor automatically display a code file, follow these steps:

1. **Select the** `MainStoryboard.storyboard` **file in the Project navigator.**

2. **Close the Utility area if it's open (and you need the space).**

3. **In Interface Builder, select the View Controller in the View Controller – Main Scene in the Dock; and then click the Assistant editor button in the Editor selector in the toolbar (see Figure 6-2).**

   The Assistant editor pane opens and displays the header file for that view controller.

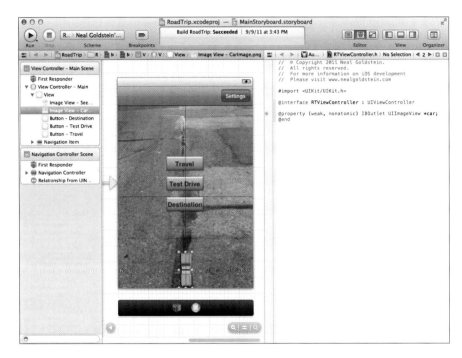

Figure 6-7: The outlet you just created.

Now you can go back to the Interface file and create outlets for the Test Drive button (name it testDriveButton) and the background image (name it backgroundImage). You drag from each of these to the ViewController Interface in the same way as you do the car image.

You won't be using `backgroundImage` in this example, but I have you put the structure in place to be able to change it in case you want to. For example, you might want to change it based on the time of the year, or from where the user is leaving.

The Connections inspector

You should also know about the Connections inspector in the Utility area because you can use the Connections inspector to make an outlet connection, with a bit more work. It's useful in that it can help you understand the connections between Interface Builder objects and your code. To use the Connections inspector, follow these steps:

1. **Select Standard editor in the View selector in the toolbar.**

   The Assistant editor closes.

Added @synthesize

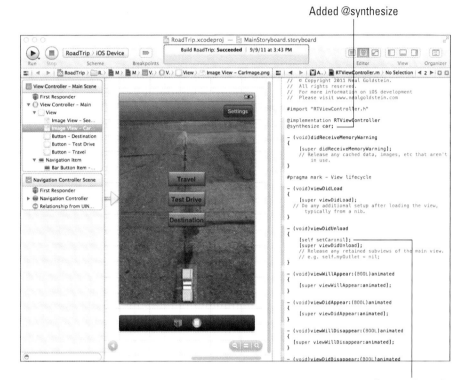

Added [self setCar:nil]

Figure 6-8: The generated code.

2. Show the Utility area by selecting it in the view selector.

 3. Select the Connections inspector by clicking its icon in the Inspector selector bar (the icon is shown here in the left margin).

4. Select the view controller in the View Controller – Main Scene.

In Figure 6-9, you can see that the view controller contains backgroundImage, car, and testDriveButton outlets (as should yours, if you followed along and created them).

You can also Control-click the view controller in the Dock to get a similar picture in the Connections window (see Figure 6-10).

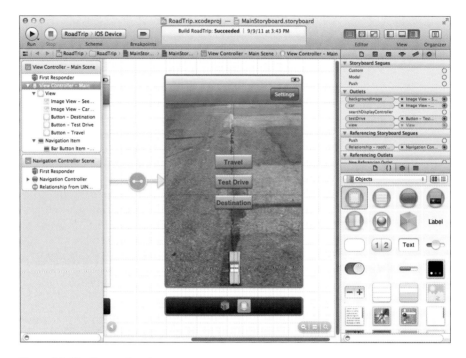

Figure 6-9: The Connections inspector.

When you add outlets, there are some memory management considerations, not to mention the entire subject of properties that I have yet to explain. But in this chapter, I'm keeping the focus on what you need to know about interacting with Interface Builder objects in a storyboard. That interaction also includes working with a design pattern called Target-Action, which I explain next.

Working with the Target-Action Design Pattern

The other requirement of a user interface that I mention at the beginning of this chapter is being able to connect a button to your code so that when a user taps the button, something happens. This requirement involves using the *Target-Action pattern,* which is one of the key design patterns in iOS programming.

You use the Target-Action pattern to let your app know that it should do something. A user might tap a button or enter some text, for example, and the app must respond in some way. The control — a button, say — sends a message (the Action message) that you specify to the target (the receiving object, which is usually a view controller object) that you have selected to handle that particular action.

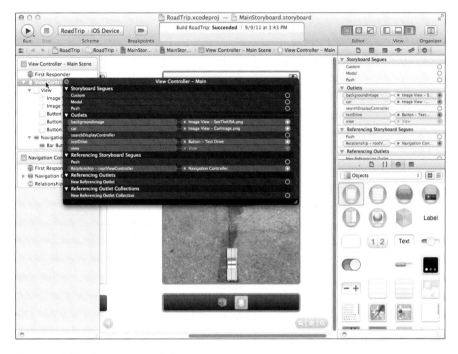

Figure 6-10: The Connections window.

Using the Target-Action pattern: It's about controls

When a user acts on the control by, say, tapping a button, the iPhone generates an event. The event triggering an action message can be anything, just as the object sending the message can be any object. For example, a gesture-recognizer object might send an action message to another object when it recognizes its gesture. However, the Target-Action pattern is usually found with controls such as buttons and sliders.

The event doesn't tell you much, but Target-Action provides a way to send an application-specific instruction to the appropriate object.

If you wanted to develop an app that could start a car from an iPhone (not a bad idea for those who live in a place like Hibbing, Minnesota in winter), you could display two buttons, Start and Heater. You could use Interface Builder to specify that when the user taps Start, the target is the `CarController` object and the method to invoke is `ignition`. Figure 6-11 shows the Target-Action mechanism in action.

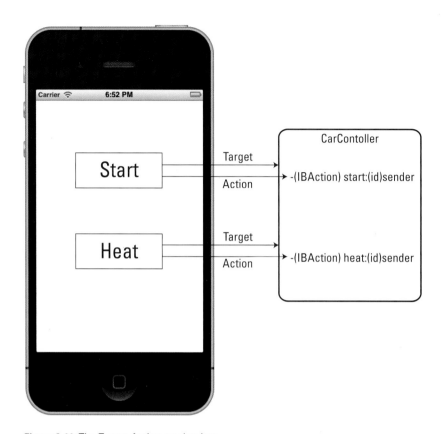

Figure 6-11: The Target-Action mechanism.

The Target-Action mechanism enables you to create a control object and tell it not only which object you want to handle the event but also the message to send. For example, if the user touches a Ring Bell button onscreen, you want to send a Ring Bell message to the view controller. But if the Wave Flag button on the same screen is touched, you want to be able to send the Wave Flag message to the same view controller. If you couldn't specify the message, all buttons would have to send the same message. It would then make the coding more difficult and more complex because you would have to identify which button sent the message and what to do in response. It would also make changing the user interface more work and more prone to errors.

You set a control's action and target using Interface Builder. You specify what method in which object should respond to a control without having to write any code.

You can also change the target and action dynamically by sending the control or its cell `setTarget:` and `setAction:` messages.

Action methods have a certain signature:

```
- (IBAction)testDrive:(id)sender;
```

The type qualifier `IBAction`, which is used in place of the `void` return type, flags the declared method as an action so that Interface Builder is aware of it. (This is similar to the IBOutlet tag, used in the "Creating the outlet" section, earlier in this chapter). And just as with outlets, you can actually make the connections in the Interface Builder editor and Xcode will generate the necessary code for you.

The sender parameter is the control object sending the action message. When responding to an action message, you may query the sender to get more information about the context of the event triggering the action message.

You can set the action and target of a control object programmatically or in Interface Builder. Setting these properties effectively connects the control and its target via the action. If you connect a control and its target in Interface Builder, the connection is archived in a nib file. When an application later loads the nib file, the connection is restored.

`IBAction` is like `IBOutlet` — it does nothing in the code but rather is a tag used by Interface Builder.

Adding an action

After you have the `RTViewController` interface displayed (as I do in Figure 6-3), by having the Assistant editor display it automatically or navigating to it using the Jump bar, creating an outlet using the Interface Builder editor is very straightforward and pretty easy. You do it by Control+dragging from the button to the `RTViewController` interface, as detailed in the following steps:

1. **In the Project navigator, select the** `MainStoryboard.storyboard` **file.**

2. **Close the Utility area.**

   You don't need it to create the action.

3. **Open the Assistant editor.**

   You should see the `ViewController.h` Interface file displayed in the Assistant editor. If it doesn't appear, navigate to it using the steps in the earlier section, "Creating the outlet."

4. **Control-drag from the Test Drive button to the** `ViewController.h` **file, just as you did to create the outlet.**

5. **In the Connection pop-up menu, select Action (see Figure 6-12).**

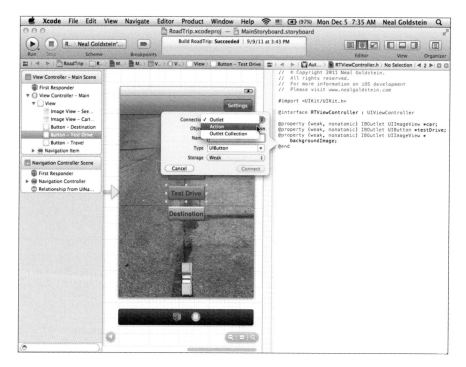

Figure 6-12: Select Action as the connection type.

6. **Leave the event as Touch Up Inside.**

   To create an Action for a control, you need to specify what event triggers the action. In the case of a button, a Touch Up Inside event is the usual choice because Touch Up Inside is the event that is generated when the last place the user touched before lifting his or her finger was inside the button. This allows a user to change his or her mind about touching the button by moving his or her finger off the button before lifting it up.

7. **Name this action Test Drive by entering Test Drive in the Name field; then click Connect.**

   As shown in Figure 6-13, a new action method called Test Drive appears.

Just as it did when you added an outlet, Xcode will also add code for you in the .m file to support, in this case, the action. To see what has been added, select the RTViewController.m file or press Control ⌘ up arrow in the file to get the counterpart. Just as with the IBOutlet, in Figure 6-14 you can see that some code has been added — in this case a new method (stub) has been added. It will be up to you to code what should be done when this message is received, and you find out how to make that decision in Chapter 10.

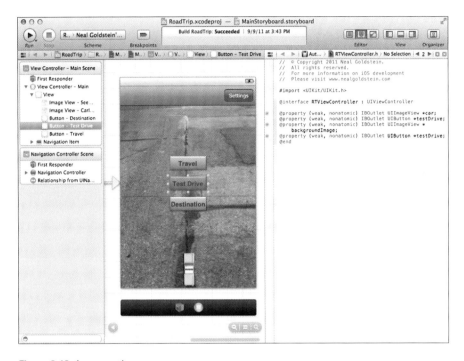

Figure 6-13: A new action message.

And just as you do with the IBOutlet, mentioned earlier in the chapter when adding an outlet is discussed, you can look at the Connections inspector in the utility area (under Received Actions) or right-click the view controller in the Dock to get a similar picture in the Connections window.

But as you notice, there are other buttons that also need connecting. You won't be using the target-action pattern to connect them. You'll be using a storyboard feature called *segues* to do that for you. I explain using segues in Chapter 11.

How Outlets and Actions Work

At the start of this chapter, I explain that you need to be able to connect the objects you added to your user interface in Interface Builder to code that enables you to access these objects (such as to an Image view to change its image) or receive a message that the user has tapped a button.

In the chapter, I show you how to create outlets and actions to do that, but I haven't really explained how all that gets connected at runtime.

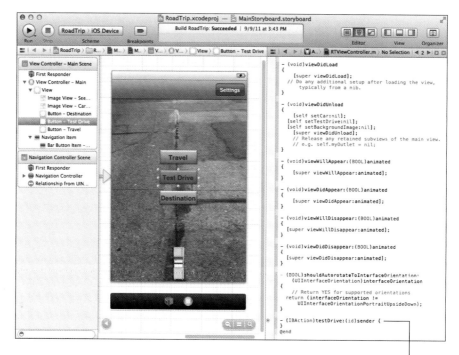

Added - (IBAction)testDrive:(id) sender {
}

Figure 6-14: The testDrive method stub.

As I explain in Chapter 4, storyboards are a collection of (resource) nib files that you use to store the user interface of your application.

A nib file is an Interface Builder document. When you use interface Builder in Chapter 4 to create your user interface, you create an *object graph* that is saved (archived) as part of the resource file. When you load the file, the object graph is then used to recreate the relationships between the objects in the file, and your program objects as well.

As I explain in Chapter 5 every storyboard file has an initial view controller. At runtime, it is loaded along with its view and all of the other Interface Builder objects you added in Chapter 5 — and you get an exact replica of the objects that were in your Interface Builder document. The nib-loading code instantiates the objects, configures them, and reestablishes any inter-object connections *including the outlets and actions* that you created in Interface Builder.

Chapter 7

Understanding the Runtime, Managing Memory, and Using Properties

In This Chapter

▷ Understanding the application life cycle

▷ Handling interruptions

▷ Using Automatic Reference Counting to manage memory

▷ Understanding the five rules of memory management

▷ Customizing framework behaviors

▷ Taking advantage of the power of declared properties

*P*revious chapters provide you with at least a basic understanding of how to graphically build your user interface. Now it's time to add some code to have your application actually do something. But before you do that, I want to explain three things about writing iPhone apps.

First, a lot of what you will be doing is customizing and extending the behavior of framework classes. You customize and extend the behavior of these classes through *subclassing*, *delegation*, and a powerful Objective-C feature called *properties*.

Second, on the iPhone, like any other device, you create objects to do your bidding — which means that you allocate memory — a scarce resource on the iPhone. Running out of memory is the main cause of applications crashing (not to mention being rejected from the App Store), so you need to understand *memory management*.

And finally, to know what message to send to what objects at what time, and what messages will be sent to your app at runtime, you need to understand the *application life cycle*.

Dealing with these three aspects of writing iPhone Apps is your pass to the Successful iPhone Programmers Secret Society, and in this chapter, you start your initiation. And because you'll find all this easier to understand if you understand the overall context, I begin with the application life cycle.

This chapter is like the "Classic Comics" version of several hundred pages of Apple documentation, reference manuals, and how-to guides. Although a lot is left unsaid (though less than you might suspect), what's in this chapter is enough to get you started and also to keep you going as you develop your own iPhone apps. It provides a frame of reference on which you can hang the concepts I throw around with abandon in upcoming chapters — as well as the groundwork for a deep enough understanding of the application life cycle to give you a handle on the detailed documentation.

So relax. Get yourself a cup of coffee (or something stronger if you want), and be prepared to be entertained.

Stepping Through the App Life Cycle

Although simple for the user, the birth, life, and death of an application is a pretty complex process. In this section, I explain what happens throughout the time that the user launches the app from the Home screen, uses the app, and then stops using the app, either because she is done or decides to respond to an interruption such as a phone call or SMS message.

The life of an iPhone app begins when a user launches it by tapping its icon on the Home screen. The system launches your app by calling its `main` function, which you can see by opening the disclosure triangle next to the Supporting files group and selecting `main.m` in the Project navigator.

The details of the implementation shown here may change, but the overall architecture will stay the same from iOS version to iOS version.

```
#import <UIKit/UIKit.h>
#import "RTAppDelegate.h"

int main(int argc, char *argv[])
{
  @autoreleasepool {
      return UIApplicationMain(argc, argv, nil,
           NSStringFromClass([RTAppDelegate class]));
  }
}
```

The `main` function is where a program starts execution. This function is responsible for the high-level organization of the program's functionality and typically has access to the command arguments given to the program when it was executed.

The `main` function does only two things:

1. Sets up an autorelease pool:

   ```
   @autoreleasepool {
   ```

   This is a piece of memory-management plumbing that you don't need to use in this book (other than here), or perhaps ever, but feel free to investigate on your own if you are interested.

2. Calls the `UIApplicationMain` function to create the application object and delegate and set up the event loop:

   ```
   return UIApplicationMain(argc, argv, nil,
               NSStringFromClass([RTAppDelegate class]));
   ```

   This is your entrance into the entire application startup process and its underlying architecture.

UIApplicationMain

The `UIApplicationMain` function creates the *Application object* (a singleton `UIApplication` object) and the *Application Delegate* (a class created for you by the Xcode template). It also sets up the *main event loop*, including the application's run loop (which is responsible for polling input sources) and begins processing events.

In the following section, I explain the role of each of them in the application lifecycle.

UIApplication *provides application-wide control*

The `UIApplication` object provides the application-wide control and coordination for an iOS application. It is responsible for handling the initial routing of incoming user events (touches, for example) as well as for dispatching action messages from control objects (such as buttons) to the appropriate target objects. The application object sends messages to its Application Delegate to allow you to respond in an application-unique way to occurrences such as application launch, low-memory warnings, and state transitions such as moving into background and back into foreground.

Delegation is a mechanism used to avoid subclassing complex `UIKit` objects, such as the `UIApplication` object. Instead of subclassing and overriding methods in a framework or other object, you use that object unmodified and put your custom code inside a delegate object. As interesting events occur, the framework or other object sends messages to your delegate object. You use these methods to execute your custom code and implement the behavior you need. I explain the delegation pattern more in "The Delegation pattern" section, later in this chapter.

The Application Delegate object is responsible for handling several critical system messages and must be present in every iOS application. The object can be an instance of any class you like, as long as it adopts the `UIApplicationDelegate` protocol. In the template you'll find it is a subclass of `UIResponder`, which enables it to respond to and handle events. (`UIApplication` is also derived from `UIResponder`.)

The methods of this protocol correspond to behaviors that are needed during the application life cycle and are your way of implementing this custom behavior. Although you aren't required to implement all the methods of the `UIApplicationDelegate` protocol, you'll often find yourself writing code to handle the following:

- Initialization in your App Delegate's `application:didFinish LaunchingWithOptions:` method.
- State transitions such as moving in and out of background and foreground. I explain these in more detail in "The Normal Processing of Your Application Is Interrupted," later in this chapter.
- Low-memory warnings, which I cover in "Observing Low-Memory Warnings," later in this chapter.

The `UIApplication` is a singleton object (there is just one). To get a reference to it, you send the class message. (In Objective-C, you can send messages to classes, which are really objects on their own.) Sending the `UIApplication` object the `delegate` message gives you a pointer to the delegate object.

```
RTAppDelegate *appDelegate =
              [[UIApplication sharedApplication] delegate];
```

You'll be doing that a lot and it will become second nature to you.

UIApplicationMain *loads the storyboard*

If the application's `Info.plist` file specifies a storyboard file (or a main nib file), as RoadTrip's does in Figure 7-1, the `UIApplicationMain` function loads it. The application's `Info.plist` file provides a map to the high-level structure of the application.

To see the `RoadTrip-Info.plist` file, select RoadTrip-Info.plist in the Project navigator, as shown in Figure 7-1. The information in the file appears in the Editor area.

A *nib* file is a resource file that contains the specifications for one or more objects and is used to graphically create your user interface using Interface Builder in applications without a storyboard. (A storyboard consists of a series of linked nib files created for you.)

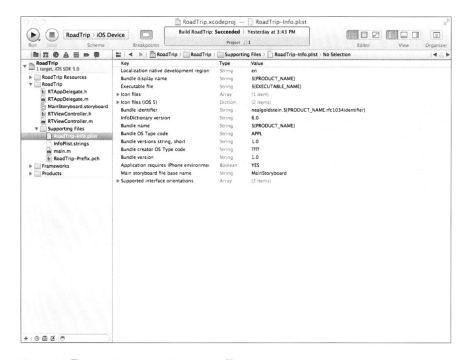

Figure 7-1: The `RoadTrip-Info.plist` file.

If you are using a storyboard, the initial view controller is instantiated. As you can see in in the Attributes inspector in Figure 7-2, that is a view controller property and is set for you by Interface Builder (you don't have to usually think about it). In this case, it is the navigation controller that you add in Chapter 5. Its root view controller (`RTViewController`) is instantiated as well.

If you created the project from the template as explained in Chapter 3, the initial view controller was the `RTViewController`. When you added the navigation controller, Interface Builder changed that for you.

UIApplication sends the application: didFinishLaunchingWithOptions: message to its delegate

If the method is implemented in the application delegate, the `application: didFinishLaunchingWithOptions:` message is sent to the App Delegate.

Launch time is a particularly important point in an application's lifecycle. In addition to the user launching an application by tapping its icon, an application can be launched to respond to a specific type of event. For example, it could be launched in response to an incoming push notification, it could be launched to open a file, or it could be launched to handle some background event that it had specified it wanted to handle (a location update for example). In all these cases, an options dictionary passed to the `application:didFinishLaunchingWithOptions:` method provides information about the reason for the launch.

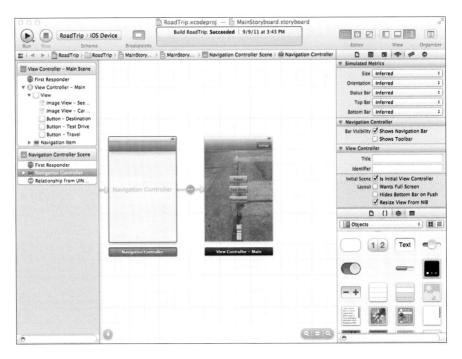

Figure 7-2: The initial view controller is specified.

The `application:didFinishLaunchingWithOptions:` message is sent to the delegate when the application has launched and its storyboard has been loaded. In this step, as you will see, you initialize and set up your application. At the time this method is called, your application is in the inactive state. At some point after this method returns, unless your application does some kind of background processing, your application will become active and will receive the `applicationDidBecomeActive:` message when it *enters the foreground* (becomes the application that the user sees on the screen), which I explain in "The Normal Processing of Your Application Is Interrupted" later in this chapter.

If your application was launched by the system for a specific reason, a `launchOptions` dictionary contains data indicating the reason for the launch. An application launched by the system for a specific reason (other than the user tapping its icon) is beyond the scope of this book.

Your goal during startup is to present your application's user interface as quickly as possible — and quick initialization equals happy users. Don't load large data structures that your application won't use right away. If your application requires time to load data from the network (or perform other tasks that take noticeable time), get your interface up and running first and then launch the task that takes a longer time on a background thread. Then you can display a progress indicator or other feedback to the user to indicate that your application is loading the necessary data or doing something important.

In the templates that don't use a storyboard, you'll see that this method allocates and initializes the window and the initial view controller, adds it to the window, and makes the window visible, as follows:

```
self.window = [[UIWindow alloc] initWithFrame:
                        [[UIScreen mainScreen] bounds]];
self.viewController = [[RTViewController alloc]
        initWithNibName:@"RTViewController" bundle:nil];
self.window.rootViewController = self.viewController;
[self.window makeKeyAndVisible];
```

In a storyboard-based application, this is all done by the storyboard for you, and the `application:didFinishLaunchingWithOptions:` is just a stub that does nothing other than return YES (the "usual" return).

You would return NO only if your application was launched because another application opened a URL that is owned by your application and your application cannot handle the URL.

I tell you more about using this method in Chapter 9.

Handling events while your application is executing

Most events sent to an application are encapsulated in an event object — an instance of the UIEvent class. In the case of touch-related events, the event object contains one or more touch objects (UITouch) representing the fingers that are touching the screen. As the user places fingers on the screen, moves them around, and finally removes them from the screen, the system reports the changes for each finger in the corresponding touch object.

Distributing and handling events is the job of responder objects, which are instances of the UIResponder class. The UIApplication, UIViewController, UIWindow, and UIView classes (and your own RTAppDelegate) all inherit from UIResponder. After pulling an event off the event queue, the application dispatches that event to the UIWindow object where it occurred. The window object, in turn, forwards the event to its first responder, designated to be the first recipient of events other than touch events. In the case of touch events, the first responder is typically the view object (UIView) in which the touch took place. For example, a touch event occurring in a button is delivered to the corresponding button object.

If the first responder is unable to handle an event, it forwards the event to its next responder, which is typically a parent view or view controller. If that object is unable to handle the event, it forwards it to its next responder, and so on until the event is handled. This series of linked responder objects is known as the *responder chain*. Messages continue traveling up the responder chain — toward higher-level responder objects, such as the window, the application, and the application's delegate — until the event is either handled or discarded if it is not handled.

The responder object that handles an event often sets in motion a series of programmatic actions by the application — such as when you drag an image of a 1959 Cadillac Eldorado Biarritz convertible across the screen as I describe in Chapter 10.

The following list provides the chronology of what actually happens when the user taps something.

1. You have an event — the user taps a button, for example.

   The touch of a finger (or the lifting of a finger from the screen) adds a touch event to the application's event queue, where that event is *encapsulated* in — placed into, in other words — a UIEvent object. A UITouch object exists for each finger touching the screen, so you can track individual touches. As the user manipulates the screen with his or her fingers, the system reports the changes for each finger in the corresponding UITouch object.

2. The run loop monitor dispatches the event.

   When something occurs that needs to be processed, the event-handling code of the UIApplication processes touch events by dispatching them to the appropriate *responder* object — the object that has signed up to take responsibility for doing something when an event happens (when the user touches the screen, for example). As mentioned previously, responder objects can include instances of UIApplication, UIWindow, UIView (and any of the subclasses) and UIViewController (and any of its subclasses). All these classes inherit from UIResponder.

3. A responder object decides how to handle the event.

   For example, a touch event occurring with a button in a view is delivered to the button object. The button object handles the event by sending an action message to another object — in this case, the UIViewController object. This enables you to use standard button objects without having to muck about in their internals — you just tell the button what method you want to have invoked in your view controller, and you're basically set.

Processing the message may result in changes to a view, a new view altogether, or some other kind of change in the user interface. When one of these results occurs, the view and graphics infrastructure takes over and processes the required drawing events.

4. Your application then returns to the run loop.

After an event is handled or discarded, application control passes back to the run loop. The run loop then processes the next event or puts the thread to sleep if it has nothing more to do.

But because your application it not alone on the device, it can be interrupted by a phone call, SMS message, or the user touching the Home button. When your application is interrupted, there are some things you'll have to take care of before control is switched to another application.

Knowing what to do when the normal processing of your application is interrupted

On an iPhone or iPod touch running iOS 4.2 or newer versions, various events besides termination can interrupt your app to allow the user to respond — for example, calendar alerts or the user pressing the Sleep/Wake button — and your app moves into the *inactive state.* If the user chooses to ignore an interruption, your app moves back into the *active state* and continues running as before. If the user decides to tap the alert to deal with it (or if the interruption was from the user touching the Home button to switch out of your application), your app the moves into its *background state,* where it is suspended to but remains in memory.

iOS sends you a number of messages to let you know exactly what's happening as well as to give you the opportunity to take actions such as save user data and state information, which means saving at the point where the user was in the application. (If an app needs to continue running, it can request execution time from the system.) Because the app is in the background (running or suspended) and still in memory, relaunching is nearly instantaneous. An app's objects (including its windows and views) remain in memory, so they don't need to be re-created when the app relaunches. If memory becomes constrained, iOS may purge background apps to make more room for the foreground app.

Because these interruptions cause a temporary loss of control by your app, touch events are no longer sent to your app. When developing your app, you need to take this fact into account. For example, if your app is a game, you should pause the game when your game is interrupted. In general, your app should store information about its current state when it moves to the inactive state and be able to restore itself to the current state upon a subsequent relaunch.

In all cases, the sequence of events starts the same way — with the `applicationWillResignActive:` message sent to your application delegate when the application is about to move from active to inactive state. In this method, you should pause ongoing tasks, disable timers, throttle down OpenGL ES frame rates (that is, you should use this method to pause the game), and generally put things on hold.

What happens after this depends on the nature of the interruption, and how the user responds to the interruption. Your application may be either moved to the background or reactivated. I explain these occurrences next.

Figure 7-3 shows the application lifecycle and how interruptions are handled.

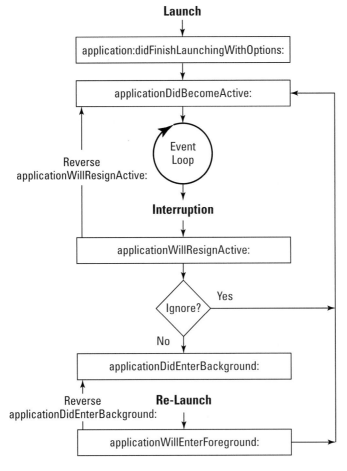

Figure 7-3: The application life cycle.

Your application is moved to the background

When the user accepts the notification or interruption, or clicks the Home button (or when the system launches another application), your application moves into the background state, where it is suspended. (If an app needs to continue running, it can request execution time from the system.)

The next two sections explain the messages your application can respond to when it is moved into background.

The applicationDidEnterBackground: message

When your app first enters the background state, it is sent the `application DidEnterBackground:` message. In this method, you should save any unsaved data or *state* (where the user is in the app — the current view, options selected, and stuff like that) to a temporary cache file or to the preferences database "on disk." (Okay, I know, Apple calls the iOS storage system a *disk* even though it is a solid-state drive, but if Apple calls it that, I probably should too, just so I don't confuse too many people.)

Even though your application enters the background state, you have no guarantee that it will remain there indefinitely. If memory becomes constrained, iOS will purge background apps to make more room for the foreground app. You need to do everything necessary to be able to restore your application in case it's subsequently purged from memory so that the next time the user launches your app, your application can use that information to restore your app to its previous state. You also have to do additional cleanup operations, such as deleting temporary files.

If your application is purged when it is in this suspended state, *it receives no notice that it is removed from memory.* You need to save any data beforehand!

When your delegate is sent the `applicationDidEnterBackground:` method, your app has an undocumented amount of time to finish things up. If the method doesn't return before time runs out (or if your app doesn't request more execution time from iOS), your app is terminated and purged from memory.

If your application requests more execution time or it has declared that it does background execution, it is allowed to continue running after the `applicationDidEnterBackground:` method returns. If not, your (now) background application is moved to the *suspended* state shortly after returning from the `applicationDidEnterBackground:` method.

If the application is in background it then may be relaunched. This can happen if the user selects the app from the Home screen or the Multitasking bar, or it is launched by the system if the app processes events in background or monitors a significant location change, for example.

The applicationWillEnterForeground: message is sent

When your application is relaunched from the background, it is sent the `applicationWillEnterForeground:` message. In this method, you need to undo what you did in the `applicationDidEnterBackground:` method (not `applicationWillResignActive;` you undo that next).

Your application is reactivated

If the user ignores the phone call, SMS, or calendar notification, or the app is relaunched from background, your application is reactivated and starts getting touch and other events.

When your application is reactivated, it is sent the `applicationDidBecomeActive:` message.

You can use the `applicationDidBecomeActive:` method to restore the application to the state it was in before the interruption. Here you undo what you did in the `applicationWillResignActive` method, such as restart any tasks that were paused (or not yet started) while the application was inactive. If the application was previously in the background, you might need to refresh the user interface.

While an application is in the suspended state, the system tracks and coalesces events that might have an impact on that application when it relaunches. As soon as your application is up and running again, the system delivers those events to it. For most of these events, your application's existing infrastructure should just respond appropriately. For example, if the device orientation changed, your application's view controllers would automatically update the interface orientation in an appropriate way.

Your application is terminated

Apps are generally moved to the background when interrupted or when the user quits. But if the app was compiled with an earlier version of the SDK, or is running on an earlier version of the operating system that doesn't support multitasking — or if you decide that you don't want your app to run in the background and you set the `UIApplicationExitsOnSuspend` key in its `Info.plist` file — iOS terminates your app.

Even if your application supports multitasking (almost all do at this point), you must still be prepared for your application to be killed without any notification. The user can kill applications explicitly using the Multitasking bar. In addition, if memory becomes constrained, the system might remove applications from memory to make more room. If it does remove your *suspended* application, *it does not give you any warning, much less notice!* However, if your application is currently running in the background state, the system does call the `applicationWillTerminate:` method of the Application Delegate.

When your App Delegate is sent the `applicationWillTerminate:` in non-multitasking applications, or those running in background, you need to do the same kinds of things you do in `applicationDidEnterBackground:`, except this time you do them knowing that your application will not be returning from background.

Your `applicationWillTerminate:` method implementation has a limited (albeit undocumented) amount of time to do what it needs to do and return. Any longer than that and your application is terminated and purged from memory. (The Terminator doesn't kid around.)

An Overview of the View Controller Life Cycle

View controllers have a life cycle just as applications do, but I don't need to go into much detail about it here. The important part to know is that certain messages are sent as views that are displayed and hidden.

The two methods you need to know about in order to work with views are the following:

- ✔ `viewDidLoad`
- ✔ `viewWillAppear:`

The `viewDidLoad` message is sent to your `RTViewController`. This method is called after the view controller has loaded its associated views into memory. This method is used to perform view initialization and is not *necessarily* called every time the view appears. If, for example, the user makes a selection in the view that causes a new view controller to load and slide its view into place, and the user then taps the Back button, this message is not sent when the originating view reappears. That is the job of `viewWillAppear:`.

The `viewWillAppear:` message is sent when the view is about to become visible. The first time it is sent is after the `viewDidLoad` message and then whenever the view reappears, such as when you tap the Back button, for example. You use this method to refresh your user interface if needed, but not for initialization.

Numerous other methods are also placed in the `RTViewController` for you as stubs. I leave you to explore them on your own.

Of course, aside from all this system stuff that happens, your application will be chugging along doing what the user wants it to do. And in responding to user requests, you'll create objects to do the user's bidding — which means that you allocate memory. And because memory is a scarce resource on the iPhone, you need to understand *memory management,* discussed in the next section.

Working within the Managed Memory Model Design Pattern

As powerful as it is, the iPhone is limited in resources, and the most critical of these resources is memory.

To truly understand how to manage memory correctly in your application, you need to understand how the iOS memory works.

Understanding memory management

Whenever you (or a framework object) create an object using Objective-C, you allocate memory for the object. Although the iPhone OS and the Mac both use what's known as *virtual memory*, unlike the Mac, virtual memory in the iPhone is limited to the actual amount of physical memory. So when it begins to run low on memory, the iPhone OS frees memory pages that contain read-only content (such as code); this way, all it has to do is load the "originals" back into memory when they're needed. In contrast to what the Mac does, the iPhone doesn't temporarily store "changeable" memory (such as object data) to the disk to free space and then read the data back later when it's needed. This state of affairs limits the amount of available memory.

So as you can see, when one object is done using memory, it is critical that the memory be released for use by other objects.

If memory continues to be limited, the system may also send notifications to the running application, asking it to free additional memory. This is one of the critical events that all applications must respond to, and I explain this process in the section "Observing Low-Memory Warnings," later in this chapter.

In Objective-C, memory is managed on the iPhone apps by reference counting — keeping the system up to date on whether an object is currently being used.

Using reference counting

In many ways, Objective-C is like the coolest guy in your school who now makes a seven-figure income surfing, bungee jumping, and skateboarding during the summers and then snowboarding around the world in the winter.

In other ways, though, Objective-C is like the nerd in your class who grew up to be an accountant and reads the *Financial Times* for fun. Memory management falls into this category.

In fact, memory management is simply an exercise in counting. To manage its memory, Objective-C (actually the iOS memory manager) uses a technique known as reference counting. Every object has its own reference count, or *retain count.*

As long as the retain count is greater than zero, the memory manager assumes that someone cares about that object and leaves it alone.

When an object's retain count goes to zero, the memory manager knows that no one needs it anymore and sends the object a `dealloc` message, and after that, its memory is returned to the system to be reused.

That process sounds pretty straightforward, but how does the retain count get incremented and decremented?

Until Xcode 4.2 and iOS 5.0, you had to manage the retain count in your application. When an object is created via `alloc` or `new` or through a `copy` or `mutableCopy` message (which creates a copy of an object but has subtleties beyond the scope of this book), the object's retain count is set to 1. When your application uses one of those methods, ownership is transferred to the "caller" — that is, the object has been retained for the caller and it becomes a nonexclusive *owner* of the object. Ownership here means that the object will be there to use until it's explicitly released by sending it a `release` message when it is longer needed (although if there are other active owners, it wouldn't be de-allocated until all of them have released it).

Before Xcode 4.2 and iOS 5.0, if you didn't create an object by one of those methods but you wanted to become an owner, thereby making sure that the object stayed around for you to use until you were done with, it was up to you to send a `retain` message to increase the retain count, and when you were done, to send a `release` message. This was because the creator of the object (which caused the retain count to be set to 1) may have auto released it — sent an object a "deferred" release message. This is useful in situations in which you want to relinquish ownership of an object but avoid the possibility of its being deallocated immediately (such as when you return an object from a method).

In either instance, you were maintaining a pointer to the object so that it could be used.

Although this approach was simple in theory, it was a real headache for programmers. The vast majority of system crashes occurred because apps ran out of memory and were shut down by the system.

In some of these cases, the application *didn't* respond to the memory warning methods and manage the low-memory warnings I explain in "Observing Low-Memory Warnings," later in this chapter.

Most of the time, however, even if the application responded to the low-memory warnings. It was limited to what it could do because the memory was *leaked*. Memory was actually available because some objects were not being used, but those objects' memory had not been released back to the system. But there were no longer pointers to these objects (for a variety of reasons), so they couldn't be released and then deallocated and the memory reused.

There are ways to manage memory automatically. One is garbage collection, which scans through memory and releases objects that have no pointers to them. Garbage collection for Objective-C is available on the Mac (and for many other languages on other platforms), but garbage collection has a few problems. Garbage collection can start up and "pause" your applications at the most inopportune time, and it affects performance and the user experience because you have no control, or any idea, when it will occur.

Having to do all this memory management in your application has all changed with the latest version of the Objective-C compiler with the introduction of automatic Reference Counting (ARC), the use of which is one of your options when you create your project in Chapter 3. ARC does for you in the compiler what you used to have to do on your own. It handles all those `releases`, `autoreleases`, and `retains` for you. I tell you much more about ARC in the next section.

Automatic Reference Counting

Automatic Reference Counting (ARC) is a compiler-level feature that simplifies the process of managing the lifetimes of Objective-C objects. Instead of your having to remember when to retain or release an object, ARC evaluates the lifetime requirements of your objects and automatically synthesizes the appropriate method calls at compile time. It is not a new runtime memory model — and it is not a garbage collector. All the action takes place in the compiler.

ARC takes care of the process of retaining and releasing objects by obeying and enforcing naming conventions. It also relies on new object pointer ownership qualifiers (more on that later).

Lest you worry, ARC is actually much faster (has better performance) than doing memory management on your own.

ARC does not automate `malloc()` and `free()` and does not automate CoreFoundation (CF) or CoreGraphics (CG). You will be using some of those kinds of functions, and I tell about them in Chapter 10.

To be able to manage memory for you, ARC imposes some restrictions — primarily enforcing some best practices and disallowing some other practices. You won't have to worry about most of this in an application that was created to use ARC. You may see some things in non-ARC samples, and this will explain how to work within the ARC restrictions.

In the following sections, I explain the rules that you have to follow to use ARC in your application.

Rule 1: Do not call the retain, release, or autorelease methods

In addition, you cannot implement custom retain or release methods.

If you are new to Objective-C programming, this rule won't mean anything to you because it is not something you will have been doing in your existing applications. You'll need to know about this rule only to understand what non ARC code is doing to manage memory. If you're an old hand, you will have been using these methods and you'll be happy to comply.

You can provide a custom implementation of `dealloc` if you need to manage other resources — but I don't have you do that for the example app developed in this book.

Rule 2: Do not store object pointers in C structures

Because the compiler must know when references come and go, you can't store object pointers in C structures. For most readers, that won't be a problem because you will be using objects.

Rule 3: Inform the compiler about ownership when using Core Foundation-style objects

In iOS applications, you use the Core Foundation framework. An example is in Chapter 10, when you add sound to your application.

Core Foundation objects are anything beginning with a CF — things like the address book functions. Although you don't use the address book in this book, you do use the audio in Chapter 10. An example of using a Core Foundation object is:

```
AudioServicesCreateSystemSoundID
  ((__bridge CFURLRef)burnRubberURL, burnRubberSoundID);
```

ARC does not automatically manage the lifetimes of Core Foundation types, and there are Core Foundation memory management rules and functions you can use such as `CFRetain` and `CFRelease` (or the corresponding type-specific variants).

In this book, and most of the time, you don't have to worry about memory management (and as you explore Core Foundation, the memory management requirements are documented) because you usually will be casting an Objective-C object to a Core Foundation type object (as shown previously, and which you will do in Chapter 10) or vice versa and with no Core Foundation memory management in your code. But you have to let the compiler know about any memory management implications.

In this book, and much of the time, you tell ARC simply not to worry by using a __bridge cast.

If you do have Core Foundation memory management, there are macros such as CFBridgingRetain or CFBridgingRelease that transfer ownership between ARC and Core Foundation. (This topic is beyond the scope of this book, however.)

Rule 4: Use the @autoreleasepool keyword to mark the start of an autorelease block

This is not something you'll be concerned about, or doing. But it is a rule.

Rule 5: Follow the naming conventions

The compiler knows whether to retain an object based on what something returns. Sometimes the object being returned by a method is retained, and sometimes it is auto released later. If the object is going to be auto released, the object needs to be retained. If it's already retained, you don't want the compiler to do anything.

The only way the compiler knows whether an object has been retained when it is returned is through certain naming conventions. Under ARC, these naming conventions are now are now part of the language, and you must follow them.

The compiler knows that a retained object has been returned when the first "word" in the first part of the selector is alloc, new, copy, mutableCopy, or init. These methods transfer ownership — with *transferred ownership* meaning that the object has been retained for you. An example is the NSString initWithFormat: method.

In addition, you cannot give a property a name that begins with new.

Just follow the rules

That's it — no retaining releasing or releasing. Just follow the rules and code to your heart's content without worrying about memory management.

Except, of course, there are some situations in which you'll need to explicitly tell the compiler what you want. In those cases, you'll have to tell the compiler explicitly about an object's lifetime. I explain how to do that in the next section.

Working with variable types according to ARC

Because the reference to an object lives in a variable, object pointers can be qualified using ownership type or lifetime qualifiers. These qualifiers determine when the compiler can de-allocate an object to which a pointer points. These qualifiers are as follows:

```
__strong
__weak
__unsafe_unretained
__autoreleasing
```

The following sections describe the function of each of these qualifiers.

__strong *variables "retain" their values*

`__strong` is the default. You almost never have to specify it and stack local variables, including parameters, are `__strong`. A `__strong` pointer to an object will cause that object to be retained while it is in scope (or not set to `nil`). No more dangling references (objects that have been de-allocated that you expect to be there)!

__weak *variables don't retain values*

`__weak` variables do not cause an object to be retained (that is, you don't use them in the reference count) and are, in fact, set to `nil` (zeroed) as soon as the referenced object starts de-allocating. You need to be concerned with these only to prevent retain cycles, which I explain shortly.

__unsafe_unretained *don't retain values and are not zeroed*

There are some Apple-provided classes (only on the Mac and some third-party libraries) that don't work with zeroing weak references. These have to be cleared in a `dealloc` method elsewhere.

Using ARC, strong, weak, and autoreleasing stack variables are now implicitly initialized with `nil`.

__autoreleasing *for indirect pointers*

These variables are not for general use. They are used for out parameters that pass values back to the calling routine They are retained and then autoreleased when they are read into, and are beyond the scope of this book.

Understanding the deadly retain cycle

ARC works very well to manage memory except in one circumstance. In this section, I explain how that circumstance can arise, and what you'll need to do to keep it from happening.

When you create an object, the compiler makes sure that ownership is transferred and all is well. The compiler will release that object when it goes out of scope, so if it is an instance variable, it will stay in scope until the object itself is de-allocated.

I take you through this process using a little program called RetainCycle that I wrote to illustrate the retain cycle.

I create a new RetainIt object in the viewDidLoad method of my Retain CycleViewController object. It will be released only when the retainIt variable goes out of scope (it is __strong by default). In this case, it will be released and then de-allocated (assuming that no other object takes ownership) at the end of viewDidLoad because the retainIt variable will go out of scope:

```
-  (void)viewDidLoad
{
   [super viewDidLoad];
   RetainIt* retainIt = [[RetainIt new] init];
}
```

When I create the RetainIt object, in the RetainIt class's initialization method, init, I create a Cycle object and assign it to the cycle instance variable I declared. As you might expect, the Cycle object will be retained until the RetainIt object is de-allocated because it is referenced by an instance variable, which stays in scope until the object is de-allocated:

```
-  (id)init
{
   self = [super init];
   if (self) {
      self.cycle = [[Cycle new] init];
      cycle.retainIt = self;
   }
   return self;
}
```

I also, however, assign to the Cycle object's retainIt property a reference back to the RetainIt object. The Cycle class looks like this:

```
@interface Cycle : NSObject

@property (strong, nonatomic) RetainIt* retainIt;

@end
```

This means that the RetainIt object will not be de-allocated until the Cycle object is de-allocated, and the Cycle object will be de-allocated only when the RetainIt object is de-allocated. Whoops!

Although this example may appear a bit contrived, it actually can occur in real life when you have one object with a back pointer to the object that creates it (either directly or through a chain of other objects, each with a strong reference to the next leading back to the first).

The __weak lifetime qualifiers for objects takes care of this. Although I haven't explained properties yet, the solution is to make the lifetime qualifier back pointer __weak.

```
@property (weak, nonatomic) RetainIt* retainIt;
```

I explain this more when I explain property attributes later in this chapter.

Observing Low-Memory Warnings

Even if you have done everything correctly, in a large application you may simply run out of memory. When that situation occurs, the system dispatches a low-memory notification to your application — and it's something you must pay attention to. If you don't, it's a reliable recipe for disaster. (Think of your low-fuel light going on as you approach a sign on the highway that says "Next services 100 miles.") UIKit provides several ways for you to set up your application so that you receive timely low-memory notifications:

- Override the viewDidUnload and didReceiveMemoryWarning methods in your custom UIViewController subclass.

- Implement the applicationDidReceiveMemoryWarning: method of your application delegate.

- Register to receive the UIApplicationDidReceiveMemoryWarningNotification: notification.

The viewDidUnload method

When a low-memory condition occurs, one way to free some memory is to remove views that are not being used. You don't have to worry about that, however, because it is handled in the view controller class from which you derive your view controllers, such as RTViewController in the RoadTrip project.

What you do have to worry about, though, is managing any references to the view or its subviews that you have. This includes managing the outlets you create in Chapter 6.

That's why Interface Builder so kindly added the following code to your project:

```
- (void)viewDidUnload
{
    [self setCar:nil];
    [self setTestDriveButton:nil];
    [self setBackgroundImage:nil];
    [super viewDidUnload];
}
```

Here you set the references to the outlets you created to nil, which will tell ARC to generate the code to release these references and which will enable them to be released from memory. You can also use this method to release any objects that you created to support the view but that are no longer needed now that the view is gone, by setting them to nil as well. You should not use this method to release user data or any other information that cannot be easily recreated.

The didReceiveMemoryWarning method

The didReceiveMemoryWarning is sent to the view controller when the application receives a memory warning. The default implementation of this method checks to see whether the view controller can safely release its view. If the view can be released, this method releases it and sends the viewDid-Unload message (see previous section).

You should override this method to release any additional memory used by your view controller, but be sure to send the [super didReceiveMemory-Warning] to allow the view controller to release its view

applicationDidReceiveMemoryWarning:

Similar to viewDidUnload, your Application Delegate should set any references to objects it can safely free to nil.

UIApplicationDidReceiveMemoryWarning Notification: notification

Low memory notifications are sent to the notification center, where all notifications are centralized. An object that wants to get informed about this notification registers itself to the notification center by telling which notification it wants to be informed about, and a block to be called when the notification is raised. A model object, for example, could then release data structures or objects it owns that it doesn't need immediately and can re-create later, by setting references to `nil`. However, this approach is beyond the scope of this book.

However for those of you who are curious, in your model object (which you create in Chapter 12), you could add:

```
[[NSNotificationCenter defaultCenter] addObserverForName:
  UIApplicationDidReceiveMemoryWarningNotification
  object:[UIApplication sharedApplication] queue:nil
  usingBlock:^(NSNotification *notif) {
//your code here
}];
```

You can test `applicationDidReceiveMemoryWarning:` and `UIApplicationDidReceiveMemoryWarningNotification:` in the simulator by choosing Hardware➪Simulate Memory Warning.

Picking the right memory-management strategy for your application

Each of these strategies gives a different part of your application a chance to free the memory it no longer needs (or doesn't need right now). How you actually get these strategies working for you depends on your application's architecture, so you'll have to explore that on your own.

Not freeing enough memory will result in iOS sending your application the `applicationWillTerminate:` message and shutting you down. For many apps, though, the best defense is a good offense, and you need to manage your memory effectively and eliminate any memory leaks in your code by following the ARC rules.

Customizing the Behavior of Framework Classes

Although you will be creating classes of your own (especially model classes), often you will want to customize the behavior of framework class. There are two ways to go about it:

- ✐ Subclassing
- ✐ Delegating

Subclassing

Objective-C, like other object-oriented programming languages, permits you to base a new class definition on a class already defined. The base class is called a *superclass;* the new class is its *subclass.* The subclass is defined only by its extension to its superclass; everything else remains the same. Each new class that you define *inherits* methods and instance variables of its superclass.

Some framework classes are expected to be subclassed. Among them are view controllers, and you will be subclassing quite a bit. Others are not expected to be subclassed, but because of the need to customize their behavior, you use *delegation* instead.

The Delegation pattern

Delegation is a pattern used extensively in the iOS frameworks, so much so that clearly understanding it is very important. In fact, when you understand it, your life will be much easier.

Delegation, as I mention in the previous section, is a way of customizing the behavior of an object without subclassing it. Instead, one object (a framework or any other object) delegates the task of implementing one of its responsibilities to another object. You're using a behavior-rich object supplied by the framework *as is,* and putting the code for program-specific behavior in a separate (delegate) object. When a request is made of the framework object, the method of the delegate that implements the program-specific behavior is automatically called.

For example, the `UIApplication` object handles most of the actual work needed to run the application. But, as you saw, it sends your application delegate the `application:didFinishLaunchingWithOptions:` message to give you an opportunity to create (model) objects that are unique to your app.

When a framework object has been designed to use delegates to implement certain behaviors, the behaviors it requires (or gives you the option to implement) are defined in a *protocol.*

Protocols define an interface that the delegate object implements. On the iPhone, protocols can be formal or informal, although I concentrate solely on the former because formal protocols include support for things like type checking and runtime checking to see whether an object conforms to the protocol.

In a formal protocol, you usually don't have to implement all the methods; many are declared optional, meaning that you have to implement only the ones relevant to your app. Before a formal protocol attempts to send a message to its delegate, the host object determines whether the delegate implements the method (via a `respondsToSelector:` message) to avoid the embarrassment of branching into nowhere if the method is not implemented.

Delegation and protocols are the preferred way to manage model views, and you create your own protocol to manage model views in Chapter 18.

Understanding Declared Properties

Although properties and instance variable access and accessors are often mushed together by programmers, I want to make sure that you understand properties and how they really work.

Whereas methods are concerned with sending message to objects to get things done, properties are concerned with the state of the object. Framework and other objects behave based on what they find in their properties; for example, a button's background image is a property you set (indirectly, in Interface Builder) in Chapter 5.

You also may want to know something about the state of the object, such as its color, or about a window's root view controller.

In Chapter 12, I discuss creating a model object — `Trip`. Your app's view controllers, which act as a bridge between the views and the model, need to be able to find the `Trip` object to get data and send it updates. All of this is done using properties.

As I discuss when creating an outlet in Chapter 6, a property looks like the following:

```
@property (strong, nonatomic) IBOutlet UIImageView *car;
```

But not all properties are outlets. If you select the `RTAppDelegate.h` file in the Project inspector, you can see that it includes a window property:

```
@property (strong, nonatomic) UIWindow *window;
```

And in Chapter 12, you add a `trip` property to `RTAppDelegate`:

```
@property (nonatomic, strong) Trip *trip;
```

The order of the attributes doesn't matter.

What comprises a declared property

A declared property has two parts: its declaration and its implementation.

The declaration uses the @property keyword, followed by an optional parenthesized set of attributes, the type information, and the name of the property.

Access to properties is implemented by accessor methods (although within the class that declares the property, they can be accessed directly, just as instance variables are). You can write your own accessor methods or you can let the compiler do it for you. To have the compiler do it for you, you use the @synthesize directive to tell the compiler to create the accessor methods. The code it generates matches the attributes you have specified. (I explain the attributes in the upcoming "Attributes" section).

The default names for the getter and setter methods associated with a property are *whateverThePropertyNameIs* for the getter and *setWhateverThe PropertyNameIs:* for the setter . In the case of trip, the getter method is trip, and the setter method is setTrip:.

To access the trip property in the appDelegate, you would use

```
RTAppDelegate* appDelegate =
              [[UIApplication sharedApplication] delegate];
Trip* thisTrip = [appDelegate trip];
```

or to set that property

```
RTAppDelegate* appDelegate =
              [[UIApplication sharedApplication] delegate];
[appDelegate setTrip:newTrip];
```

As I said, the UIApplication is a singleton object (there is just one). To get a reference to it, you send the class message (in Objective-C, you can send messages to classes, which are really objects on their own). Sending the UIApplication object the delegate message gives you a pointer to the delegate object.

Using dot syntax

Objective-C provides a dot (.) operator that offers an alternative to square bracket notation ([]) to invoke accessor methods. You use dot syntax in the same way as you would to access a C structure element:

```
Trip* thisTrip = appDelegate.trip;
```

or to set that property

```
appDelegate.trip = newTrip;
```

When used with objects, however, dot syntax acts as "syntactic sugar" — it is transformed by the compiler into an accessor message. Dot syntax does not directly get or set an instance variable. The code examples using it are the exact equivalent to using the bracket notation.

Many programmers like the dot syntax because it may be more readable than when you are accessing a property that is a property of another object (that is a property of another object, and so on). The real advantage of dot syntax, though, is that the compiler will generate an *error* when it detects an attempt to write to a read-only declared property instead of an undeclared method *warning* because you invoked a nonexistent setter method, with the app subsequently failing at runtime.

When you use the compiler to create accessor methods for you, the compiler will create an instance variable of the type you have declared that it will use to store and retrieve the property value with the name of the property. For example, in the following:

```
@synthesize car;
```

an instance variable with the name of `car` and the type of `UIImage` is generated.

You can, however, specify the instance variable name. For example, in `RTAppDelegate.m` in Xcode, you will find

```
@synthesize window = _window;
```

You'll see this quite a bit, and I have you specify the instance variable name this way as well. By prefixing an underscore, you can distinguish between a local variable and direct access to a property that's not using an accessor method.

Setting attributes for a declared property

As I said, you can set certain property attributes when you declare a property. I cover some of those attributes in this section.

Setter semantics/ownership

- ✔ `strong` (similar to `retain`, which was used previous to ARC) creates an accessor method that means that the object this property points to will be retained while it is in scope (or not set to nil or some other value).

✔ weak (similar to assign, which was used previous to ARC) creates an accessor that uses simple assignment. This attribute is the default, and you typically use this attribute for scalar types such as NSInteger and CGRect, or (in a reference-counted environment) for objects you don't own, such as delegates and to avoid retain cycle problems, as I explain in "Understanding the deadly retain cycle," earlier in this chapter.

✔ copy specifies that a copy of the object should be used for assignment. The previous value is sent a release message.

The copy is made by invoking the copy method. This attribute is valid only for object types, which must implement the NSCopying protocol (and is beyond the scope of this book).

For object properties, you must explicitly specify one of these; otherwise, you get a compiler warning. So you need to think about what memory management behavior you want, and type the behavior explicitly.

Writability

These attributes specify whether a property has an associated set accessor. They are mutually exclusive.

✔ readwrite indicates that the property should be treated as read/write. This attribute is the default. If you use the @synthesize directive, the getter and setter methods are synthesized; otherwise, both a getter and setter method are required.

✔ readonly indicates that the property is read-only. If you use the @synthesize directive, only a getter method is synthesized. Otherwise, only a getter method is required. If you attempt to assign a value using the dot syntax, you get a compiler error.

Accessor method names

The default names for the getter and setter methods associated with a property are propertyName and setPropertyName:, respectively. For example, for the property trip, the accessors are trip and setTrip:. You can, however, specify custom names instead. They are both optional and can appear with any other attribute (except for readonly in the case of setter =):

✔ getter = getterName specifies the name of the get accessor for the property. The getter must return a type matching the property's type and take no parameters.

✔ setter = setterName specifies the name of the set accessor for the property. The setter method must take a single parameter of a type matching the property's type and must return void.

Typically, you should specify accessor method names that are key-value coding compliant (which is beyond the scope of this book). A common reason for using the getter decorator is to adhere to the isPropertyName convention for Boolean values.

Atomicity

You can use this attribute to specify that accessor methods are not atomic. (There is no keyword to denote atomic.) If you specify nonatomic, a synthesized accessor for an object property simply returns the value directly. Otherwise, a synthesized get accessor for an object property uses a lock and retains and autoreleases the returned value. You use nonatamic throughout this book and on the iPhone in general.

Writing your own accessors

You don't have to use the assessors generated by the compiler, and sometimes it makes sense to implement them yourself (although such times don't arise in this book). If you implement the accessor methods yourself, you should ensure that your approach matches the attributes you have declared. (For example, if you specify copy, you must make sure that you do copy the input value in the setter method).

For example, if there is a lot of overhead to create an object that might not be used, you can create your own getter accessor that creates the object the first tine it is accessed. In addition, writing your own accessor means you don't have to have an instance variable associated with the property. The UIView frame property, for example, is actually computed based on the bounds and center properties.

Accessing instance variables with accessors

If you do not use self., you access the instance variable directly. In the following example, the set accessor method for currentDestinationIndex is not invoked:

```
currentDestinationIndex = [[NSUserDefaults
  standardUserDefaults]objectForKey:CurrentDestinationKey];
```

The preceding is not the same as

```
self.currentDestinationIndex = [[NSUserDefaults
  standardUserDefaults]objectForKey:CurrentDestinationKey];
```

To use an accessor, you must use self.

Hiding Instance Variables

When properties were first developed, they were looked at as a way to avoid the tedium of writing accessors for instance variable based properties.

People used to think about properties as a way to access instance variables. In fact, instance variables should not be equated to properties, and more important, instance variables should not be made public. (Doing so violates the object-oriented principle of encapsulation, but that's a conversation for a different time). In fact, Apple's new approach is to put instance variable declarations in the implementation file of the class.

Before the new Objective-C compiler that comes with Xcode 4.2 came about, programmers declared instance variables in the header file in the `@interface` class declaration. In the old times, you would have added the following bolded code to the `RTViewController.h` file:

```
@interface RTViewController : UIViewController
                      <DestinationControllerDelegate> {

    AVAudioPlayer *backgroundAudioPlayer;
    SystemSoundID burnRubberSoundID;
    BOOL touchInCar;
}
```

This approach made instance variables (ivars) visible to everyone and every thing and was, as I mentioned, at odds with the principle of encapsulation (even if the variables couldn't be accessed).

In Xcode 4.2, you can hide instance variables by declaring them in the implementation file in one of two ways. The first is as a *class extension,* which you create by adding a second interface block in the implementation file followed by open and close parenthesis:

```
@interface RTViewController () {

  AVAudioPlayer *backgroundAudioPlayer;
  SystemSoundID burnRubberSoundID;
  BOOL touchInCar;
}
@end
```

The second way is by declaring the instance variable in the @implementation block of the class:

```
@implementation RTViewController

AVAudioPlayer *backgroundAudioPlayer;
SystemSoundID burnRubberSoundID;
BOOL touchInCar;
```

A class extension is a variation of an Objective-C category, which is beyond the scope of this book.

The approach you use is your choice; I prefer the class extension because I think it makes the variables easier to distinguish.

You can also use class extensions to have a publicly declared set of methods and to then have additional methods declared privately for use solely by the class:

```
@interface RTViewController () {

  AVAudioPlayer *backgroundAudioPlayer;
  SystemSoundID burnRubberSoundID;
  BOOL touchInCar;
}
- (void) privateMethod;
@end
```

Part IV

Finishing the Basic Application Structure

The 5th Wave   By Rich Tennant

"Other than this little glitch with the landscape view, I really love my iPhone."

*A*fter you have the foundation in place, you need to make all those controls do something, such as when a user taps a button.

In this part, you start the actual coding process to turn a good idea (an app that you use when you take a road trip) into a real working app.

You start by adding animation and sound to the opening screen of your app so that when the user taps the Test Drive button, the '59 Cadillac Eldorado Biarritz convertible takes off with a screech and then drives up and down the screen with a satisfying engine purr.

You also create the application model — the part of your application that manages the content. The content includes where the user is going, what to see when he or she gets there, and how to find out what the weather is like at that location.

You also add navigation to the application, including a screen that shows the features and functions available. In the process, you learn how to customize the appearance of the controls provided by the framework to make your application a thing of beauty.

And because your app will be using the Internet — a lot! — you also learn how to determine whether the Internet is available and how to alert the user when it is not.

Chapter 8

Working with the Source Editor

In This Chapter

▶ Using the Standard Source editor to add code

▶ Fixing syntax errors as you code

▶ Getting the help you need from the documentation and other forms of help

▶ Searching and finding symbols

*I*f you've been reading through the chapters in order, you may be beginning to hate me because I haven't shown you much in the way of coding yet. Isn't developing apps about coding? Well, yes and no.

Think of painting a room in your house. So much time and effort needs to be spent in the prep work because you know that if you prepare correctly, the job will take you less time in the long run by saving you a lot of rework.

That's what the chapters in this book have been doing so far— preparing you to code by showing you the ins and out of Xcode and the UIKit framework. At this point, all you have left to do is learn about the Xcode Source editor and a few other features. After that you'll be ready to code, and take my word for it, you will.

In this chapter, I tell you how to navigate the files in your project using the Jump bar and the navigators, as well as how to work with the Source editor to enter code. And for when you are confused, or simply just curious, I explain how to access the documentation and Xcode's help system. This chapter finishes the explanation on how to use Xcode, and you learn what you need to know to make it easy to start coding in the next chapter.

Navigating in the Xcode Source Editors

In previous chapters, I give you quite a bit of information about the Xcode Workspace, albeit primarily focusing on storyboards. I tell you a little about the Assistant as well, and in this chapter I want to extend that knowledge and describe most of the rest of the tasks you need to be able to do in Xcode.

As you've seen, most development work in Xcode is done in the Editor area, the main area that is always visible within the Workspace window. The Editor area can also be further configured, with the Standard editor pane always shown, as well as an optional Assistant pane that shows related content. (If you select an interface [.h] header file, the Assistant pane shows the corresponding in the Jump bar above the Assistant editor). As you can see in Figure 8-5, the choices offered depend on the type of file being edited (a source file, for example, as shown, or the storyboard).

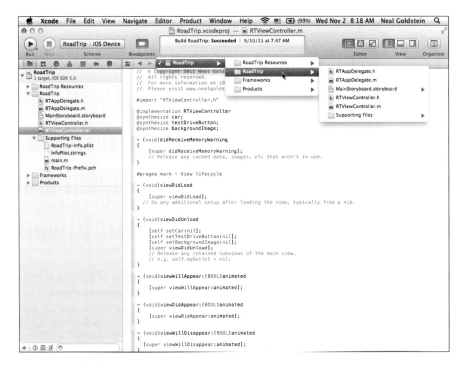

Figure 8-3: A file hierarchy.

In Manual mode, you select the file to display in the Assistant pane. (As mentioned previously, you can also split the Assistant editor pane to create multiple assistant editors.)

Hold down the Option key when selecting an item in the Navigation bar to open the Assistant and display that item in the Assistant editor pane.

If you have any questions about what something does, just position the mouse pointer above the icon; a tooltip appears to explain it.

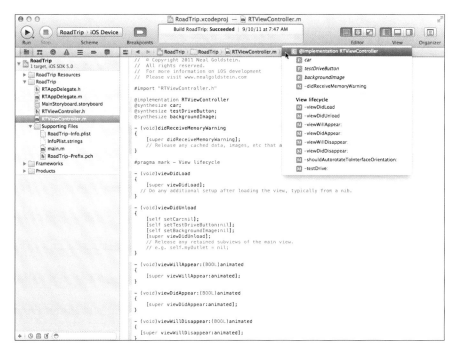

Figure 8-4: A tour of `RTViewController.m`.

Organizing your code using the #pragma mark statement

While you're here, this is a good time to introduce the `#pragma mark` statement. As you can see in Figure 8-4, this statement helps you group things in your file; such statements are also displayed in the list of symbols.

You use the `# pragma mark` statement with a label (such as `View life cycle` or `Animation`) to add a category header in the Methods list so that you can identify and keep separate the methods that fit logically in the list.

For example, in Figure 8-4, the template added

```
#pragma mark - View lifecycle
```

The first part of the statement (with a space and a dash) places a horizontal line in the Methods list. The second one places the text "View life cycle" in the Methods lists.

This is a useful trick for finding code sections, organizing your code, and adding new code in the proper sections.

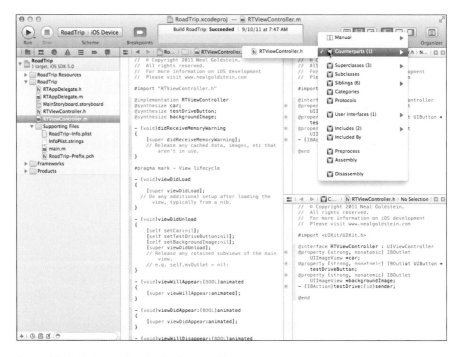

Figure 8-5: Assistant options in the Source editor.

Using the Xcode Source Editor

The main tool you use to write code for an iPhone application is the Xcode Source editor, which appears as the Standard editor pane in the editor area on the right side of the Xcode Workspace window after you select a source code file in the Project navigator. It also appears as the Assistant editor in a second pane if you click the Assistant Editor button — the middle Editor selector button in the top-right corner of the Workspace window.

Apple has gone out of its way to make the Source editor as useful as possible by including the following:

✔ **Code completion:** Code completion is a feature of the editor that shows symbols — arguments, placeholders, and suggested code — as you type statements. Code completion can be really useful, especially if you're like me and forget exactly what the arguments are for a function. When code completion is active (as it is by default), Xcode uses the text you typed, as well as the context within which you typed it, to provide inline suggestions for completing what it thinks you're *going to* type. You can accept inline suggestions by pressing Tab or Return. You also see a pop-up list of suggestions by clicking an item in the suggestion list or clicking the up and down arrows to select an item. As you do so, the inline suggestion changes depending on what you selected. Press the Esc key, or Control+Spacebar, to cancel a code completion operation. You can turn off code completion, or set options for code completion, by choosing Xcode⊕Preferences and clicking the Text Editing tab.

✐ **Automatic indenting, formatting, and closing braces:** As I explain in Chapter 3 in the section on preferences, the Source editor indents the text you type according to the rules you can set in the Text Editing preferences pane. It also uses fonts and colors for the various syntax elements (variables, constants, comments, and so on) according to the settings in the Fonts & Colors pane of Xcode preferences. After typing an opening brace ({), you can continue typing, and Xcode automatically adds a closing brace (}) — unless you've deactivated the Automatically Insert Closing "}" option in the Text Editing preferences.

✐ **Code Folding in the focus ribbon:** With Code Folding, you can collapse code that you're not working on and display only the code that requires your attention. You do this by clicking in the Focus ribbon column to the left of the code you want to hide (between the gutter, which displays line numbers and breakpoints, and the editor). A disclosure triangle appears, and clicking it hides or shows blocks of code.

✐ **Opening a file in a separate window:** Double-click the file in the Project navigator to open the file in a new window.

Using Live Issues and Fix-it

The Apple LLVM compiler engine wants to be your best friend, so *Live Issues* continuously evaluates your code in the background and alerts you to coding mistakes. Before this feature came along, you had to build your app first, and trust me, this new way saves lots of time and effort.

But not only is Live Issues happy to point out your mistakes (like someone else I know, but I won't go there) *Fix-it* will also offer (when it can) to fix the problem for you. Clicking the error displays the available Fix-its, such as correcting an assignment to a comparison, repairing a misspelled symbol, or appending a missing semicolon. With a single keyboard shortcut, you can instantly have the error repaired, and you can continue coding. Fix-it marks syntax errors with a red underline or a caret at the position of the error and with a symbol in the gutter.

For example, in Figure 8-6, the semicolon is missing after the `[super view DidLoad]` statement (notice the error indicator in the Activity viewer). Pressing Return will automatically fix this problem. This is a very useful feature and will cut down your debugging time significantly (especially if you use it).

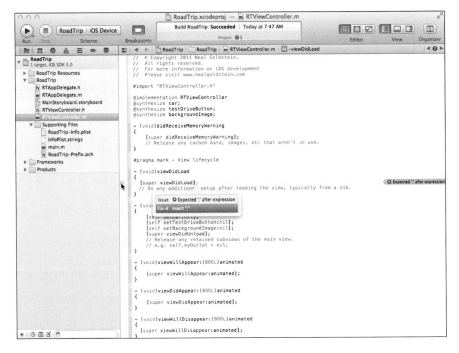

Figure 8-6: Live Issues and Fix-it.

Compiler warnings

Although Xcode and the compiler working together are very good at you giving warnings and errors, sometimes they are a little slow on the uptake when you fix the problem. So don't be surprised by random warning and errors, especially if the compiler for some reason can't find header file.

If you see a warning or error that you are sure you have fixed, you can press Run. Xcode and compiler will reset and the warning will go away. (Unless, of course, it was right and you were wrong.)

The Issue navigator

The Issue navigator is one of the navigators provided by Xcode. The error displayed in Figure 8-6, shown previously, also appears in the Issue navigator, as shown in Figure 8-7.

To get to the Issue navigator, you select it in the Navigator selector bar.

If, in spite of Live Issues and Fix-it (or any other) warnings, you decide to compile the program, the Issue navigator will automatically launch for you.

Scope bar

Issue list

Issue stepper

Filter bar

Figure 8-7: An error message displayed by the Issue navigator.

The Issue navigator displays the error and warning messages generated in a Project or Workspace and is similar to the other navigators you have used so far.

When you select a warning or error in the Issue navigator, an editor displays the item with the issue, and if the error occurs in a source file, the issue message is placed on the line of code with the issue.

Place the pointer over an issue message that ends with an ellipsis (which appears if the pane is too narrow to display the entire message) to get a complete description of the issue.

You can display issues by file or by type using the buttons in the Scope bar (see Figure 8-7), filter the issue list with the Filter bar, and step through issues using the issue stepper in the Jump bar. Use the Next and Previous buttons in the Jump bar to jump to the previous and next issues.

As you may recall from Chapter 3, I changed Xcode preferences to have the Issue navigator displayed and a sound played when a build fails.

Accessing Documentation

The ability to quickly access documentation is a major feature of Xcode, and one you'll want to use regularly. If you have no idea how to do something, or how something works, you can often find the answer in the documentation.

Being able to figure out what is going on will make your life easier. You saw that Xcode will complete your code for you, which is useful when you can't quite remember the method signature and parameters, but what if you don't even have a clue?

Or, like many developers, you may find yourself wanting to dig deeper when it comes to a particular bit of code. That's when you'll really appreciate Xcode's Quick Help, the Documentation pane in the Organizer window, header file access, Help menu, and Find tools. With these tools, you can quickly access the documentation for a particular class, method, or property.

To see how easy it is to access the documentation, say that you have selected `RTViewController.h` as shown in Figure 8-9. (I've hidden the Assistant to have more room). What if you wanted to find out more about UIViewController?

Getting Xcode help

The Quick Help section of the Utility area provides documentation for a single symbol. (To see the Utility area, click the rightmost view selector button in the top-right corner of the Workspace window), and in the Inspector selector bar, select the second button). In an editor, click anywhere in the symbol or select the entire symbol, as shown in Figure 8-8.

The Quick Help section of the Utility area shows a description of the symbol and provides links to more information. For example, you can click the `UIViewController` Class Reference link near the bottom of the Quick Help section (refer to Figure 8-8) to bring up the class reference definition in the iOS Library Reference in the Documentation pane of the Organizer window, as shown in Figure 8-9. I use class references a lot!

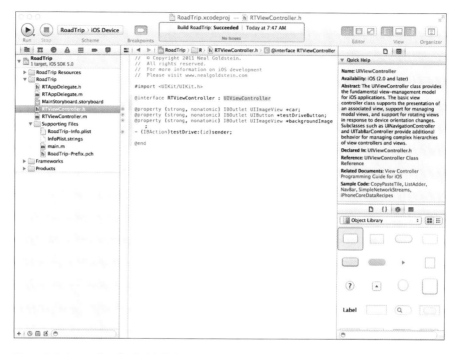

Figure 8-8: Accessing the Quick Help section of the Utility area.

With the Quick Help section open, information is available for three types of elements in your project, depending on your selection in the open editor:

- **Symbols**, in the Source editor
- **Interface objects**, in Interface Builder
- **Build settings**, in the Project editor

It may be more convenient to use a Quick Help window if, for example, you prefer to work with the Utility area hidden. To do so, press Option and click one of the following in the open editor:

- **Symbols**, in the Source editor
- **Build settings**, in the Project editor

As you can see in Figure 8-10, a Quick Help window appears with the pointer indicating the item you selected (in this case, the symbol UIView Controller):

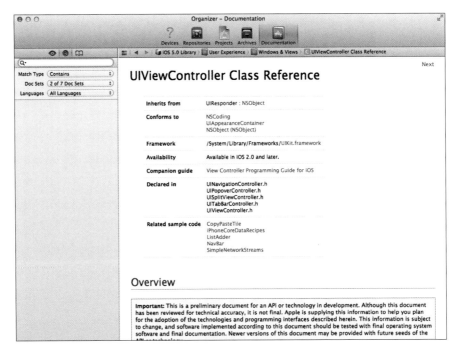

Figure 8-9: The Class reference in the Organizer window.

If you are like me and want to go directly to the class reference, press Option and double-click the symbol instead.

The Organizer window

You can have only one Organizer window (shown in Figure 8-11). You use the organizers in this window to manage all the development resources (projects, the Workspace, repositories, and so forth) on your local system in addition to using documentation and managing devices, and archives.

To display the Organizer window, click the Organizer button in the Workspace window's toolbar or choose Window⇨Organizer. The window includes five individual organizers, whose tasks I describe in the following list:

- ✔ **Devices organizer:** Provision a device, manage your developer profile, install iOS on the device, and work with your application and its data. This organizer is present only if the iOS SDK is installed.

- ✔ **Repositories organizer:** Create, view, and manage Git and Subversion repositories for your Workspace in a single consistent interface.

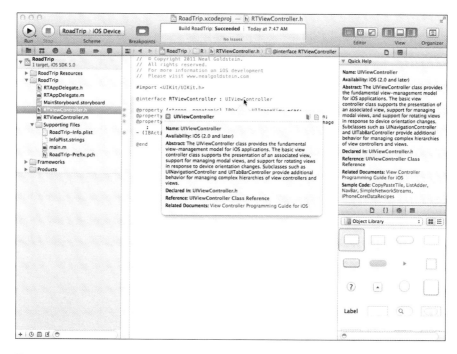

Figure 8-10: The Quick Help window.

- ✏ **Projects organizer:** Find, view, and manage an open project or Workspace, its derived data, and its snapshots.

- ✏ **Archives organizer:** View and manage build product archives resulting from your distribution scheme.

- ✏ **Documentation organizer:** Find documentation and sample code and use them within Xcode. You can search and explore documentation and set bookmarks, and I suggest that you explore these topics further.

Each of these organizers includes task-oriented contextual help articles that you can view by choosing the Organizer, and clicking in its content pane while pressing Control.

I explain a bit more about some of the other organizers as you use them in upcoming chapters.

Organizers

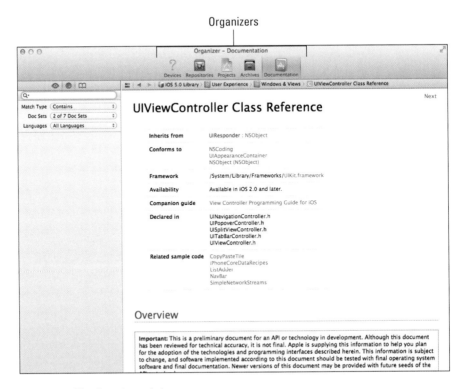

Figure 8-11: The Organizer window.

The Help menu

The Help menu's search field (in the Xcode menu bar) also lets you search Xcode Help, the Xcode User Guide, and Documentation and API Reference, all of which open the Documentation pane of the Organizer window. You can also choose Quick Help for Selected Item, which displays a Quick Help panel above the selected symbol in the editor.

Finding and Searching in Your Project

You'll find that, as your classes get bigger, sometimes you'll want to find a symbol of some other text in your project. Xcode provides a number of ways to do that.

Using the Find command to locate an item in a file

You'll likely discover that, as your classes get bigger, you'll sometimes want to find a single symbol or all occurrences of a symbol in a file or class. You can easily locate what you're looking for by choosing Edit⇨Find⇨Find or pressing CMD+F, which opens a Find toolbar above the editor pane to help you search the file in the editor.

For example, as shown in Figure 8-12, I entered **viewDidLoad** on the Find toolbar. Xcode found both instances of viewDidLoad in the Source editor and highlighted them.

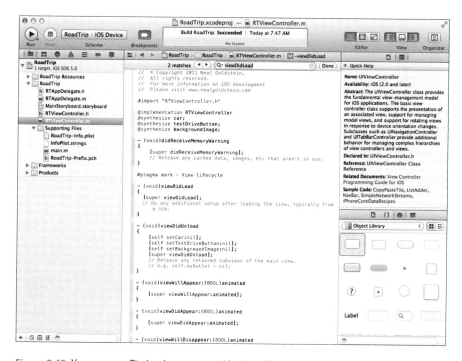

Figure 8-12: You can use Find to locate something in a file.

 You can jump from one instance to the next by pressing CMD+G. Or you can use the Previous and Next buttons (left and right arrows) on the Find bar.

Clicking the Find pop-up menu on the Find bar lets you do a file-level replace.

Click the magnifying glass in the Search field to display a menu that allows you to show or hide the Find options. For example, you can choose to ignore or match the case of the text in the Search field. Changes you make to this set of options remain persistent for future searches.

Using the Search navigator to search your project or framework

Whereas the Find command works for locating an item in a file or class, you use the Search navigator (the third button from the left in the Project navigator) to find items in your project or even frameworks.

In Figure 8-13, I entered @synthesize in the search filed. I also clicked the magnifying glass to display search options (clicking in the Find pop-up menu) will also let you perform a global search and replace).

After you obtain the initial results of your search, if you want to filter the Results list further, you can enter text into the field at the bottom of the pane. Any items that do not match the text are removed from the Results list.

To go directly to where the search term appears in a file, click an entry under the file's name in the Search navigator, as shown in Figure 8-13. The file appears in the editor pane on the right, open to the location where the search term appears.

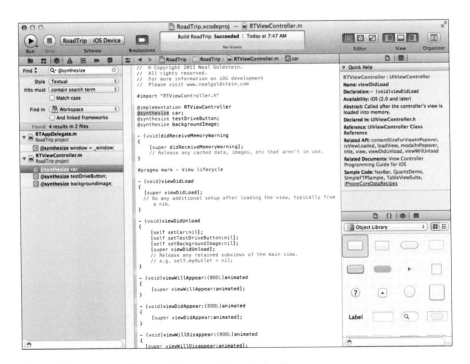

Figure 8-13: See a specific use of the search term in the file.

Using the Symbol Navigator

 The Symbol navigator allows you to browse through the symbols in your project — just click the Symbol button in the navigator selector bar. Note that you need to wait until Xcode finishes indexing your project before you can use this feature.

You can display symbols in a hierarchical or flat list using the buttons at the top of the Symbol navigator.

You can specify which symbols are displayed by using the buttons at the bottom of the navigator. Buttons are blue when on and black when off. Use the buttons in any combination:

✔ The first button on the Symbol navigator shows only class symbols and hides global symbol types.

✔ The middle button shows only symbols in this project.

✔ The third button shows only containers (classes and categories).

You can refine the Results list yet more by using the filter field at the bottom of the navigator. If you select a symbol to display, its header file definition will be displayed in the Source editor. In Figure 8-14, I have hidden everything but the member symbols. In the resulting list, I selected the `viewDidLoad` method, and its definition was highlighted in the Source editor.

You're Finally Ready to Code!

Yes, it's finally time to code, and from here on, it's full steam ahead.

Filter bar

Show Only Class Symbols

Show Only Symbols in This Project

Show Only Containers

Figure 8-14: The Symbol navigator.

Chapter 9

It's (Finally) Time to Code

*Y*es, it's finally time to start coding, although this chapter doesn't get you going on the RoadTrip app functionality itself yet (the example app developed in this book). In this chapter, I show you some code you have to include to make sure that your app isn't rejected out of hand by Apple.

I also show you how to spruce up the Main view by customizing how controls appear, and finally I give you an introduction to your new friend, the debugger. Although some of you out there (but not me) may code perfectly, most developers make some mistakes as they develop an application (me included). Fortunately, the debugger in Xcode 4.2 starts helping you right from the start — so you want to understand how to use it as soon as you start coding.

Checking for Network Availability

One of the easiest ways to get your app rejected by Apple is to fail to make sure that you have an Internet connection when your app needs it, and therefore failing to notify the user that the functionality that requires the connection will be unavailable (or even worse, having your app just hang there).

Downloading the Reachability sample

Apple provides a sample application on how to determine whether you have an Internet connection (as well as quite a bit of additional network information I won't be going into), and you will be using that code (which is what many other developers do as well) in the RoadTrip app developed in this book.

1. **Download the Reachability sample from Apple by clicking Sample Code at** http://developer.apple.com/devcenter/ios/.

2. **Type** Reachability **in the Search field.**

3. **Click Reachability in the search results and then click the Download Sample Code button.**

4. **In Safari download, double-click the Reachability folder to open it.**

5. **Open the disclosure triangle next to the Classes folder, and drag the** `Reachability.m` **and** `Reachability.h` **files into your project (I put them in my Frameworks group).**

   Be sure to select the Copy Items into Destination Group's Folder option (if not already selected).

In order for you to be able to use this code, you need to add the SystemConfiguration framework. To do so, follow these steps:

1. **In the Project navigator, select the Project icon at the top of the Project Navigator area (RoadTrip) to display the Project editor.**

2. **In the TARGETS section, select RoadTrip.**

3. **In the Summary tab, scroll down to the Linked Frameworks and Libraries section.**

4. **Expand the Linked Frameworks and Libraries section if it is not already expanded (see Figure 9-1) by clicking the disclosure triangle.**

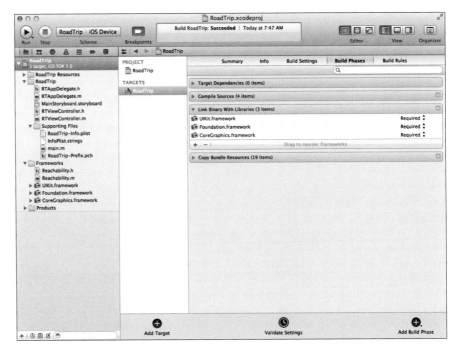

Figure 9-1: Adding a framework.

5. **Click the + (plus sign) button underneath the list of current project frameworks.**

   A list of frameworks appears.

6. **Scroll down and select the** `SystemConfiguration.framework`, **as shown in Figure 9-2.**

7. **Click the Add button.**

   You'll see the framework added to the Linked Frameworks and Libraries section.

8. **Close the Linked Frameworks and Libraries section.**

9. **In the Project navigator (don't do this from the Linked Frameworks and Libraries section!), drag the** `SystemConfiguration.framework` **file to the Frameworks group (see Figure 9-3).**

You can also add a framework by clicking the Build Phases tab, expanding the Link Binary With Libraries section, and following the same procedure.

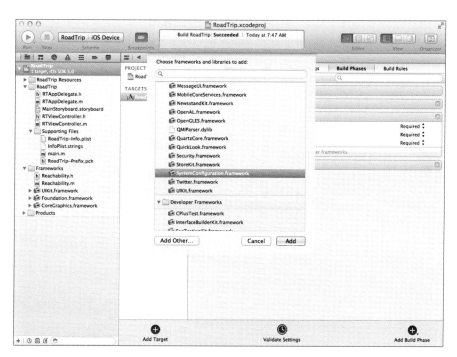

Figure 9-2: Select the `SystemConfoguration.framework`.

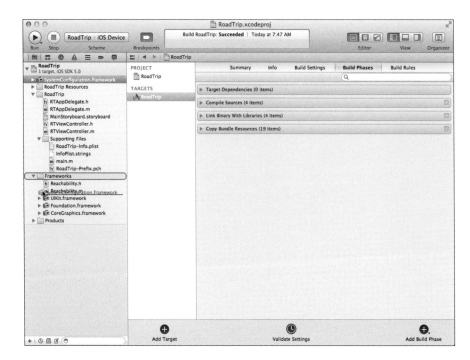

Figure 9-3: Drag in the Project navigator!

When I wrote this chapter, the Reachability sample application had not yet been updated to use ARC, which is okay, because it gives me a chance to show you how to use both ARC and non-ARC files in your project.

In order to have both ARC and non-ARC code in a single project, the following steps allow you to remove a file from ARC:

1. **In the Project navigator, select the Project icon at the top of the Project Navigator area (RoadTrip) to display the Project editor.**

2. **In the TARGETS section, select RoadTrip.**

3. **Click the Build Phases tab.**

   This is one of the few reasons you would have for using any of the other tabs in the Project editor.

4. **Expand the Compile Sources section (see Figure 9-4).**

5. Double-click the Reachability.m file.

A window appears.

6. In the window's text box, enter –fno-objc-arc, **as shown in Figure 9-4; then click Done.**

You may also have to choose Product ➪ Clean if you tried to compile the project without doing Steps 1-6 because you wanted to see how many errors it would generate.

You have now told the compiler not to use ARC in Reachability.h and .m and that memory management is done by the Reachability code (which it has been doing pre-ARC).

You also need to add the bolded code in Listing 9-1 to Reachability.h.

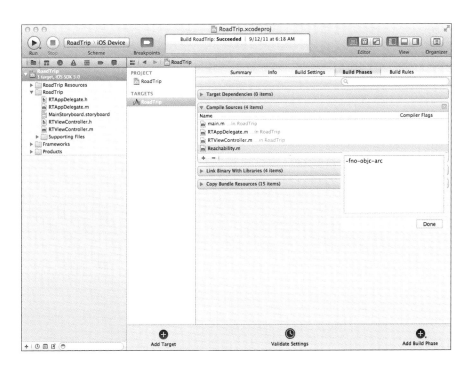

Figure 9-4: Don't use ARC for this file.

Listing 9-1: Update the `Reachability` interface.

```
#import <Foundation/Foundation.h>
#import <SystemConfiguration/SystemConfiguration.h>
#import <netinet/in.h>
```

Adding the code to check for reachability

The place to check for whether you have access to the Internet is right when you start up. The method to do that in is the Application Delegate protocol method `application:didFinishLaunchingWithOptions:`.

You also need to include the `Reachability.h` file to be able to use Reachability, so add the bolded code in Listing 9-2 to the beginning of the `RTAppDelegate.m` file.

Listing 9-2: Updating the RTAppDelegate Implementation and `application:didFinishLaunchingWithOptions:`

```
#import "RTAppDelegate.h"
#import "Reachability.h"

@implementation RTAppDelegate

@synthesize window = _window;

- (BOOL)application:(UIApplication *)application
    didFinishLaunchingWithOptions:
                        (NSDictionary *)launchOptions
{
  NetworkStatus networkStatus =
    [[Reachability reachabilityForInternetConnection]
                        currentReachabilityStatus];
  if (networkStatus == NotReachable) {
    UIAlertView *alert = [[UIAlertView alloc]
      initWithTitle:@"Network Unavailable"
      message:@"RoadTrip requires an internet connection"
      delegate:nil
      cancelButtonTitle:@"OK"
      otherButtonTitles:nil];
    [alert show];
  }
  return YES;
}
```

You start by creating a `Reachability` object and then send it the `current-ReachabilityStatus` message.

```
NetworkStatus networkStatus =
  [[Reachability reachabilityForInternetConnection]
                            currentReachabilityStatus];
```

`reachabilityForInternetConnection` is an initializer that creates a
`Reachability` object that checks for the availability of an Internet connection. As I said, Reachability has a lot of functionality, but all you really care
about is whether you can reach the Internet.

Next, check to see whether you have network access:

```
if (networkStatus == NotReachable) {
```

If you don't have network access, you post an alert:

```
UIAlertView *alert = [[UIAlertView alloc]
      initWithTitle:@"Network Unavailable"
      message:@"RoadTrip requires an internet connection"
      delegate:nil
      cancelButtonTitle:@"OK"
      otherButtonTitles:nil];
[alert show];
```

This is the standard way to configure and then show an alert. You have filled
in the various (self-explanatory) parameters required by the initialization
method. Configured this way, the alert will have a single button.

The `show` message to the `alert` object causes the alert to be displayed in
the window, and when the user touches Cancel, the alert dismisses itself.

If you had added other buttons to give the user a choice of responses,
you would have had to make the object posting the alert (the
`RTAppDelegate`, in this case) a `UIAlertViewDelegate` assigned
the delegate parameter to `self`, and added the title of the other buttons using a `nil` terminated list. You would then have to implement the
`alertView:clickedButtonAtIndex:` method in the delegate.

Explaining how `Reachability` works is beyond the scope of this book, but
by examining the code, you will easily be able figure out how to get any other
network status information you want.

If you run the application now, and either turn off your Internet connection
on the computer if you are running the Simulator or turn on Airplane Mode
on the phone, you see Figure 9-5.

Figure 9-5: Checking the network connection.

Of course, in a real app, you would want to do something further here, such as give the user options and so on. I'll leave that up to you.

Congratulations! It's time for your first adventure in coding land.

Sprucing Up the Main View

Now that you have some code written, it's time to pick up the pace. If you look underneath the alert in Figure 9-5, or if you dismiss the alert, you can see that you are close to the User Interface I show you in Chapter 4, but not quite there. Although some of what you need to do to get to the user interface I show you in Chapter 4 could be accomplished in Interface Builder, some can't, and I want to explain how to set the appearance of controls programmatically in your app.

Users appreciate consistency of the user interface on their iPhone. If you just use the interface objects "as is," however, your app looks sort of generic.

To allow developers to spice up the look of their apps, Apple provides three basic ways to customize a control's appearance:

- **By setting properties in Interface Builder.** You use this approach you create the custom button in Chapter 5, in the section about adding user interface objects.

- **By setting properties in your program.** These include some of the same properties that you could have set in Interface Builder, and some that can only be set programmatically.

- **By customizing the appearance of an entire class.** An example is a UIButton, which you can customize by using the UIAppearance protocol to get the appearance proxy for a class and then customize the appearance of instances of a class by sending appearance modification messages to the class's appearance proxy.

In this section, I show you how to use the last two approaches.

You start by adding the bolded code in Listing 9-3 to the application:did FinishLaunchingWithOptions: method that you add in Listing 9-2, which appeared previously. In this method, you work on changing the appearance of the Navigation bar and the bar's button items.

Listing 9-3: Updating `application:didFinishLaunchingWithOptions:`

```
- (BOOL)application:(UIApplication *)application
          didFinishLaunchingWithOptions:
                             (NSDictionary *)launchOptions
{
  NetworkStatus networkStatus =
  [[Reachability reachabilityForInternetConnection]
                          currentReachabilityStatus];
  if (networkStatus == NotReachable) {
    UIAlertView *alert = [[UIAlertView alloc]
      initWithTitle:@"Network Unavailable"
      message:@"RoadTrip requires an internet connection"
      delegate:nil
      cancelButtonTitle:@"OK"
      otherButtonTitles:nil];
    [alert show];
  }
[[UIApplication sharedApplication] setStatusBarStyle:UIStatus
          BarStyleBlackOpaque animated:NO];
```

(continued)

Listing 9-3 *(continued)*

```
UINavigationController *navigationController =
  (UINavigationController *)
                          self.window.rootViewController;
navigationController.navigationBar.barStyle =
                                      UIBarStyleBlack;
[navigationController.navigationBar
  setTitleTextAttributes:
    [NSDictionary dictionaryWithObject:
      [UIColor yellowColor]
      forKey:UITextAttributeTextColor]];
[navigationController.navigationBar
  setBackgroundImage:
    [UIImage imageNamed:@"NavBarImage.png"]
    forBarMetrics:UIBarMetricsDefault];
[[UIButton appearance] setTitleColor:
    [UIColor greenColor] forState:UIControlStateNormal];
[[UIBarButtonItem appearanceWhenContainedIn:
    [UINavigationBar class], nil]
  setTitleTextAttributes:
    [NSDictionary dictionaryWithObject:
      [UIColor yellowColor]
      forKey:UITextAttributeTextColor]
  forState:UIControlStateNormal];
[[UIButton appearanceWhenContainedIn:
  [UIAlertView class], nil] setTitleColor:
  [UIColor whiteColor] forState:UIControlStateNormal];
return YES;
}
```

These changes are for the Navigation bar elements, and other application-wide classes. The fact that they are application wide makes it convenient to set them all up here.

Here's what this code is all about. The first chunk shows you how to customize a control's appearance by setting properties in your program.

To start with, you set the status bar at the very top of the window to black:

```
[[UIApplication sharedApplication]
  setStatusBarStyle:UIStatusBarStyleBlackOpaque
                                      animated:NO];
```

You send the `setStatusBarStyle:animated` message to the `UIApplication` object, which "owns" the status bar. As you may recall from Chapter 7, there is only one `UIApplication` object. You get a reference to it by sending the class message `sharedApplication` (also explained in Chapter 7, in the section about declared properties).

In Objective C, a every class is also an object, so you can define methods that are responded to by the class.

`setStausBarStyle:animated` allows you to set the status bar to the default (white), black translucent, and black opaque, either with an animated action or immediately. I choose the latter here.

Next, you set some of the properties of the Navigation bar, which means that you'll need a reference to the Navigation bar object. The Navigation bar is a property of the navigation controller, which means that you need a reference to the navigation controller. (I learned all this by going through the Xcode documentation for each of the classes, which I did by pressing Option and clicking the class name in the Source editor. I recommend that you explore those classes as well.)

You could have created an outlet for the navigation controller using Interface Builder as you did for other outlets in Chapter 6 — but if you don't need to create an outlet, then don't. In this case, I can get the navigation controller reference from the window object, which I already have reference to because it is one of the `UIApplicationDelegate` properties.

```
UINavigationController *navigationController =
    (UINavigationController *)
                        self.window.rootViewController;
```

Note that I had to cast the property here to `UINavigationController`, because normally it is a view controller. But as you may recall from Chapter 5, I have you embed the `RTViewController` in a navigation controller in that chapter, so now that navigation controller is the `rootViewController`.

Now you set the Navigation bar style to black:

```
navigationController.navigationBar.barStyle =
                                    UIBarStyleBlack;
```

This code sets not only the Navigation bar style but also the bar button elements (such as the back button) to black

Now that you have a nice black Navigation bar, set the title text to yellow. Setting the title text requires creating a dictionary to pass the parameters for the title text. Each key in the dictionary corresponds to a different text style attribute. (You can discover such facts by pressing Option while double-clicking the `setTitleTextAttributes` symbol in the Source editor to read the method documentation.) Here's the code that sets the title text to yellow:

```
[navigationController.navigationBar
    setTitleTextAttributes:
      [NSDictionary dictionaryWithObject:
        [UIColor yellowColor]
        forKey:UITextAttributeTextColor]];
```

Several different title text attributes are available for you to set, including font, text shadow color, and a text shadow offset, each with its own key. In this case, you specify a text color.

The `UITextAttributeTextColor` key specifies a text color and requires a `UIColor` object as its value.

A `UIColor` object represents color and can also represent opacity (alpha value). `yellowColor` (along with a number of similar methods) is a class method that returns a color object whose RGB values are 1.0, 1.0, and 0.0 and whose alpha value is 1.0. There are similar class methods for other colors such as `redColor`, `clearColor`, and so on, as I discovered by pressing Option while double-clicking `UIColor` and reading the class reference documentation. You should be getting the picture by now, so I won't belabor the point.

I also don't like the boring black background for the Navigation bar that I get when I set the bar style to black. To remedy that situation, you have the option of adding a background image. `setBackgroundImage: forBarMetrics:` as you might guess, enables you to set a background image. You have to provide the image using `UIImage` (as you do in Chapter 5 in the section about adding user interface objects).

```
[navigationController.navigationBar
    setBackgroundImage:
    [UIImage imageNamed:@"NavBarImage.png"]
  forBarMetrics:UIBarMetricsDefault];
```

You use the `imageNamed:` method to find an image in your program's bundle (which contains the application executable and any resources used by the application, such as the application icon and aforementioned image). The `imageNamed:` method first looks to see whether the image has already been loaded (because you have used it previously) and cached. If not, it loads the image data, caches it, and then returns the resulting object.

On a device running iOS 4 or later, the behavior is identical if the device's screen has a scale of 1.0. If the screen has a scale of 2.0, this method first searches for an image file with the same filename with an @2x suffix appended to it. For example, if the file's name is `button`, the method first searches for `button@2x`. If it finds an image with `2x` in the filename, it loads that image and sets the scale property of the returned `UIImage` object to 2.0. Otherwise, it loads the unmodified filename and sets the scale property to 1.0.

`UIBarMetricsDefault` says use this image for both Landscape and Portrait mode. You can set a different image for Landscape mode if you would like.

After you have your background image installed (if you want one), you can customize the appearance of your controls using the following code. Up until know, you have been customizing a control's appearance by setting properties in your program. In this next chunk of code, I show you how to customize a control's appearance by customizing the appearance of an entire class.

```
[[UIButton appearance] setTitleColor:
    [UIColor greenColor] forState:UIControlStateNormal];
```

This code takes advantage of a feature in `UIKit` called Custom Appearance for `UIKit` Controls. It enables you to customize the appearance of many `UIKit` views and controls to give your application a unique look and feel. You can set the tint color, background image, and title position properties (among others) on a number of objects, including toolbars, navigation bars, search bars, buttons, sliders, and some other controls.

You set the default attributes to use for a class by using an *appearance proxy* — an object supplied by `UIKit` that you can use to modify the default appearance of views and controls in classes that adopt the `UIAppearance` protocol. (You can see whether a class conforms to the `UIAppearance` protocol by looking in the class reference for the class. If you were to look up the `UIButton` class, as shown in Figure 9-6, you would see that it does conform.

To modify the default appearance of such a class, you need to first get its appearance proxy object by sending the `appearance` class message to the class:

```
[UIButton appearance]
```

Next, you send a message to the appearance proxy object to set new default values. For example, you can use a proxy object to change the default `title` color of the `UIButton` class to green by using `setTitleColor`, as follows:

```
[[UIButton appearance] setTitleColor:
    [UIColor greenColor] forState:UIControlStateNormal];
```

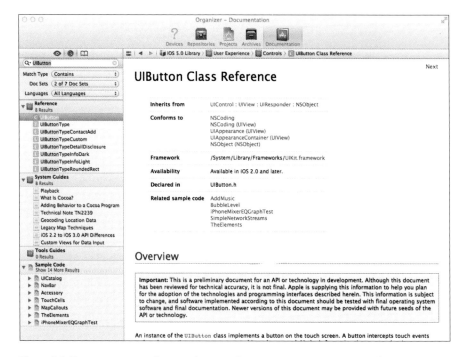

Figure 9-6: The `UIButton` class conforms to the `UIAppearance` protocol.

This statement modifies the `titleColor` for all buttons. This approach works well if you want all buttons to have this title color. It also means that *every* button title, including the Back button in the Navigation bar and the OK button in the alert you post when you don't have an Internet connection, will be green. But you can fix that situation if you don't want to include those items.

If you want the text for all Bar Button Items (such as the Back button) in the alert to be yellow and not green, or to be set to any other color you want instead of the one you're using for the `appearance` object, you can use the `appearanceWhenContainedIn:` object to set the tint color, background, image, and title position properties (among others) for all Bar Button Items that are *subviews* (not subclasses, contained in a Navigation bar) of the `UINavigationBar` to yellow:

```
[[UIBarButtonItem appearanceWhenContainedIn:
    [UINavigationBar class], nil]
  setTitleTextAttributes:
    [NSDictionary dictionaryWithObject:
      [UIColor yellowColor]
      forKey:UITextAttributeTextColor]
  forState:UIControlStateNormal];
```

To make the title of the OK button in an alert another color (white, for in this example), you can use the `appearanceWhenContainedIn:` object again:

```
[[UIButton appearanceWhenContainedIn:
  [UIAlertView class], nil] setTitleColor:
  [UIColor whiteColor] forState:UIControlStateNormal];
```

This code sets the font color for all Bar Button Items that are subviews of the `UIAlertView`.

Finally, you also want to be able to set the title in the Navigation bar for the view. You could have done that in Interface Builder, but I'm showing you how to do it programmatically because you will be doing it that way for the rest of the view controllers in this book's example application. In some cases, I take this route because you will be setting the title of the view based on where the user is going; in others, I go the programmatic route because I like to set view titles in code *I find that doing it that way makes it easy to keep track of and change).

To set the `RTViewController` object title, add the bolded code in Listing 9-4 to `viewDidLoad` in `RTViewController.m`.

Listing 9-4:   Updating viewDidLoad

```
- (void)viewDidLoad
{
  [super viewDidLoad];

  self.title = @"Road Trip";
}
```

`title` is a `UIViewController` property that represents the tile of the view that this controller manages.

How did I know to put it here? As I explain in Chapter 7, `viewDidLoad` is the message sent when the view is loaded for the first time, but before it is displayed, so you want to see the title here, before the view is displayed.

Understanding Autorotation

One of the responsibilities of the `UIViewController` class is to work with the application's window to handle device rotation (a.k.a. device orientation changes). Although the `UIViewController` class itself already includes the functionality to animate the transition from the current orientation to the new one (and which you can override if you need to layout the view again for the new orientation), it must also communicate to the application window whether it in fact wants to support a particular orientation.

This communication is accomplished through the `UIViewController` method `shouldAutorotateToInterfaceOrientation:`. The `should-AutorotateToInterfaceOrientation:` message, with the new orientation as a parameter, is sent to the view controller when the user rotates the device. If the view controller supports that orientation, it returns `YES`; if it does not, it returns `NO`.

When you use the Single View Application template to create your project, that template generates a view controller that supports all orientations except upside down, as you can see in Listing 9-5.

Listing 9-5: The Single View Application Template's `shouldAutorotateToInterfaceOrientation:`

```
- (BOOL)shouldAutorotateToInterfaceOrientation:
            (UIInterfaceOrientation)interfaceOrientation
{
    // Return YES for supported orientations
  return (interfaceOrientation !=
          UIInterfaceOrientationPortraitUpsideDown);
}
```

In the case of this book's example app, RoadTrip, however, you won't include support for Landscape orientation (except (optionally) in events, as I explain in Chapter 15, and in mapping, as I explain in Chapter 16). So you want to change the user interface orientation supporting by the `RTViewController` by deleting the commented-out code and adding the code in bold in Listing 9-6 to `shouldAutorotateToInterface Orientation:` in `RTViewController.m`.

Listing 9-6: Updating `shouldAutorotateToInterfaceOrientation:` to Remove Landscape Orientation

```
- (BOOL)shouldAutorotateToInterfaceOrientation:
            (UIInterfaceOrientation)interfaceOrientation
{
    // Return YES for supported orientations
  //return (interfaceOrientation !=
              UIInterfaceOrientationPortraitUpsideDown);
  return (interfaceOrientation ==
                      UIInterfaceOrientationPortrait);

}
```

Writing Bug-Free Code

Although some developers think that writing code is where they spend the vast majority of their time when they are developing an app, debugging is actually right up there as a very close second.

Because that is the case, there are two things I want to explain in this section.

The first is how to write code with fewer bugs. The second is how to use the debugger to track down any bugs you do have as efficiently as possible.

With the release of Xcode 4, Apple has made it easier to both write code with fewer bugs, as well as use the debugger to track down bugs you do have.

Because the best defense is a good offense, I want to start with the tools that Xcode provides that help you to write less buggy code.

The best way to make sure your code has as few bugs as possible is by fixing it as you code. How do you do that? Pay attention to the compiler warnings! By taking advantage of the Live Issues and Fix-it features, which I explain in Chapter 8, you'll catch many of your errors before you even run your program, and fixing them will be easy (well, some of them, at least). Live Issues continuously evaluates your code in the background and alerts you to coding mistakes, and Fix-it will also offer to fix the problem for you. I suggest that unless you are crystal clear about what you are doing, don't run your app without first resolving any outstanding compiler warnings.

Of course, Live Issues and Fix-it are really only good at fixing syntax errors — they are usually not much help in detecting logic errors or coding mistakes that cause runtime errors (such as dividing by zero). For those errors, you need to become facile at using the debugger — or, more precisely, the Debug area and the Debug navigator.

Working in the Debug Area and Debug Navigator

The Debug area consists of the Debug bar and Variables and Console panes, each of which has pop-up menus. You usually use the Debug area in conjunction with the Debug navigator.

You access the Debug area by selecting it in the Xcode toolbar's View selector (as shown in Figure 9-7). You select the Debug navigator by showing the Navigator area and then selecting the Debug navigator in the Navigator selector bar. But there is nothing much to see in the Debug area or Debug navigator unless your application is actually running. And although the Debug area's Variables and Console panes will retain the results from your last program execution, the Debug navigator shows content only when your application is paused. It is often useful, however, to be able to hide the Debug area using the toolbar's View selector.

Figure 9-7: Managing
the Debug area.

If you get a runtime error (or if you click the Pause button or a breakpoint
is triggered), the Debug area and the Debug navigator are opened
automatically.

Figure 9-8 show what happens when you hit a breakpoint (which I explain
shortly) in your program.

Figure 9-8: Hitting a breakpoint displays the Debug area and Debug navigator.

What you see in the Debug area is controlled by using the Debug area scope
bar, shown in Figure 9-9. You use this bar to toggle between the Variables
pane only (left button), both Variables and Console panes (center button),
and Console pane only (right button).

Figure 9-9: Use the Debug area scope bar to control what pane you see in the Debug area.

Scope bars are also available in the Variables pane and Console pane.

The pop-up menu in the Variables pane Scope bar lets you display:

- ✔ **Auto:** Recently accessed variables
- ✔ **Local:** Local variables
- ✔ **All:** All variables and registers

The pop-up menu in the Console pane Scope bar lets you display:

- ✔ **All Output:** Target and debugger output
- ✔ **Debugger Output:** Debugger output only
- ✔ **Target Output:** Target output (program logging to the debugger, for example) only

There are also other controls and filters for what gets displayed that I encourage you to explore on your own.

Managing breakpoints

You can use the Debugger to pause execution of your program at anytime and view the state of the running code.

As mentioned previously, you won't find much to see in the Debug area and Debug navigator unless your program is stopped at a breakpoint or paused (and not much at those points, either). The Debugger will be more useful to you if you set breakpoints to stop at known points and then view the values of the variables in your source code. So I'll show you how to set a breakpoint and explain what a breakpoint is.

A *breakpoint* is an instruction to the Debugger to stop execution at a particular program instruction. By setting breakpoints at various methods in your program, you can step through its execution — at the instruction level — to see exactly what it's doing. You can also examine the variables that the program is setting and using. If you're stymied by a logic error, setting breakpoints is a great way to break that logjam.

To set breakpoints, open a file in the Source editor and click in the gutter next to the spot where you want execution to stop. You can toggle the state (on or off) of all the breakpoints in your program at any time by clicking the Breakpoints button in the Xcode toolbar.

You can also disable an individual breakpoint by clicking its icon. You can also view all breakpoints in the Breakpoint navigator, and you can select a given breakpoint in the Breakpoint navigator to display it in the Source editor (where you can also edit it).

To get rid of a breakpoint, simply drag it off to the side. You can also right-click (or Ctrl+click) the breakpoint and choose Remove Breakpoint from the pop-up menu that appears.

In Figure 9-10, I have added a breakpoint to the statement after I check network status. I have also selected the Breakpoint navigator in the Navigator selector bar.

Figure 9-10: Setting a breakpoint and displaying the Breakpoint navigator.

You can set several options for each breakpoint, such as a condition, the number of times to pass the breakpoint before it's triggered, or an action to perform when the breakpoint is triggered.

To set breakpoint actions and options, Option+click the breakpoint and choose Edit Breakpoint from the shortcut menu, as shown in Figure 9-11.

With the Edit Breakpoint window open, you can set the actions and the options for the breakpoint in the Breakpoint editor. As shown in Figure 9-12, you can set a condition for a breakpoint, ignore it a set number of before stopping, add an action, and automatically continue after evaluating actions.

In Figure 9-13, I clicked the Click to Add an Action check box and then chose to add a sound. I also set a condition that I want the breakpoint to be triggered only if the `networkStatus` is not equal to `notReachable`.

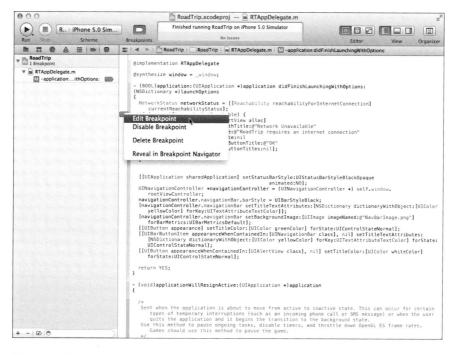

Figure 9-11: Editing a breakpoint.

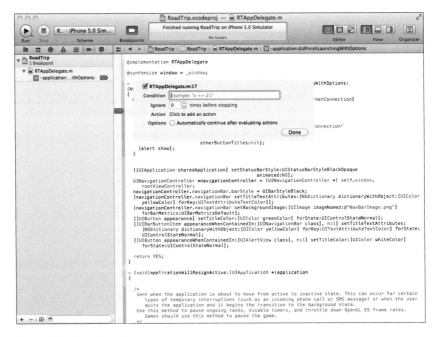

Figure 9-12: Some breakpoint options.

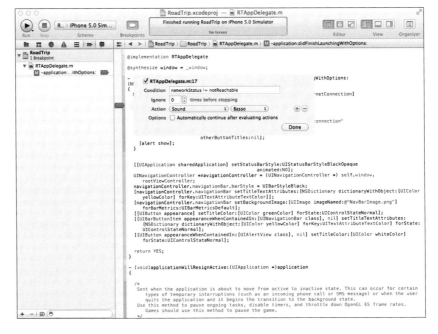

Figure 9-13: Fine-tuning the breakpoint.

Set this breakpoint and run your program in Xcode. As you can see in Figure 9-14, you'll be stopped at the breakpoint.

As you can see in the figure, when the breakpoint is reached, the Debug area is displayed and the Debug navigator opened automatically. (As I mention in Chapter 2, you can change that response in the Behaviors tab of Xcode Preferences.)

What you find in the Debug area

As you can see in Figure 9-14, on one side you have the Variables pane (which displays the values of variables), and on the other the Console pane. That is the configuration I have selected in the Debug area scope bar (the middle button).

The Variables pane

The Variables pane displays the variables you're interested in. You need to click the disclosure triangle next to `self` to see the instance variables in the object. The local variables to a method are displayed as well. You can specify which items to display using the pop-up menu in the top-left corner of the variables pane:

Figure 9-14: The compiler stops at the breakpoint I set.

✔ **Auto:** Displays only the variables you're most likely to be interested in, given the current context

✔ **Local:** Displays local variables

✔ **All:** Displays all variables and registers

You can also use the search field to filter the items displayed in the variables pane.

The Console pane

The Console pane displays program output. Again, you can specify the type of output you see in the console by using the pop-up menu in the top-left corner of the Console pane:

✔ **All Output:** Displays target and debugger output

✔ **Debugger Output:** Displays debugger output only

✔ **Target Output:** Displays target output only

When you are stopped at the breakpoint you set earlier, what you see is a lot of boilerplate and then:

```
2011-09-11 11:54:23.635 RoadTrip[1149:f803] Reachability Flag
         Status: -R -----l- networkStatusForFlags
Current language:  auto; currently objective-c
(gdb)
```

Not much interesting, but in Chapter 12 you learn how to "print" the contents of a variable to the Console pane, and in Chapter 14 you have the opportunity to examine some runtime error messages.

What you see here is the result of an NSLog statement in Reachability.

```
2011-09-11 11:54:23.635 RoadTrip[1149:f803] Reachability Flag
         Status: -R -----l- networkStatusForFlags
```

NSLog allow you to display information in the Console pane during execution. For example

```
NSLog(@"Number of sights %i", [sightsData count]);
```

Would display

```
2011-09-11 11:56:05.041 RoadTrip[1048:12503] Number of sights
    1
```

In the Console pane

NSLog is pretty useful and uses the same formatting as NSString's string-WithFormat and other formatting methods.

What you find in the Debug navigator

Xcode opens the Debug navigator automatically, which also shows you the thread list and the call stack for each thread.

Selecting an item in the debug navigator causes information about the item to be displayed in the Source editor. For example selecting a method displays the method in the Source editor.

Each application within iOS is made up of one or more *threads,* each of which represents a single path of execution through the application's code. Every application starts with a single thread, which runs the application's main function. The main thread encompasses the application's main run loop, and it's where the NSApplication object receives events. Applications can add (spawn) additional threads, each of which executes the code of a specific method.

Threads per se are way beyond the scope of this book, but that's okay: Here you're only concerned with the main thread.

Every time you send a message (or make a function call), the Debugger stores information about it in a *stack frame,* and then it stores all such frames in the *call stack.* When you're thrown into the Debugger because of an error (or if you pause the application by clicking the Pause button in the toolbar), Xcode displays the Thread list, and within each thread the call stack for that thread, putting the most recent call at the top. The call stack shows a trace of the objects and methods that got you to where you are now.

If you select a method in the Debug navigator, you see the source code for that function.

There's a lot more you can do as far as threads are concerned, but again, that's outside of the scope of this book. (If you don't know whether to be disappointed or relieved, hold that thought.)

Although the trace isn't really all that useful in this particular context, it can be *very* useful in a more complex application — it can help you understand the path that you took to get where you are. Seeing how one object sent a message to another object — which sent a message to a third object — can be really helpful, especially if you didn't expect the program flow to work that way.

Getting a look at the call stack can also be useful if you're trying to understand how the framework does its job, and in what order messages are sent. As you will see, you can stop the execution of your program at a breakpoint and trace the messages sent up to that point.

Displaying variables in the Source editor

In the Debugger window, you can move your pointer over an object or variable in the source editor to show its contents and move your pointer over disclosure triangles to see even more information.

In Figure 9-15, I moved the pointer over `networkStatus` to see its value (information about the current status of the Internet connection).

TIP

When you move your pointer over a variable, its contents are revealed — and if more disclosure triangles appear, you can move your pointer over them to see even more information (which I explain in more detail in Chapter 12).

You see the value of the variable in the variable pane as well.

In the next section, I show you now to step through your program after it's stopped at a breakpoint.

Figure 9-15: Showing the `networkStatus`.

Tiptoeing through your program

When you build and run the program with breakpoints, the Debug bar appears in the Workspace window as the program runs in the Simulator. The program stops executing at the first breakpoint.

To control the execution, you use the Debug bar (located at the top of the Debug area that you see in Figure 9-16). The Debug bar includes buttons to

- ✔ **Open or close the Debug area:** As mentioned previously, you can hide the Debug area.

- ✔ **Pause or resume execution of your code:** Stop your program from executing or continue execution after it stopped when it entered the Debugger.

- ✔ **Step Over:** The *process counter* (PC), which is identified by the green arrow in the gutter, moves to the next line of code to be executed. If that line of code sends a message, it sends the message (and run the method) — but then, from your perspective, it just moves to the next line of code.

- ✔ **Step In:** In this case, the process counter moves to the next line of code to be executed and, if the line of code sends a message to a method in your source code, the debugger steps to the method and then returns to the next line of code after the line that sends the message.

- ✔ **Step Out:** Steps out of the current function or method. The Source editor then displays the method that sent the message or the function's caller.

Hide the debug area

Pause/resume program execution

Step over

Step into

Step out

Simulate location

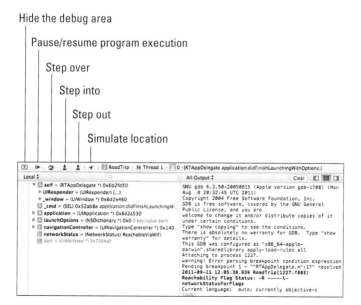

Figure 9-16: The Debug area and Debug bar.

I step you through line by line.

When I select Step In, the screen shown in Figure 9-17 appears.

You can see that the instruction was executed and the Debugger has paused the program at the next instruction:

```
[[UIApplication sharedApplication]
    setStatusBarStyle:UIStatusBarStyleBlackOpaque
                                        animated:NO];
```

The Debugger stepped in here because the condition in the `if` statement was not met. Of course you knew that, having displayed the value of the `net-workStatus` as reachable in Figure 9-15.

This concludes your introduction to the Debugger and Debug navigator. There are a couple of more things I do want to show you, but I need to have you add more code to have them make sense. In Chapter 12, I show you how to "print" the contents of a variable in the Console pane, and then in Chapter 14 I show you a couple of my favorite runtime errors.

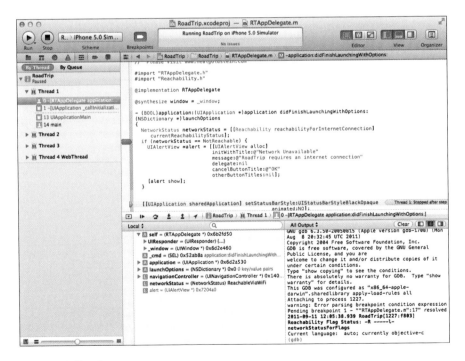

Figure 9-17: Step in.

Chapter 10

Adding Animation and Sound to Your App

*A*lthough it may take some time before you go on your road trip, as well as complete the building of the app I'm showing you in this book, the least I can do is show you how to take a test drive in your '59 pink Cadillac Eldorado convertible.

In this chapter, you find out how to make the car move up the screen, turn around, and move back to its original position — and with appropriate sound effects.

I also show you how to drag the car on the screen to position the ride from wherever you'd like. And to add just a little more pizazz, I show you how to make the TestDrive button blink.

This chapter provides you with a very good base for understanding animation and sound, and explains how to manage touches on the screen.

Understanding Animation on the iPhone

Fortunately, most of what you need to do as far as animation is concerned is already built into the framework. Some view properties are animatable (the center point, for example), which means that you just need to tell the view where to start, where to end, and a few other optional parameters, and you're done. The view will take care of moving the image. To give you some context in which to understand how animation on the iPhone works, I need to explain a little more about views, their properties, and the coordinate systems on the iPhone.

View geometry and coordinate systems

The default coordinate system in UIKit has its origin in the top-left corner and has axes that extend down and to the right from the origin point. Coordinate values are represented using floating-point numbers, and you don't have to worry about the screen resolution; the frameworks take care of that automatically. Figure 10-1 shows this coordinate system relative to the screen. In addition to the screen coordinate system, views define their own local coordinate systems that allow you to specify coordinates relative to the view instead of relative to the screen.

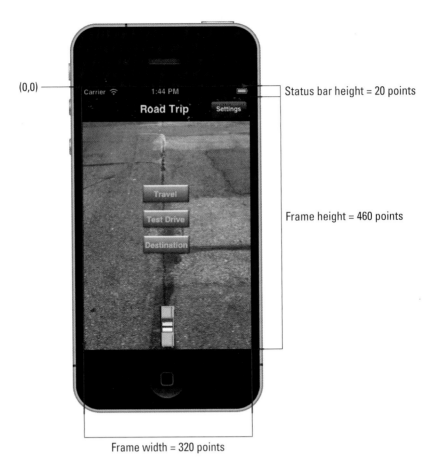

Figure 10-1: The coordinate system.

Because every view and window defines its own local coordinate system, whenever you are drawing or dealing with coordinates, you'll need to pay attention to which coordinate system you are using. I know that sounds ominous, but it's really not after you get into the rhythm of working with the coordinate systems.

Points versus pixels

Where does the high-resolution display come in?

In iOS, all coordinate values and distances are specified using floating-point values in units referred to as *points*. The measurable size of a point varies from device to device and is largely irrelevant. The main concept to understand about points is that they provide a fixed frame of reference for drawing.

For example, the screen dimensions (width x height) for the iPhone and iPod touch is 320 x 480 *points* and the iPad is 768 x 1024 *points*.

So although an iPhone with a retina display has a 960-by-640-*pixel* resolution (pixel density of 326 pixels per inch (ppi)) and a nonretina's display has a 480-by-320 *pixel* resolution (163 ppi screen), as long as you design your interface to fit the screen sizes *in points*, your views will display correctly on the corresponding type of device.

So don't worry about the resolution; concentrate on points and you'll be fine.

A view's size and position

A view object's location in a coordinate system is determined using either its `frame` or its `center` properties.

- ✔ The `frame` property contains the frame rectangle, which specifies the size and location of the view in *its super view's coordinate system* (if you are still hazy on the whole super view sub view thing check out Chapter 4).

- ✔ The `center` property contains the known center point of the view *in its super view's coordinate system*.

- ✔ The `bounds` property contains the bounds rectangle, which specifies the size of the view (and its content origin) in *the view's own local coordinate system*. I mention it here for completeness, but you won't use it in this book.

Figure 10-1 shows the frame of the main view (not the image view I have you add in Chapter 5) with an origin of x=0.0 and y=20.0. Its size is width = 320.0 and height = 460.0 The reason that its origin is y=20 is that its frame is in its window coordinates (its super view) and it has to share the window with the status bar which is, as you might deduce, is 20 pixels high.

There are some data structures you need to understand as you work with views.

The frame is a CGRect — a struct with an origin and a size that are comprised of CGPoints. The following code shows the CGRect struct.

```
struct CGRect {
  CGPoint origin;
  CGSize size;
};
```

An origin is a CGPoint with an x and y value, and a CGSize is a CGPoint with a width and height value. The following code shows the CGPoint struct.

```
struct CGPoint {
  CGFloat x;
  CGFloat y;
};

struct CGSize {
  CGFloat width;
  CGFloat height;
};
```

Similarly, the center property is a CGPoint. And that's all you need to know about the data structures you'll be using.

Animating a View

Whenever you assign a new value to certain view properties (such as the frame, center, and bounds properties, as explained in the previous section), the view is immediately redrawn and the change is immediately visible on the screen.

In addition, changes to several view properties (such as those just mentioned) can be animated. This means that changing the property creates an animation that conveys the change to the user over a short period of time — and it's all handled for you by the UIView class. What's more, it takes only one method call to specify the animations to be performed and the options for the animation.

The following properties of the UIView class are animatable (the first three are explained previously):

- frame
- bounds
- center
- transform: Explained later in the chapter.
- alpha: The degree of transparency. If you animate it, you can get views to fade in and fade out.
- backgroundColor: Allows you to transition from one color to another.
- contentStretch: Controls how a view's content is stretched to fill its bounds when the view is resized and is often used to animate the resizing of a buttons and controls.

Finally, More Code

In this section, you add the code to animate the car and have it travel up the screen, turn around, travel back down the screen, and then turn around again so that it's back to its original position. First you declare some methods. Add the bolded code in Listing 10-1 to RTViewController.h.

Listing 10-1:   Updating the **RTViewController.h** interface with the Methods to Animate the Car

```
#import <UIKit/UIKit.h>

@interface RTViewController : UIViewController

@property (weak, nonatomic) IBOutlet UIImageView *car;
@property (weak, nonatomic) IBOutlet UIButton
          *testDriveButton;
@property (weak, nonatomic) IBOutlet UIImageView
          *backgroundImage;

- (IBAction)testDrive:(id)sender;
- (void)rotate;
- (void)returnCar;
- (void)continueRotation;

@end
```

Implementing the `testDrive` Method

In Chapter 5, I tell you how to create an action for the TestDrive button using Interface Builder, which generates a method stub for you. In this chapter, it's time to fill that stub with code.

Add the bolded code in Listing 10-2 to the `testDrive:` method in `RTViewController.m`. You also add the stubs for code that you will be adding later so that you can run your program before you are completely finished with the back and forth of the animation.

Listing 10-2: Updating `testDrive:` to Move the Car Up the Screen

```
- (IBAction)testDrive:(id)sender {

  CGPoint center = CGPointMake(car.center.x,
      self.view.frame.origin.y + car.frame.size.height/2);
  [UIView animateWithDuration:3 animations:^ {
      car.center = center;
  }
  completion:^(BOOL finished){
      [self rotate];
  }];
}

- (void)rotate {
}

- (void)returnCar {
}

- (void)continueRotation {
}
```

Now, run your program, and click or touch the TestDrive button. Your car moves up the screen and you're on your way!

In the testDrive method, you start by creating the coordinate (`CGPoint` of where you would like the car to end up.

A car is just another view.

```
CGPoint center = CGPointMake(car.center.x,
    self.view.frame.origin.y + car.frame.size.height/2);
```

You use the center and frame properties primarily for manipulating the view. If you are changing only the position of the view (and not its size), the center property is the preferred way to do so.

CGPointMake is a function that creates a point for you when you specify the y and x coordinates as parameters (you set the car's new center point).

You can leave the x coordinate as is. Doing so makes the car drive right up the center of the screen.

```
car.center.x
```

Here's the y coordinate:

```
self.view.frame.origin.y + car.frame.size.height/2)
```

self.view.frame.origin.y is the top of the view, but if you have the center there, half the car is off the screen. To keep it all on the screen, you add back half the car's height by including car.frame.size.height/2.

Notice I am *adding* to the y coordinate because y increases as you move down the screen from the origin.

So, how do you get the sucker to actually move? Use the following code:

```
[UIView animateWithDuration:3 animations:^ {
  car.center = center;
}
```

animateWithDuration:animations:completion: is a UIView class method that allows you to set an animation duration and specify what you want animated as well as a completion handler that is called when the animation is complete.

First you specify that you want the animation to take three seconds:

```
animateWithDuration:3
```

and then you pass in an animation *block* with what you want animated:

```
animations:^ {
  car.center = center;
}
```

This sets the new center you just computed, taking three seconds to move it from start to finish.

If the preceding syntax seems mysterious (and it probably should), don't worry: I explain blocks in the next section.

Although that's all there is to getting the car to move across the screen, you're not done. You want it to rotate and then drive back across the screen and then rotate again. That's where the completion handler comes in.

Although you can use a completion handler to simply let you know that an animation is finished, using a completion handler is the primary way that you link multiple animations.

The completion handler that you specify:

```
completion:^(BOOL finished){
    [self rotate];
}
```

causes the `rotate` message to be sent when the animation is complete. You do the actual rotation in the `rotate` method.

Of course, right now, the rotate method does nothing. I have you add it so that the app would compile and run. I have you add `returnCar` and `continueRotation` to eliminate the Incomplete implementation `RTViewContoller.m` compiler warning.

`animateWithDuration:animations:completion:` is only one of a number of block-based methods that offer different levels of configuration for the animation block. The other methods are the following:

```
animateWithDuration:animations:
```

```
animateWithDuration:delay:options:animations:completion
```

`animateWithDuration:animations:` has no completion block, as you can see.

Both `animateWithDuration:animations:completion:` and `animateWithDuration:animations:` run only once, using an ease-in, ease-out animation curve. If you want to change the default animation parameters, you must use the `animateWithDuration:delay:options:animations:completion:` method, which lets you customize the following:

  ✔ The delay to use before starting the animation

  ✔ The type of timing curve to use during the animation

  ✔ The number of times the animation should repeat

✔ Whether the animation should reverse itself automatically when it reaches the end

✔ Whether touch events are delivered to views while the animations are in progress

✔ Whether the animation should interrupt any in-progress animations or wait until those are complete before starting

As you probably noticed (and I even admitted to) one of the things I slid over was an explanation of the animation syntax:

```
[UIView animateWithDuration:3 animations:^ {
  car.center = center;
}
```

Animations use blocks. A *block* is a primary design pattern in the iPhone and is becoming increasingly more important.

So before I get to the `rotate` completion handler, I want to explain blocks.

Understanding Blocks

Although delegation is extremely useful, it's not the only way to customize the behavior of a method or function.

Blocks are like traditional C functions in that blocks are small, self-contained units of code. They can be passed in as arguments of methods and functions and then used when they're needed to do some work. Like many programming topics, understanding block objects is easier when you use them, as you do in the previous section.

With iOS 4 and newer versions, a number of methods and functions of the system frameworks are starting to take blocks as parameters, including the following:

✔ Completion handlers

✔ Notification handlers

✔ Error handlers

✔ Enumeration

✔ View animation and transitions

✔ Sorting

Here you are using a block-based method to animate the car, but block objects also have a number of other uses, especially in Grand Central Dispatch and the `NSOperationQueue` class, the two recommended technologies for concurrent processing. But because concurrent processing is beyond the scope of this book (*way* out of the scope, in fact), I leave you to explore that use on your own.

One of the values of using blocks is that you can access local variables, which you can't do in a function or a call back. You don't have to pass data around, and a block can modify variables to pass data back (which is beyond the scope of this book as well) In addition, if you need to change something, there is no API to change, with its concomitant ripple effect.

In the animation explained in the previous section, you passed a block as the argument to a method. You created the block *inline*, because there wasn't that much code, and that is often the way it is done. But sometimes it is easier to follow what is happening by declaring a block variable and passing that as the argument to the method. The declaration syntax, however, is similar to the standard syntax for function pointers, except that you use a caret (^) instead of an asterisk pointer (*).

If you look the `animateWithDuration:animations:completion:` in the UIView class reference, you see

```
+ (void)animateWithDuration:(NSTimeInterval)duration
    animations:(void (^)(void))animations
    completion:(void (^)(BOOL finished))completion;
```

While this may seem a bit advanced for a *For Dummies* book, I cover it here because Apple is now treating blocks as a primary design pattern, up there with inheritance and delegation, so don't be surprised to find blocks being used more and more.

So I go through this slowly, and by the end, I promise you'll be comfortable with blocks, despite the really weird syntax.

To start, the `animations` is defined as a block that has no parameters and no return value:

```
void (^)(void))animations
```

Completion is defined as a block that has no return value and takes a single Boolean argument parameter and no return value:

```
(void (^)(BOOL finished))completion
```

When you create a block inline, you just use the caret (^) operator to indicate the beginning of a block with the code enclosed within the normal braces. Hence the code you entered previously:

```
animations:^ {
  car.center = center;
}
```

and

```
completion:^(BOOL finished){
  [self rotate];
}
```

Although in this example you use blocks inline, you could also declare them like any other local variable, as you can see in Listing 10-3.

Listing 10-3:   Using Declared Blocks

```
- (IBAction)testDrive:(id)sender {

  CGPoint center = CGPointMake(car.center.x,
    self.view.frame.origin.y + car.frame.size.height/2);

  void (^animation)() = ^(){

    car.center = center;
  };

  void (^completion)(BOOL) = ^(BOOL finished){
    [self rotate];
  };

    [UIView animateWithDuration:3 animations:animation
                                 completion:completion];
}
```

When you declare a block you use the caret (^) operator to indicate the beginning of a block with the code enclosed within the normal braces, and a semicolon to indicate the end of a block expression.

The declaration in Listing 10-3 is pretty much the same as you saw in the `animateWithDuration:animations:completion:` method declaration, except with the identifiers moved around a little. I have bolded both to make that a little easier to see:

```
+ (void)animateWithDuration:(NSTimeInterval)duration
    animations:(void (^)(void))animations
    completion:(void (^)(BOOL finished))completion;
```

Here, you are declaring two block variables by using the ^ operator, one with the name of animations that has no return value, and one with the name of completion that has no return value and takes BOOL as its single argument:

```
void (^animation)()
void (^completion)(BOOL)
```

This is like any other variable declaration (int i = 1, for example), in which you follow the equal sign with its definition.

You use the ^ operator again to indicate the beginning of the block literal — the definition assigned to the block variable. The block literal includes argument names (finished) as well as the body (code) of the block and is terminated with a semicolon:

```
void (^animation)()  =  ^(){
  car.center = center;
};

void (^completion)(BOOL) = ^(BOOL finished){
  [self rotate];
};
```

Although the code you add in Listing 10-2 creates the blocks inline, you should actually replace the testDrive method with the code in Listing 10-3 because that is the way I have you use blocks for the rest of this book. Inline blocks work fine for small blocks; for large blocks, however, I find that declaring the block makes the code easier to follow.

You use blocks a bit more in this book so at some point (despite the weird syntax), you will become comfortable with them; frankly it took me a while myself. After you do get the hang of them, you'll find all sorts of opportunities to use them to simplify your code, as you discover in Chapter 18.

Rotating the Object

In this section, I show you how to rotate a view (in this case, turn the car around). To do so, you update the rotate code stub with the bolded code in Listing 10-4.

Listening 10-4: Updating `rotate`

```
- (void)rotate {

  CGAffineTransform transform =
          CGAffineTransformMakeRotation(M_PI);

  void (^animation)()  =  ^(){
    car.transform = transform;
  };

  void (^completion)(BOOL) = ^(BOOL finished){
    [self returnCar];
  };

  [UIView animateWithDuration:3 animations:animation
          completion:completion];
}
```

This method uses the block declarations that I explain in the previous section.

The `CGAffineTransform` data structure represents a matrix used for affine transformations — how points in one coordinate system map to points in another coordinate system. Although `CGAffineTransform` has a number of uses (such as scaling and translating a coordinate system), the only one covered here is the rotation method you used in Listing 10-4.

```
CGAffineTransformMakeRotation(M_PI)
```

To rotate a view, you specify the angle, in radians, to rotate the coordinate system axes. Whereas degrees are numbers between 0 and 360, radians, though similar, range from 0 to 2*pi. So, when you create a rotation that turns an object around one half-circle, that rotation in radians is pi (`M_PI` is a system constant that represents pi).

Just to make your life interesting, you should note that in iOS, positive is counterclockwise but on Mac OS X, positive is clockwise.

The end result is that the car will rotate 180 degrees in three seconds, and when it is done, you send the `returnCar` message in the completion handler.

To return the car back to its original position, add the bolded code in Listing 10-5 to the `returnCar` method stub in `RTViewController.m`.

Listing 10-5: Updating `returnCar`

```
- (void)returnCar {

    CGPoint center = CGPointMake(car.center.x, self.view.frame.
             origin.y + self.view.frame.size.height - car.
             frame.size.height/2 );


    void (^animation)()  =  ^(){
      car.center = center;
    };

    void (^completion)(BOOL) = ^(BOOL finished){
      [self continueRotation];
    };

    [UIView animateWithDuration:3 animations:animation
                                  completion:completion];
}
```

This approach is pretty much the same as that of the `testDrive` method except that the new `center` is back where the car started. You put the `center` back by computing the bottom of the view:

```
self.view.frame.origin.x + self.view.frame.size.height
```

and then subtracting half the car's height, as shown in Listing 10-5.

But you're not done yet. You need to rotate the car back to its original position (unless you want to drive in reverse from California to New York). Add the bolded code in Listing 10-6 to the `continueRotation` method stub in `RTViewController.m`.

Listing 10-6: Updating `continueRotation`

```
- (void)continueRotation {

    CGAffineTransform transform =
                         CGAffineTransformMakeRotation(0);

    void (^animation)() = ^(){
      car.transform = transform;
    };

        [UIView animateWithDuration:3 animations:animation
                                  completion:nil];
}
```

You need to understand that the transform is still there; that is, you created a transform to rotate the car 180 degrees. If you want to get the car back to the original position, you need to return the transform to 0.

You could extend this action by having the car drive around the perimeter of the screen — but I'll leave that up to you.

Working with Audio on the iPhone

Cars make noise, and a '59 Cadillac certainly does not disappoint in that respect. So in this section, I show you how to add some sound to the RoadTrip app so that everyone can hear your car coming down the road.

I discuss using two different ways to implement audio available in iOS in this section. One is an instance of the `AVAudioPlayer` class, called an audio player, which provides playback of audio data from a file or memory. You use this class unless you are playing audio captured from a network stream or require very low I/O latency. This class offers quite a lot of functionality, including playing sounds of any duration, looping sounds, playing multiple sounds simultaneously, and having one sound per audio player with precise synchronization among all the players in use. It also controls relative playback level, stereo positioning, and playback rate for each sound you are playing.

The `AVAudioPlayer` class lets you play sound in any audio format available in iOS. You implement a delegate to handle interruptions (such as an incoming phone call) and to update the user interface when a sound has finished playing. The delegate methods to use are described in `AVAudioPlayerDelegate` Protocol Reference.

The second way to play sound is by using System Sound Services, which provides a way to play short sounds and make the device vibrate.

You can use System Sound Services to play short (30 seconds or shorter) sounds. The interface does not provide level, positioning, looping, or timing control and does not support simultaneous playback: You can play only one sound at a time. You can use System Sound Services to provide audible alerts. On some iOS devices, alerts can include vibration.

To add sound to your app, you start by adding the frameworks. If you need a refresher on how to do that in more detail than I give here, see the section in Chapter 8 about network availability. Or just follow these steps:

1. **In the Project navigator, select the Project icon at the top of the Project Navigator area (RoadTrip) to display the Project editor.**

2. **In the TARGETS section, select RoadTrip.**

3. **In the Summary tab, scroll down to the Linked Frameworks and Libraries section.**

4. **Expand the Linked Frameworks and Libraries section If it is not already expanded by clicking the disclosure triangle.**

5. **Click the + (plus sign) button underneath the list of current project frameworks.**

   A list of frameworks appears.

6. **Scroll down and select the** AVFoundation.framework and AudioToolbox.framework **from the list of frameworks.**

7. **Click the Add button.**

   You see the framework added to the Linked Frameworks and Libraries section.

8. **Close the Linked Frameworks and Libraries section.**

9. **In the Project navigator (don't do this from the Linked Frameworks and Libraries section!), drag the** AVFoundation.framework **and** AudioToolbox.framework **files to the Frameworks group).**

The sound files you need are already in the Resources folder that you added to your project (see Chapter 3 if you haven't already done this).

You can use Audacity, a free, open source software for recording and editing sounds, to create your own sound files. It is available for Mac OS X, Microsoft Windows, GNU/Linux, and other operating systems.

You start by importing the necessary the audio player and system sound services headers, and then you add the instance variables you'll be using. To accomplish all this, add the bolded code in Listing 10-7 to RTViewController.m.

Listing 10-7: Updating the RTViewController Implementation

```
#import "RTViewController.h"
#import <AVFoundation/AVFoundation.h>
#import <AudioToolbox/AudioToolbox.h>

@interface RTViewController () {

  AVAudioPlayer *backgroundAudioPlayer;
```

```
     SystemSoundID burnRubberSoundID;

}
@end


@implementation RTViewController
```

As you can see, I am having you take advantage of being able to put instance variables in the implementation file to keep them hidden (as I explain in Chapter 7).

Next, you need to set up the audio player and system sound services. Add the bolded code in Listing 10-8 to `viewDidLoad` in `RTViewController.m`.

Listing 10-8:   Updating `viewDidLoad`

```
- (void)viewDidLoad
{
  [super viewDidLoad];
  self.title = @"Road Trip";

  NSURL* backgroundURL = [NSURL fileURLWithPath:
    [[NSBundle mainBundle]pathForResource:
                          @"CarRunning" ofType:@"aif"]];
  backgroundAudioPlayer = [[AVAudioPlayer alloc]
          initWithContentsOfURL:backgroundURL error:nil];
  backgroundAudioPlayer.numberOfLoops = -1;
  [backgroundAudioPlayer prepareToPlay];

  NSURL* burnRubberURL = [NSURL fileURLWithPath:
    [[NSBundle mainBundle] pathForResource:
                          @"BurnRubber" ofType:@"aif"]];
  AudioServicesCreateSystemSoundID((__bridge
          CFURLRef)burnRubberURL, &burnRubberSoundID);
}
```

In Listing 10-8, the first thing you do is load the sound file from the resources in your bundle:

```
NSURL* backgroundURL = [NSURL fileURLWithPath:
  [[NSBundle mainBundle]pathForResource:
                        @"CarRunning" ofType:@"aif"]];
```

`fileURLWithPath` is an NSURL class method that initializes and returns an NSURL object as a file URL with a specified path. The NSURL class includes the utilities necessary for downloading files or other resources from web and FTP servers and from the file system.

The sound file you use is a resource, and pathForResource: is an NSBundle method that creates the path needed by the fileURLWithPath: method to construct the NSURL. Just give pathForResource: the name and the file type, and it returns the path that gets packed in to the NSURL and loaded.

"What bundle?" you say? Well, when you build your iPhone application, Xcode packages it as a bundle — one containing the following:

✔ The application's executable code

✔ Any resources that the app has to use (for instance, the application icon, other images, and localized content — in this case, the plist, .html files, and .png files)

✔ The RoadTrip-Info.plist, also known as the information property list, which defines key values for the application, such as bundle ID, version number, and display name

Pretty easy, huh?

Be sure that you provide the right file type; otherwise, this technique won't work.

Next, create an instance of the audio player:

```
backgroundAudioPlayer = [[AVAudioPlayer alloc]
    initWithContentsOfURL:backgroundURL error:nil];
```

and initialize it with the audio file location (NSURL). Ignore any errors.

Then set the number of loops to -1 (which will cause the audio file to continue to play until you stop it) and tell the player to get ready to play:

```
backgroundAudioPlayer.numberOfLoops = -1;
[backgroundAudioPlayer prepareToPlay];
```

prepareToPlay prepares the audio player for playback by preloading its buffers; it also acquires the audio hardware needed for playback. This preloading minimizes the lag between calling the play method and the start of sound output. Without this preloading, although the player would still play when you send the play message (later) in viewDidLoad, you'll likely notice a lag as it sets up its buffers.

Similarly, you set up the NSURL for the BurnRubber sound:

```
NSURL* burnRubberURL = [NSURL fileURLWithPath:
  [[NSBundle mainBundle] pathForResource:
                        @"BurnRubber" ofType:@"aif"]];
```

You then call a core foundation method to create a system sound object that you later use to play the sound:

```
AudioServicesCreateSystemSoundID((__bridge
            CFURLRef)burnRubberURL, &burnRubberSoundID);
```

CFURLRef (as I explain in Chapter 7 in the section about automatic reference counting) is a Core Foundation object, and ARC does not automatically manage the lifetimes of Core Foundation types. And although you can use certain Core Foundation memory management rules and functions, you don't need to do that here. That's because all you are doing is casting an Objective-C to a core foundation type object, and you won't need to use any Core Foundation memory management in your code. You have to let the compiler know about any memory management implications, however, so you need to use the __bridge cast.

In testDrive, you play both of the sounds created so far. To do so, add the bolded code in Listing 10-9 to testDrive in RTViewContoller.m.

Listing 10-9:   Updating testDrive

```
- (IBAction)testDrive:(id)sender {

  AudioServicesPlaySystemSound(burnRubberSoundID);
  [self performSelector:@selector(playCarSound)
                        withObject:self afterDelay:.2];

  CGPoint center = CGPointMake(car.center.x,
                              self.view.frame.origin.y +
            car.frame.size.height/2 );

  void (^animation)() = ^(){

    car.center = center;
  };

  void (^completion)(BOOL) = ^(BOOL finished){
    [self rotate];
  };

  [UIView animateWithDuration:3 animations:animation
          completion:null];
}
```

You also need to add the code in Listing 10-10.

Listing 10-10: Adding `playCarSound`

```
- (void)playCarSound {

    [backgroundAudioPlayer play];
}
```

You play the BurnRubber sound first, followed by the CarRunning sound. If you don't wait until the BurnRubber is complete before you play the CarRunning sound, the BurnRubber sound gets drowned out by the CarRunning sound.

To play the BurnRubber sound, you use a function call to system sound services:

```
AudioServicesPlaySystemSound(burnRubberSoundID);
```

After this sound is done, you start the CarRunning sound by using a very useful method that will enable you to send the message to start the audio player after a delay. That method is performSelector:withObject: afterDelay:, and it looks like this:

```
[self performSelector:@selector(playCarSound)
                        withObject:self afterDelay:.2];
```

performSelector:withObject:afterDelay: sends a message that you specify to an object after a delay. The method you want invoked should have no return value, and should have zero or one argument.

In Listing 10-10, this method meets these rules:

```
- (void)playCarSound {

    [backgroundAudioPlayer play];
}
```

@selector(playCarSound) is a compiler directive that returns a selector for a method name. A selector is the name used to select a method to execute for an object; it becomes a unique identifier when the source code is compiled.

Selectors really don't do anything. What makes the selector method name different from a plain string is that the compiler makes sure that selectors are unique. Selectors are useful because at runtime they act like a dynamic function pointer that, for a given name, automatically point to the implementation of a method appropriate for whichever class they're used with.

`withObject:` is the argument to pass to the method when it is invoked. In this case, you are passing `nil` because the method does not take an argument.

`afterDelay:` is the minimum time before which the message is sent. Specifying a delay of 0 does not necessarily cause the selector to be performed immediately. When you send the `performSelector:withObject:` message, you specify .2 seconds because that is the duration of the `BurnRubber` sound.

Sometimes you may need to cancel a selector. The method `cancelPerformSelectorsWithTarget:` cancels all outstanding ordered performs scheduled with a given target.

Several other variations exist on the `performSelector:withObject:aft erDelay:` method. Those variations are part of the `NSObject` class, which is the root class of most Objective-C class hierarchies. It provides the basic interface to the runtime system and the ability to behave as Objective-C objects.

Finally, to play the sound in the `playCarSound` method, you send the audio player the `play` message:

```
[backgroundAudioPlayer play];
```

The `play` message plays a sound asynchronously. If you haven't already sent the `prepareToPlay` message, `play` will send that for you as well (although you should expect a lag before the sound is played)

Next, you need to stop playing the sound in the `continueRotation` animation's completion block (or it gets really annoying). To stop playing the sound, add the bolded code in Listing 10-11 to `continueRotation` in `RTViewContoller.m`.

Listing 10-11: Updating `continueRotation` to Stop the Sound

```
- (void)continueRotation {

    CGAffineTransform transform =
            CGAffineTransformMakeRotation(-0);

    void (^animation)() = ^(){
      car.transform = transform;
    };

    void (^completion)(BOOL) = ^(BOOL finished){
      [backgroundAudioPlayer stop];
      [backgroundAudioPlayer prepareToPlay];
    };

    [UIView animateWithDuration:3 animations:animation
                                   completion:completion];
}
```

In the code in Listing 10-11, you also set the audio player up to play again.

And there you have it. Run your project and you'll notice some very realistic sound effects when you touch the TestDrive button.

Tracking Touches

While Skippy (the inspiration for the RoadTrip app) was pretending to drive across country, he said that it would be nice to be able to drag the car and place it anywhere on the screen. And because his wish is my command, in this section I explain how to code for dragging an object, as well as how touches work on the iPhone.

The touch of a finger (or lifting it from the screen) adds a touch event to the application's event queue, where it's encapsulated in a `UIEvent` object. A `UITouch` object exists for each finger touching the screen, which enables you to track individual touches.

The `touchesBegan:withEvent:` message is sent when one or more fingers touch down in a view. This message is a method of the `RTViewController`'s superclass, `UIResponder`, from which the view controller is derived (I explain this in Chapter 7, in the section about `UIApplicationMain`).

As the user manipulates the screen with his or her fingers, the system reports the changes for each finger in the corresponding `UITouch` object, thereby sending the `touchesMoved:withEvent:` message. The `touchesEnded:withEvent:` message is sent when one or more fingers lift from the associated view, or when the `touchesCancelled:withEvent:`

message is sent when a system event (such as a low-memory warning) cancels a touch event.

In this app, you need be concerned only with the first two methods just described.

To begin the process of responding to a touch event, add a new instance variable (bolded in Listing 10-12) to the `RTViewController.m` implementation file.

Listing 10-12:   Updating the `RTViewController` Implementation

```
@interface RTViewController () {

  AVAudioPlayer *backgroundAudioPlayer;
  SystemSoundID burnRubberSoundID;
  BOOL touchInCar;
}
```

Next, add the `touchesBegan:` method in Listing 10-13 to `RTView Controller.m` to start tracking touches. You are actually overriding this method because you have inherited it from the `UIResponder` base class.

Listing 10-13:   Overriding `touchesBegan:`

```
- (void)touchesBegan:(NSSet *)touches withEvent:
                                      (UIEvent *)event
{
  UITouch *touch = [touches anyObject];
  if (CGRectContainsPoint(car.frame,
                      [touch locationInView:self.view]))
    touchInCar = YES;
  else  {
    touchInCar = NO;
    [super touchesBegan:touches withEvent:event];
  }
}
```

As mentioned previously, the `touchesBegan:withEvent:` message is sent when one or more fingers touch down in a view. The touches themselves are passed to the method in an `NSSet` object — an unordered collection of distinct elements.

To access an object in the `NSSet` object, use the `anyObject` method — it returns one of the objects in the set. For the purpose here, you are assuming just one — but you might want to explore this issue further on your own so that you can learn to handle additional possibilities. The following code shows how that is done:

Listing 10-15 *(continued)*

```
backgroundAudioPlayer = [[AVAudioPlayer alloc]
        initWithContentsOfURL:backgroundURL error:nil];
backgroundAudioPlayer.numberOfLoops = -1;
[backgroundAudioPlayer prepareToPlay];

NSURL* burnRubberURL = [NSURL fileURLWithPath:[[NSBundle
        mainBundle] pathForResource:@"BurnRubber"
        ofType:@"aif"]];
AudioServicesCreateSystemSoundID((__bridge CFURLRef)
        burnRubberURL, &burnRubberSoundID);
[testDriveButton setBackgroundImage:[UIImage
        animatedImageNamed:@"Button" duration:1.0 ]
        forState:UIControlStateNormal];
}
```

In Chapter 5, I show you how to add a custom button with a Button background image. You could have also programmatically added the background image by sending the button the `setBackgroundImage:forState:` message (Chapter 5 explains the control state as well). Normally, you might think of making the background image a single image. However, `animatedImageNamed:duration:` and some similar methods use a series of files, each displayed for a duration you specify, instead. This type of method enables you to animate (this time in place) not only a button but any image by simply supplying a series of images:

```
[testDriveButton setBackgroundImage:
  [UIImage animatedImageNamed:@"Button" duration:1.0]
                        forState:UIControlStateNormal];
```

In the `animatedImageNamed:` method, you supply a *base* name of an image to animate. The method will append a zero to the base name and load that image (in this case, `Button0`). After the time that you specify in `duration` has elapsed, the `animatedImageNamed:` method appends the next number (in this case, 1) to the base image name and attempts to load it and the remainder of images (up to 1,024 images) until it runs out of images, and then it starts over.

In the Project navigator, open the disclosure triangle for the RoadTrip Resources group that you created in Chapter 3. If you look in the RoadTrip Resources group, you see two images, Button0 and Button1 — with Button being the base name you specified. This is an "in place" animation, so all images included in the animated image should share the same size and scale.

If you select each image in the Project navigator, you can see that they are slightly different colors, and each will display for 1.0 seconds (`duration:1.0`). This makes the button blink and certainly adds some life to the Main view.

Chapter 11

Finishing the Basic Application Structure

*I*n earlier chapters, I've waxed poetic about storyboards, but I haven't really (completely) shown you why I find them so appealing. Now it's time for you to experience the reason yourself.

As I say earlier in the book, the storyboard is basically about working with view controllers. In this chapter, I show you how to extend your storyboard to lay out the flow, or the *user experience architecture* of most of your application, or at least the big pieces of the app, such as the Content controller, which lets you choose what you want to do. You also add the structure for the user to find out the weather forecast for the destination, find events that are happening at the destination, bring up a map, and find a location on a map.

Extending the Storyboard to Add More Functionality to Your App

You start by selecting the storyboard in the Project navigator and showing the Utility area by selecting it in the Xcode toolbar's View selector. Next, hide the Project navigator by selecting it in the Xcode toolbar's View selector (remember, as I explain in Chapter 2, it's a toggle). Doing so gives you a little more real estate onscreen. (If you have large monitor, though, you can keep the Project navigator open.)

Select the Attributes inspector in the Inspector selector bar in the Utility area. Close all the disclosure triangles in the Dock to give you a little more room to work in.

To add the ContentController (the table view that gives you access to RoadTrip's main functionality) you need to do the following:

1. **Select Objects in the Utility area's Library pane and drag a new Table view controller into your storyboard by selecting a Table view controller in the Library pane.**

   A new scene is created. (If you are hazy on how storyboards work, please check out Chapter 5.) The storyboard will automatically make room for the new scene, as you can see in Figure 11-1.

2. **Select the Travel button in the Main View Controller and Control+drag from the Travel button in the Main View controller to the Table view controller, as shown in Figure 11-2.**

3. **Select Push from the Storyboard Segues pop-up menu, as shown in Figure 11-3.**

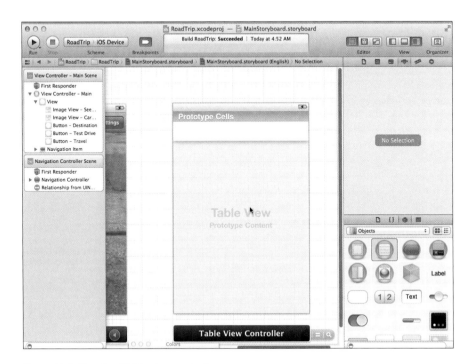

Figure 11-1: Drag in a Table view controller.

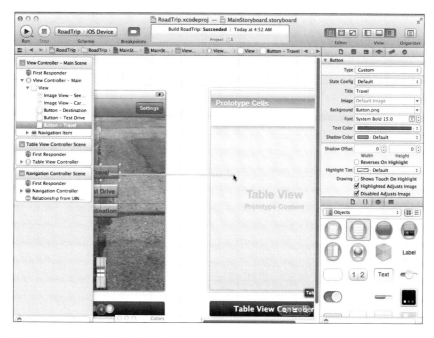

Figure 11-2: Drag from the Travel button to the Table view controller.

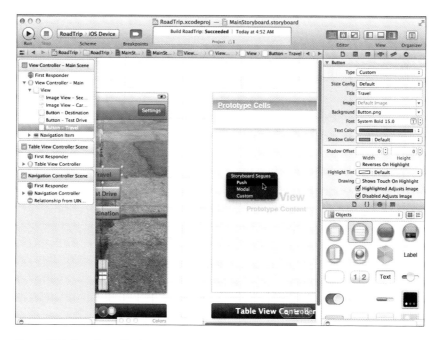

Figure 11-3: Creating a Push segue.

You create a segue, as I explain in Chapter 5, when you want to create a transition from one view controller to another. A segue performs the visual transition between two view controllers and supports push (navigation), modal, and custom transitions. All you have to do (as you just saw) is Control+click from a button or table view cell and drag to the view controller you want displayed.

A Push segue causes the new view controller with a back button to slide into place when the user taps a button, and the Navigation bar items are updated appropriately (see Chapter 5 for more about adding a Navigation controller).

In contrast to a Push segue, a Modal segue presents the view controller modally, with the transition style you specify, and requires the user to do something (tap Save or Cancel, for example) to get back to the previous view controller. Segues support the standard visual transition styles such as Cover Vertical, Flip Horizontal, Cross Dissolve, and Partial Curl.

In addition, segue objects are used to prepare for the transition from one view controller to another. Segue objects contain information about the view controllers involved in a transition. When a segue is triggered, but before the visual transition occurs, the storyboard runtime calls the current view controller's `prepareForSegue:sender:` method so that it can pass any needed data to the view controller that is about to be displayed.

4. **Select the segue and make sure that *Push* appears in the Style menu in the Attribute inspector (see Figure 11-4). Enter** Content **in the Identifier field. You won't always use the identifier, but it is good practice to name it so that you can identify it.**

Press Return.

The field in the storyboard is not updated until you press Return, or sometimes until you click in another field *in that inspector*.

5. **In the Dock, open the disclosure triangle next to the Table view controller in the new scene and select the Table view. Change the Content field from Dynamic Prototypes to Static Cells, as shown in Figure 11-5.**

As I explain in Chapter 18, Table views usually require a *data source* and a *delegate*. The data source supplies the content for the Table view and provides the content for each cell (or row). The delegate manages the appearance and behavior of the Table view and determines what to do when the user selects a cell (or row) — for example, push a view controller onto the stack, as I explain in Chapter 5 in the section about adding a Navigation controller.

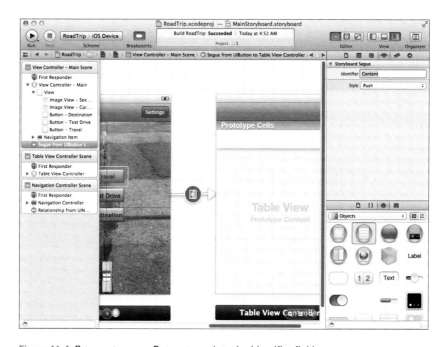

Figure 11-4: Be sure to press Return to update the Identifier field.

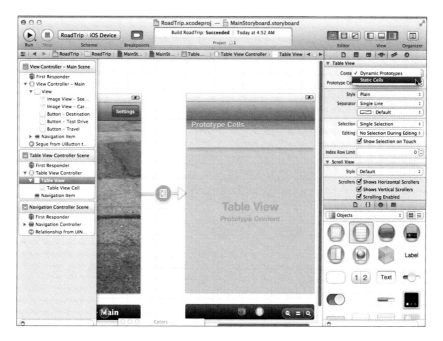

Figure 11-5: Select Static Cells for the Table view.

If you are using the Table view only as a type of "table of contents" for your application, selecting Static Cells lets you create the cell content in Interface Builder (as I show you how to do next) and use storyboard segues to specify what happens when a user selects a cell. Much easier and a lot less work than coding it yourself! I explain more about this in Chapter 18.

The following steps show you how to customize your Table view.

1. **In the Attributes inspector, enter** 2 **(or you can use the Stepper control) in the Sections pop-up menu (changing it from 1) and Grouped in the Style pop-up menu (changing it from Plain).**

   Table views come in two basic styles:

   - **Plain:** The default style is called *plain* and looks really unadorned — plain vanilla. It's a list: Just one darn thing after another. You can index it, though, just as the Table view in the Contacts application is indexed, so it can be a pretty powerful tool.

     A plain view can also have section titles (as I describe shortly) and footers.

   - **Grouped:** The other style is the *grouped* Table view; unsurprisingly, it allows you to clump entries into various categories.

     Grouped tables cannot have an index.

     When you configure a grouped Table view, you can also have header, footer, and section titles. I show you how to do section titles shortly.

   You see two sections with three Rows each (see Figure 11-6).

   The details of what you have just done may change as the storyboard defaults are changed, but you get the picture.

2. **Open the disclosure triangle next to the Table view in the Dock and notice the Table view sections under it. Select the first section and change the Rows Field in the Attributes inspector to 2 (or delete one of the cells entries in the Dock) and enter Destination in the Header field.**

3. **Select the second section, delete one of the cells, and enter** Getting Around **in the Header field. (See Figure 11-7.)**

4. **Click in the first Table View Cell in the Dock** and select Basic in the Style menu.

   The Style menu provides a number of options for how the cell is formatted. Each one formats the text in the cell a little differently in the label(s) it adds to the cell to display the text (or you can leave it as Custom, and drag in a label(s), and format the label any way you want).

   When you select Basic, you see a new disclosure triangle next to Table View Cell in the Dock. If you open it, you see that a single label has been added for you.

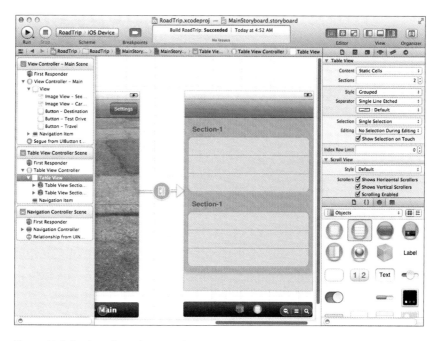

Figure 11-6: Static cells and two sections.

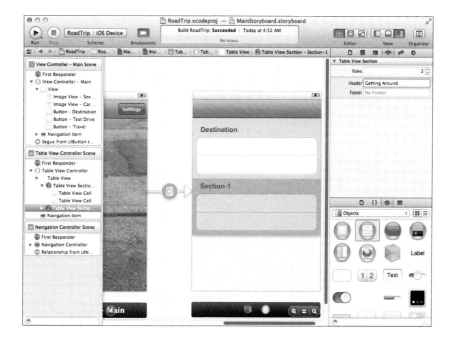

Figure 11-7: Setting the number of rows and sections with headers that you want.

5. **Select the label.**

   The Attributes inspector displays the label properties, including the Text, which you can change to your heart's content. (Selecting the text icon in the Font field allows you to change the font as well.)

   In Figure 11-8, I have entered Weather in the Text field in the Attributes inspector and changed the Font to System from System Bold.

6. **Repeat Steps 4 - 5 to format the next two cells (the second Table View Cell in this Table View Section and the first Table View Cell in the second Table View Section), this time entering Events and Map respectively in the Text field in the Attributes inspector.**

   You have to treat the last cell a little differently. Leave the cell type as Custom. Because the user will enter the place he or she wants to find in the cell, you have to format it on your own.

7. **Drag in a Label from the Library pane into the cell, as shown in Figure 11-9.**

8. **Enter** Find: **in the Text field in the Attributes Inspector.**

9. **Drag in a Text Field from the Library pane and position it and the Label as shown in Figure 11-10.**

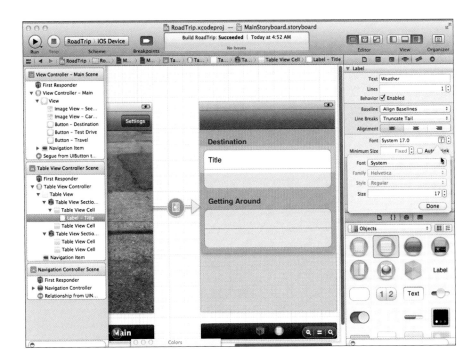

Figure 11-8: Updating the cell label.

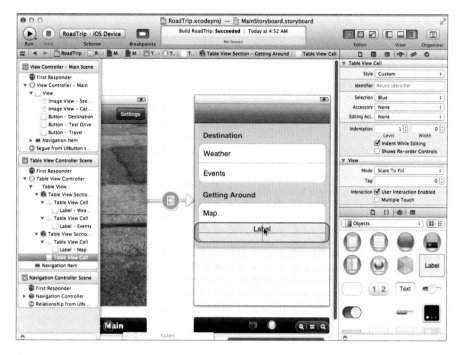

Figure 11-9: The Find Cell label.

10. **In the Attributes Inspector, enter** Enter address or place **in the Placeholder field to help the user understand what this text field is for.**

11. **In the Attributes inspector, select the first Border Style (no Border) in the Text Field section. The text field will seem to disappear, but you can always select it again in the Dock.**

    Text fields enable the user to enter small amounts of text, which is exactly what you need here.

12. **Finally, select the Table View controller and enter** Content **in the Title and Identifier Fields in the View Controller section. Specifying a Title and Identifier isn't always necessary, but you will need to use them under certain circumstances, and it's good to make a habit of adding them. Your Table View controller should look more or less like mine does in Figure 11-11.**

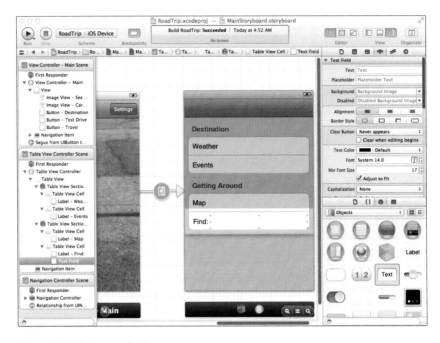

Figure 11-10: Add a text field.

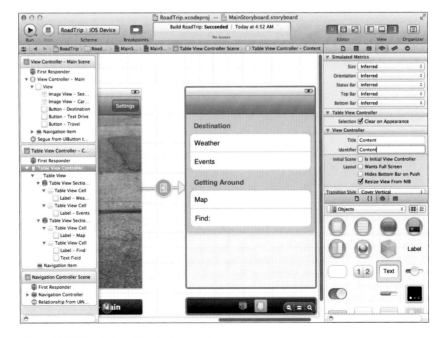

Figure 11-11: The finished Content controller.

If you Run RoadTrip and click or touch the Travel button, the screen shown in Figure 11-12 displays. Clicking or tapping in a cell doesn't get you anything yet, but I show you how to take care of that next.

Figure 11-12: The latest additions to the RoadTrip app.

Of course, this user interface is not particular exciting; in fact, it is rather pedestrian. You fix that in Chapter 13 by including a view title that is dynamically generated based on the destination the user chooses.

Adding the Remaining Elements You Need in Your Storyboard

In this section, I show you how to add the rest of the scenes you need in your storyboard for the RoadTrip app. There will be some other view controllers in the storyboard that are not launched by the storyboard, and you'll add those as needed.

1. **Add another *view controller* — not a table view controller — to the storyboard.**

2. **In the view controller's Title field, enter** Weather, **and in its Identifier field, enter** Weather **as well.**

3. **Control+drag from the Weather cell in the Content controller to the Weather view controller (see Figure 11-13).**

   It is easier to do from the Dock because you need to drag from the cell, rather than from the label that was generated when you set the Style to Basic (as you did earlier in this chapter).

4. **Select the segue and set its identifier to Weather, as shown in Figure 11-14. You can also see that Push has been selected in the storyboards Segues menu.**

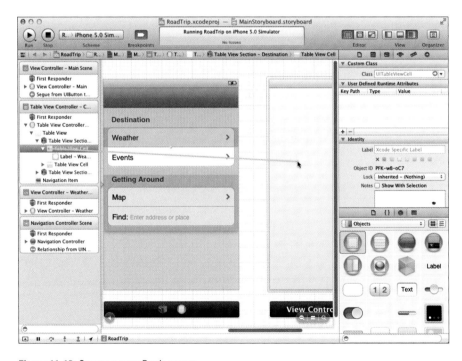

Figure 11-13: Create a new Push segue.

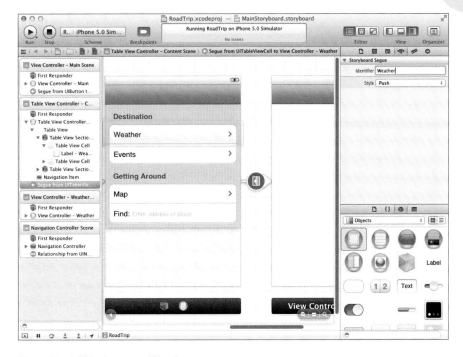

Figure 11-14: Title the segue Weather.

5. **Select the Weather Table View cell, and in the Accessory field, change the selection from Disclosure Indicator to None.**

6. **Repeat Steps 1-2 and 5 to add the Events, Map and Find view controllers to your storyboard. In each of the view controller's Title and Identifier fields, enter Events, Map, and Find respectively**

7. **Add segues for the Events and Map cells to the Events and Map view controllers by performing Steps 2-4. Be sure to title the segues Events and Map.**

   You won't be using a segue to launch the Find view controller. I show you a different way to launch a view controller in Chapter 18.

   The final result of what has been added to the storyboard so far should look like Figure 11-15.

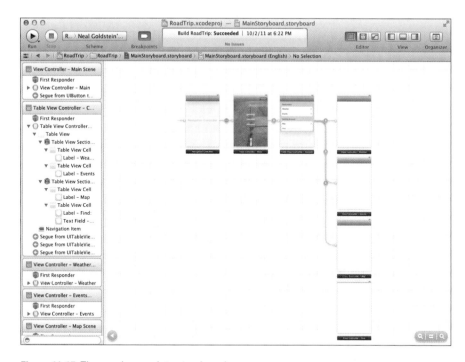

Figure 11-15: The nearly complete storyboard.

When you run RoadTrip, you'll be able to click the Travel button and then click in each of the Content Controller cells to see a new view controller (they'll all look the same) and be able to return to the Content Controller and subsequently the Main Controller.

Although what you have in your app so far may not seem all that impressive, for all of us who used to have to write all that code before Xcode 4.2, it is a giant leap forward in developing iPhone apps.

The Content view is still missing a background image as well as the name of the destination. But in order to add those elements, you have to create a model to own that data. I show you how to create that model in Chapter 12. Meanwhile, in the next section, you find out how to add another essential element to your app: the recognition of user gestures on the iPhone.

Add a Gesture Recognizer

One thing important to understand about the iPhone user experience is the importance of gestures. The use of gestures is one of features that make the use of device an intimate experience for the user, as I explain in Chapter 1.

UIKit includes gesture recognizers that you can use in your app to make it work the same way as the ones that are used by Apple in its apps.

In this section, you add a gesture recognizer to the Main view so that the user can swipe to the left to make the Content view appear.

Adding the gesture recognizer is easy. In RTViewController.m, add the bolded code in Listing 11-1 to viewDidLoad.

Listing 11-1: Adding a Gesture Recognizer

```
- (void)viewDidLoad
{
  [super viewDidLoad];

  self.title = @"Road Trip";
  NSURL* backgroundURL = [NSURL fileURLWithPath:[[NSBundle
          mainBundle]pathForResource:@"CarRunning"
          ofType:@"aif"]];
  backgroundAudioPlayer = [[AVAudioPlayer alloc]
          initWithContentsOfURL:backgroundURL error:nil];
  backgroundAudioPlayer.numberOfLoops = -1;
  [backgroundAudioPlayer prepareToPlay];
  NSURL* burnRubberURL = [NSURL fileURLWithPath:[[NSBundle
          mainBundle] pathForResource:@"BurnRubber"
          ofType:@"aif"]];
  AudioServicesCreateSystemSoundID((__bridge CFURLRef)
          burnRubberURL, &burnRubberSoundID);
  [testDriveButton setBackgroundImage:[UIImage
          animatedImageNamed:@"Button" duration:1.0]
          forState:UIControlStateNormal];

  UISwipeGestureRecognizer *swipeGesture =
    [[UISwipeGestureRecognizer alloc] initWithTarget:self
                  action:@selector(handleSwipeGesture:)];
  swipeGesture.direction =
                  UISwipeGestureRecognizerDirectionLeft;
  [self.view addGestureRecognizer:swipeGesture];
  }
}
```

UISwipeGestureRecognizer is a subclass of UIGestureRecognizer — the abstract base class for concrete gesture-recognizer classes. The gesture recognizer does the hard work of recognizing a specific gesture and then sends an action message (that you specify) to the target (that you also specify) to do something.

Besides the UISwipeGeture, there are gesture recognizers for

- **Tap:** UITapGestureRecognizer
- **Pinch:** UIPinchGestureRecognizer
- **Rotation:** UIRotationGestureRecognizer
- **Swipe:** UISwipeGestureRecognizer
- **Pan:** UIPanGestureRecognizer
- **Touch and hold:** UILongPressGestureRecognizer

A window delivers touch events to a gesture recognizer before it delivers them to the hit-tested view attached to the gesture recognizer — the gesture recognizer is attached to the view and is not part of the responder chain. Generally, if a gesture recognizer does not recognize its gesture, the touches are passed on to the view. If a gesture recognizer does recognizes its gesture, the remaining touches for the view are cancelled.

UISwipeGestureRecognizer is a concrete subclass of UIGestureRecognizer that looks for swiping gestures in one or more directions. Because a swipe is a discrete gesture, the action message is sent only once per gesture.

UISwipeGestureRecognizer recognizes a swipe when the specified number of touches (numberOfTouchesRequired) have moved mostly in an allowable direction (direction) far enough to be considered a swipe. You can configure the UISwipeGestureRecognizer recognizer for the number of touches (the default is 1) and the direction (the default is right), as follows:

```
UISwipeGestureRecognizer *swipeGesture =
  [[UISwipeGestureRecognizer alloc] initWithTarget:self
                    action:@selector(handleSwipeGesture:)];
```

Here, you have created a swipe gesture with a target of self and an action of handleSwipeGesture:.

Next, you set the direction to left from the default right, as follows:

```
swipeGesture.direction =
                UISwipeGestureRecognizerDirectionLeft;
```

To handle the swipe, add the code in Listing 11-2 to RTViewController.m.

Listing 11-2: Adding `handleSwipeGesture` to `RTViewController.m`

```
- (IBAction)handleSwipeGesture:(id)sender {

  UIStoryboard *storyboard =
    [UIStoryboard storyboardWithName:
                            @"MainStoryboard" bundle:nil];
  UIViewController *viewController =
    [storyboard instantiateViewControllerWithIdentifier:
                                        @"Content"];
  [[self navigationController]
        pushViewController:viewController animated:YES];
}
```

What you do here is find the storyboard in the bundle:

```
UIStoryboard *storyboard =
  [UIStoryboard storyboardWithName:
                          @"MainStoryboard" bundle:nil];
```

Then you create the `ContentViewController` yourself. This is the same thing that the storyboard does (in the segue logic) when you select the Travel button:

```
UIViewController *viewController =
  [storyboard instantiateViewControllerWithIdentifier:
                                      @"Content"];
```

Here's where the identifier I nag you about entering comes in handy. It's the only way you can find the View controller that you have configured in the storyboard.

Next, you tell the Navigation controller to push the View controller onto the stack (note that this method also updates the Navigation bar) and have it slide into place. (If the `animated` parameter is YES, the view is animated into position; otherwise, the view is simply displayed in place.)

```
[[self navigationController] pushViewController:
                              viewController animated:YES];
```

This is what would have been done for you in the segue logic generated by the storyboard.

I've made the point (several times) that the model is about the data. So where does the data come from?

The easy answer is . . . any place you'd like.

Given the iPhone model, however, there are several approaches you can take:

- ✔ **Option 1:** Download the data from a web service (or ftp site) and have the model control it in a file or have Core Data (Core Data is an iOS object persistence mechanism outside the scope of this book) manage it.

- ✔ **Option 2:** Have a web service manage your data and get what you need as you need it.

- ✔ **Option 3:** Include the data as an application resource.

- ✔ **Option 4:** Access the data on the web as an HTML page.

Although I really like Option 2 (and explain that in my upcoming book *iOS Cloud Development For Dummies*), it is beyond the scope of this book, so the Trip model uses both Options 3 and 4.

Although the preceding answers most of the model's "Show Me the Data" responsibility, there is yet another question to be answered: How does the model know where the data is?

The answer to that question lies in a very useful structure that is used extensively by not only iOS but also applications — property lists (or more commonly known as *plists*).

The RoadTrip plist that you are about to create will have both data used by the `Trip` model object (Option 3), as well as the URLs for the data you download as HTML pages (Option 4).

Adding the Model Data

For situations in which you need to store small relatively amounts of persistent data — say, less than a few hundred kilobytes — a *property list* offers a uniform and convenient means of organizing, storing, and accessing the data.

Using property lists

A property list (or *plist*) is perfect for storing small amounts of data that consist primarily of strings and numbers. What adds to its appeal is the ability to easily read it into your program, use the data, and (although you won't be doing it in the RoadTrip application), modify the data and then write the property list back out again (see the "Using plists to store data" sidebar, later in this chapter). That's because iOS provides a small set of objects that have that behavior built right in.

Applications and other system software in Mac OS X and iOS use property lists extensively. For example, the Mac OS X Finder stores file and directory attributes in a property list, and iOS uses them for user defaults. You also get a Property List editor with Xcode, which makes property list files easy to create and maintain in your own programs.

Figure 12-1 shows a property list that I show you how to build — one that contains the data necessary for the RoadTrip app.

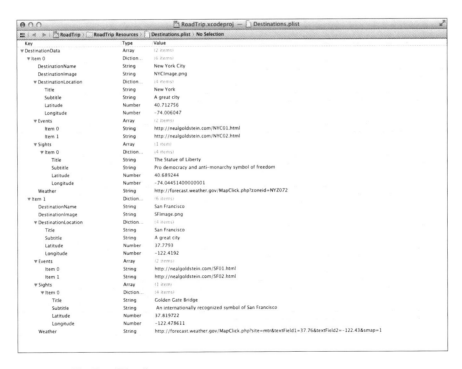

Figure 12-1: The RoadTrip plist.

After you figure out how to work with property lists, it's actually easy, but like most things, getting there is half the fun.

Property lists hold serializable objects. A *serializable object* can convert itself into a stream of birts so that it can be stored in a file; it can then reconstitute itself into the object it once was when it is read back in (yes, the phenomenon of "beam me up, Scotty" does exist, at least on your computer).

These objects, called *property list objects,* that you have to work with are as follows, and there are two types (which I explain in an upcoming paragraph):

Primitives:

- NSData and NSMutableData
- NSDate
- NSNumber
- NSString and NSMutableString

Containers:

- NSArray and NSMutableArray
- NSDictionary and NSMutableDictionary

As shown in the plist in Figure 12-1, shown previously, this plist is actually an NSDictionary. It has one entry — DestinationData, which is an array of dictionaries — and the data for each one of the destinations is held in a dictionary in that array (Item 0 and Item 1). If you are a little hazy on arrays and dictionaries, check out *Objective-C For Dummies,* by me (Wiley) or the Apple documentation.

Now for that explanation of two kinds of property list objects, as follows:

- **Primitives:** The term *primitives* is not a reflection on how civilized these property list objects are; rather, it describes the simplest kind of object. They are what they are.
- **Containers:** Containers can hold primitives as well as other containers.

One important feature of property list object containers (NSArray, NSDictionary), besides their ability to hold other objects, is that they both have a `writeToFile:` method that writes the property list to a file, and a corresponding `initWithContentsOfFile:`, which initializes the object with the contents of a file. So, if I create an array or dictionary and fill it chock full of objects of the property list type, all I have to do to save that array or dictionary to a file is tell it to go save itself — or create an array or dictionary and then tell it to initialize itself from a file.

`NSString` and `NSData` and their mutable counterparts also can write and the read themselves to and from a file.

`NSData` and `NSMutableData` are wrappers (an object whose basic purpose is to turn something into an object) in which you can dump any kind of data and then have that data act as an object.

The containers can contain other containers as well as the primitive types. Thus, you might have an array of dictionaries, and each dictionary might contain other arrays and dictionaries as well as the primitive types.

Adding a property list to your project

Given the versatility of property lists, you're sure to turn to them time and time again. Follow these steps to incorporate a plist into your Xcode project:

1. **In the Project navigator, select the RoadTrip Resources group and right-click and then choose New File or choose File⇨New⇨New File from the main menu (or press ⌘+N) to get the New File dialog.**

2. **In the left column of the dialog, select Resource under the iOS heading, select the Property List template in the top-right pane, and then click Next.**

3. **Enter *Destinations* in the Save As field.**

4. **Click Create (and make sure that the Target field has the RoadTrip text box selected).**

5. **Right-click in the Property List editor (the blank page) to show the context-sensitive menu; then choose Add Row, as shown in Figure 12-2.**

   You can also choose Editor⇨Add Item to add a row.

   A new row appears, as shown in Figure 12-3.

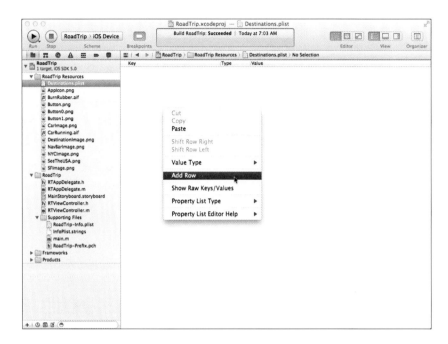

Figure 12-2: Add a row to the new plist file.

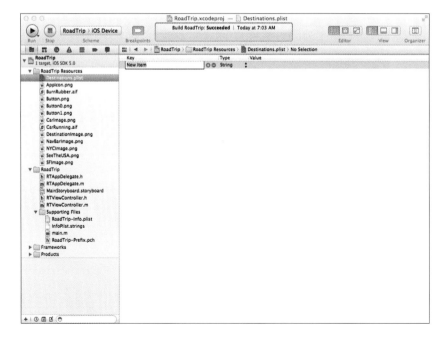

Figure 12-3: A new row.

6. **In the Type pop-up menu, change the type from** `String` **to** `Array` **and the Key to** `DestinationData`**, as shown in Figure 12-4.**

7. **Click the disclosure triangle in front of the** `DestinationData` **key and click the plus button, as shown in Figure 12-5.**

A new entry appears.

When you have the disclosure triangle pointing down, or open, adding a new row adds it as a child of the entry. When the disclosure triangle is pointing to the right, the new row is added as a sibling.

`DestinationData` is an array of dictionaries that will hold all your destination-specific information, with Item 0 being the first one.

In Figure 12-5, I have added the row and you can see the plus button in the new row.

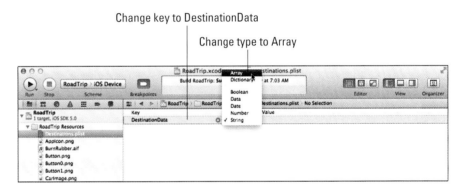

Figure 12-4: Change the New Item to Array.

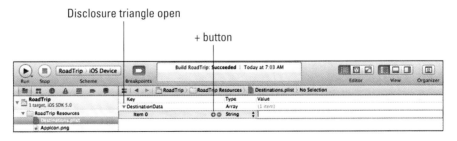

Figure 12-5: Add an entry.

8. **Make Item 0 a dictionary by selecting Dictionary in the Type pop-up menu (in the same way you select Array in Step 6).**

   Your new entry is made into a dictionary, as shown in Figure 12-6.

9. **Click the disclosure triangle in front of the Item 0 key so that it points down, and click the plus icon as you did in Step 7 to add a new entry to the dictionary.**

   You see a new entry under the dictionary like the one in Figure 12-7.

   These disclosure triangles work the same way as those in the Finder and the Xcode editor. The Property List editor interprets what you want to add based on the triangle. So, if the items are revealed (that is, the triangle is pointing down), the editor assumes that you want to add a subitem or *child*. If the subitems are not revealed (that is, the triangle is pointing sideways), the editor assumes that you want to add an item at that level *(sibling)*. In this case, with the arrow pointing down, you add a new entry — a subitem — to the dictionary. If the triangle were pointing sideways, you would be entering a new entry under the root.

   Only arrays and dictionaries have children.

10. **In the Key field, enter** DestinationName, **leave the Type as** String, **and then double-click (or tab to) the Value field and enter** New York City, **as shown in Figure 12-8.**

    It can be any of the property list objects I talk about at the beginning of this chapter, but String, which is already selected, is the one you want here.

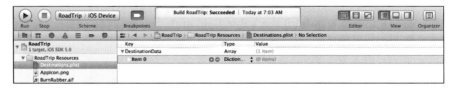

Figure 12-6: A dictionary entry.

New item

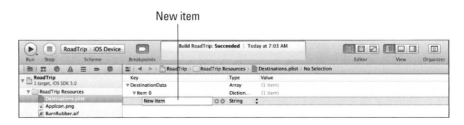

Figure 12-7: A new entry in the dictionary.

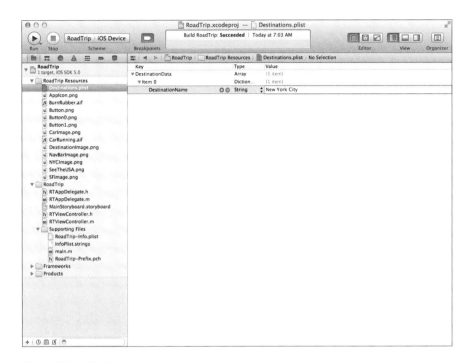

Figure 12-8: A dictionary entry.

11. **Click the Add button in the row you just entered, and you get a new entry (a sibling of the previous row). In the Key field, enter** DestinationImage, **leave the Type as** `String`, **and then double-click (or tab to) the Value field and enter NYCImage.png.**

12. **Click the add button in the row you just entered and you get a new entry (a sibling of the previous row). In the Key field, enter** `DestinationLocation` **and select Dictionary in the Type pop-up menu.**

13. **Click the disclosure triangle in front of the** `DestinationLocation` **Key so it is facing down, and click the add button as you did in Step 9.**

    You see a new entry under the dictionary, as you can see in Figure 12-9.

14. **In the Key field, enter** Title, **and enter** New York City **in the Value field. Add three more entries for the Keys:** Subtitle, Latitude, Longitude; **and three more for the Values:** A great city, 40.712756, **and** -74.006047 (the latter two fields should be Type Number). **When you are done, your plist should look like Figure 12-10.**

Change key to DestinationName

Change value to New York City

Figure 12-9: A new dictionary with its first entry.

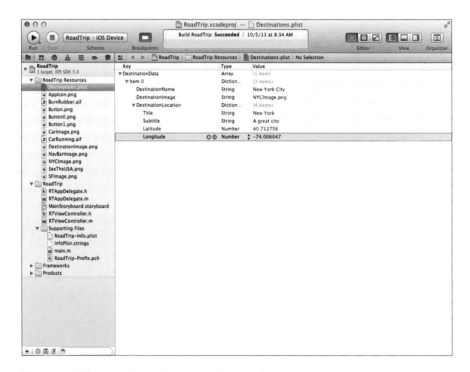

Figure 12-10: The `DestinationLocation` entries.

15. **Click the disclosure triangle to hide the** `DestinationLocation` **Dictionary entries, and add a new array named** Events **as a sibling of the** `DestinationLocation`, **as shown in Figure 12-11.**

As explained previously, when the disclosure triangle is closed, you add a sibling entry.

Continue filling out the plist to make it match Figure 12-12.

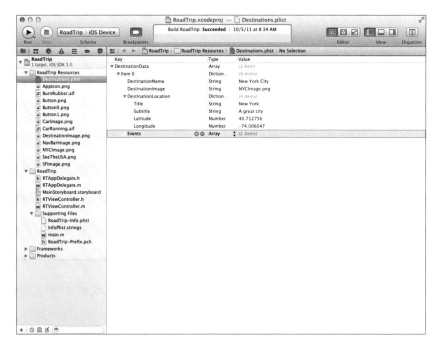

Figure 12-11: The `Events` dictionary entry is an array.

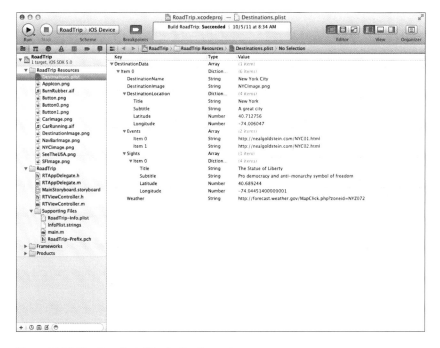

Figure 12-12: The New York City destination entry.

The keys and values are displayed in the following table.

Key	Type	Value
DestinationName	String	New York City
DestinationImage	String	NYCImage.png
DestinationLocaton		
Title	String	New York
Subtitle	String	A great city
Latitude	Number	40.712756
Longitude	Number	-74.006047
Events		
Item 0	String	`http://nealgoldstein.com/ NYC01.html`
Item 1	String	`http://nealgoldstein.com/ NYC02.html`
Sights		
Item 0		
Title	String	The Statue of Liberty
Subtitle	String	Pro democracy and anti-monarchy symbol of freedom
Latitude	Number	40.689244
Longitude	Number	-74.044514
Weather	String	http://forecast.weather.gov/ MapClick.php?zoneid=NYZ072

After you finish entering these items, close Item 0 under `DestinationData` and go through Steps 8 through 15 again to add the San Francisco entry using the keys and values in the following table. If you want to save some typing, you can copy and paste Item 0 and then expand the new Item 1 and simply replace the values (that's what I did).

Key	Type	Value
DestinationName	String	San Francisco
DestinationImage	String	SFImage.png
DestinationLocaton		
Title	String	San Francisco
Subtitle	String	A great city
Latitude	Number	37.7793
Longitude	Number	-122.4192
Events		
Item 0	String	http://nealgoldstein.com/SF01.html
Item 1	String	http://nealgoldstein.com/SF02.html
Sights		
Item 0		
Title	String	Golden Gate Bridge
Subtitle	String	An internationally recognized symbol of San Francisco
Latitude	Number	37.819722
Longitude	Number	-122.478611
Weather	String	http://forecast.weather.gov/MapClick.php?site=mtr&textField1=37.76&textField2=-122.43&smap=1

Make sure that you spell the entries *exactly as specified* or else you won't be able to access them using the examples in this book. Be especially careful of trailing spaces.

When you're done, refer to Figure 12-1 to see how your plist should look.

You also may wonder why you're using this specific data (title and subtitle for example). You'll understand that when you explore maps in Chapter 16.

Using plists to store data

Although you won't do it here, you can also modify a plist to store data. The only restriction of note is that you can't modify a plist you've created in your bundle. You need to save it in the file system instead. For example:

```
NSArray *paths = NSSearchPathForDirectoriesInDomains
                        (NSDocumentDirectory, NSUserDomainMask, YES);
NSString *documentsDirectory = [paths objectAtIndex:0];
NSString *filePath = [documentsDirectory
                        stringByAppendingPathComponent:state];
[updatedDestinations writeToFile:filePath atomically:YES];
```

Now that you have the information needed by the model to locate the data it is responsible for, it's time to start adding some model classes, which I cover in the following section.

Adding the First Model Class

The first model class I have you add is the `Trip` class. This will become the only model object visible to the view controllers. Although the `Trip` object will use other objects to carry out its responsibilities, hiding them behind the `Trip` object results in the loose coupling I explain in the next section and in the "Importance of loose coupling" sidebar.

1. **Create a new group to keep your model classes in by going to the Project navigator, selecting the RoadTrip group (*not* the RoadTrip project, which is at the top), and either right-clicking and choosing New Group or choosing File⇨New⇨New Group. Name your new group *Model Classes*.**

   To change a file's group, select the file and drag it to the group you want it to occupy. The same goes for groups as well (after all, they can go into other groups).

2. **In the Project navigator, select the Model Classes group and either right-click and then choose New File or choose File⇨New⇨New File from the main menu (or press ⌘+N) to open the New File dialog.**

3. **In the left column of the dialog, select Cocoa Touch under the iOS heading; next, select the Objective-C class template in the top-right pane; then click Next.**

4. **In the Class field, enter** Trip. **In the Subclass Of drop-down menu, select** NSObject. **Click Next.**

5. **In the Save sheet, click Create.**

6. **Repeat Steps 2–6 to create the Destination class.**

You also will be using the MapKit and CoreLocation frameworks, so add them as well:

1. **In the Project navigator, select the Project icon at the top of the Project Navigator area (RoadTrip) to display the Project editor.**

2. **In the TARGETS section, select RoadTrip.**

3. **In the Summary tab, scroll down to the Linked Frameworks and Libraries section.**

4. **Expand the Linked Frameworks and Libraries section, if it is not already expanded, by clicking the disclosure triangle.**

5. **Click the + (plus sign) button underneath the list of current project frameworks.**

   A list of frameworks appears.

6. **Scroll down and select the** both the MapKit.framework and CoreLocation.framework **from the list of frameworks.**

7. **Click the Add button.**

   You'll see the framework added to the Linked Frameworks and Libraries section.

8. **Close the Linked Frameworks and Libraries section.**

9. **In the Project navigator (don't do this from the Linked Frameworks and Libraries section!), drag the** SystemConfiguration.framework **file to the Frameworks group).**

If you make a mistake and want to delete a file, right-click and choose Delete or select the file and press Delete. You will see the dialog in Figure 12-13.

Remove References Only will remove the file from the Project navigator but leave it in your project folder on the disk. You will not be able to copy a new file with that name to that project until you delete that file from your project on the disk as well.

Figure 12-13: What would you like to do?

When you use the template to create a class, it will add the methods it thinks you may need. As a result, there will be some methods you won't need and that appear to sit around doing nothing. You can delete them or just leave them in case you do need them. This is especially true of initialization methods because initialization in this app will be (mostly) taken care of by the storyboard.

Understanding the Trip Interface

Following is what the Trip Interface will eventually become:

```
#import <Foundation/Foundation.h>
#import <MapKit/MapKit.h>
@class Annotation;

@interface Trip : NSObject

- (UIImage *) destinationImage;
- (NSString *) destinationName;
- (CLLocationCoordinate2D) destinationCoordinate;

- (id)initWithDestinationIndex:(int)destinationIndex;
- (NSString *)weather;
- (int)numberOfEvents;
- (NSString *)getEvent:(int)index;
- (NSArray *)createAnnotations;
- (NSString *)mapTitle;
- (void)addLocation:(NSString *)findLocation
    completionHandler:(void (^)(Annotation *annotation,
                              NSError* error)) completion;
@end
```

As you can see, this code contains a lot of stuff, and I explain it as you add functionality to the `Trip` class along the way.

Earlier in the chapter, I mentioned that `Trip` is the model interface, and I say this because in many cases more than one class will be involved in delivering the necessary functionality of the model. For example you just added a `Destination` class (in this chapter) that will be responsible for the information about your destination. An `Events` class in Chapter 14 will be responsible for managing the list of things going on at your destination, and an `Annotation` class (coming in Chapter 16) will provide the information you need to plot annotations (places to see) on a map. Hiding additional model objects behind the Trip object is known as *loose coupling* and is an important object-oriented design principle (see the Importance of lose coupling sidebar).

You might be tempted to have the view controllers create the model classes they'll use (for example, a `WeatherController` would create the `Weather` object, and so on). The problem with that approach is that it makes the coupling between controller objects and the model much tighter.

One advantage of the Model-View-Controller design pattern that I explain in Chapter 4 is that it allows you to assign (most) classes into one of three groups in your application and work on them individually. If each group has a well-defined interface, it encapsulates many of the kinds of changes that are often made so that they don't affect the other groups. This little fact is especially true of the model and view controller relationship.

If the view controllers have minimal knowledge about the model, you can change the model objects with minor impact on the view controllers.

So although the Trip class will provide this functionality to the various view controllers, as I said, it won't be doing all the work on its own.

What makes this possible is a well-defined interface, which I showed you at the start of this section. You create an interface between the model and the controllers by using a technique called *composition,* which is a useful way to create interfaces.

I'm a big fan of composition because it's another way to hide what's really going on behind the curtain. It keeps the objects that use the composite object (in this case, `Trip` is the composite object) ignorant of the objects that the composite object uses and actually makes the components ignorant of each other, allowing you to switch components in and out at will.

So you will have `Trip` will create the model objects, encapsulating the knowledge of what objects make up the model from the object that uses it.

`Trip` hides all implementation knowledge from a view controller; it will know only about the `Trip` object. This setup makes everything *loosely coupled* and makes your app more extensible and easier to change.

The importance of loose coupling

While there have been millions of words spoken about how to design object oriented applications, one of the most important is loose coupling.

A loosely coupled system is one in which each of its components has little or no knowledge (or makes no use of the knowledge it may have) of other components. The term *loose coupling* refers to the degree of direct knowledge that one class has of another. This is not about encapsulation or to one class's knowledge of another class's attributes or implementation, but rather knowledge of that other class *itself*.

Applying loose coupling means presenting a minimum interface to other objects. The client deals with the fewest number of objects as possible. So although you may want to break down a function into smaller pieces (for example, by using composition), you never want the client to know that. Clients are happy dealing with one object, even if that object then turns around and redistributes that work to other objects.

Implementing the Trip Class

In this chapter, I show you how to implement the `Trip` model functionality that will enable you to choose between multiple destinations (although you won't be doing the choosing until Chapter 18). You also implement the `Trip` functionality that will be needed by the Content controller (you add that in Chapter 13) — the name of the destination and its background image.

Start by adding the bolded code in Listing 12-1 to `Trip.h`.

Listing 12-1:   Updating the `Trip` Interface

```
#import <Foundation/Foundation.h>
#import <MapKit/MapKit.h>


@interface Trip : NSObject

- (id)initWithDestinationIndex:(int)destinationIndex;
- (UIImage *) destinationImage;
- (NSString *) destinationName;
- (CLLocationCoordinate2D) destinationCoordinate;
@end
```

As you can see, the code in the listing contains an initialization method. This method will enable the `Trip` object to get itself set up for the selected destination (and allow me to explain initialization and a few other things).

Initialization is the logical place to start, but first you need to add some instance variables and import the `Destination` header file if you are going to use it (which you are, in the `Trip` implementation). Add the bolded code in Listing 12-2 to `Trip. m`.

Listing 12-2: Updating the `Trip` Implementation

```
#import "Trip.h"
#import "Destination.h"

@interface Trip () {
  NSDictionary *destinationData;
  NSMutableArray *sights;
  Destination* destination;
}
@end

@implementation Trip
```

No you can add the `initWithDestinationIndex:` method in Listing 12-3 to `Trip.m`.

Listing 12-3: Adding `initWithDestinationIndex:`

```
- (id)initWithDestinationIndex:(int)destinationIndex {

  if (self = [super init]) {

    NSString *filePath = [[NSBundle mainBundle]
        pathForResource:@"Destinations" ofType:@"plist"];
    NSDictionary *destinations =
      [NSDictionary dictionaryWithContentsOfFile:filePath];
    NSArray *destinationsArray =
        [destinations objectForKey:@"DestinationData"];
    destinationData =
      [destinationsArray objectAtIndex:destinationIndex];
    destination = [[Destination alloc]
        initWithDestinationIndex:destinationIndex];
  }
  return self;
}
```

Before I explain the logic in these listings, I want to explain initialization in general. And yes, there are compiler warnings and you'll be fixing them as you go along.

Initializing objects

Initialization is the procedure that sets the instance variables of an object (including pointers to other objects) to a known initial state. Essentially, you need to initialize an object to assign initial values to these variables. Initialization is not required in every class in every app; if you can live with all the instance variables initialized to 0 and nil, you need to do nothing. Trip, however, will need to create the objects it will be using, and you'll do that during initialization.

An initialization method doesn't have to include an argument for every instance variable, because some will become relevant only during the course of your object's existence. You must make sure, however, that all the instance variables your object uses, including other objects that it needs to do its work, are in a state that enables your object to respond to the messages it receives.

You may think that the main job in initialization is to, well, initialize the variables in your objects (hence the name), but more is involved when you have a superclass and a subclass chain.

To see what I mean, start by looking at the initializer I use for the Trip class in Listing 12-3 (shown previously).

By convention, initialization methods begin with the abbreviation init. (This is true, however, only for *instance* — as opposed to *class* — methods.) If the method takes no arguments, the method name is just init. If it takes arguments, labels for the arguments follow the init prefix.

As you can see, the initializer in Listing 12-3 has a return type of id. You discover the reason for that in the next section.

Initialization involves these three steps:

1. Invoke the superclass's init method.

2. Initialize instance variables.

3. Return self.

The following sections explain each step.

Invoking the superclass's init method

Here is the type of statement you use to get the init method up and running:

if ((self = [super init]))

[super init] does nothing more than invoke the superclass's init method. By convention, all initializers are required to assign self. self is the "hidden" variable accessible to methods in an object that points its instance variables to whatever object you get back from the superclass initializer, which explains the ((self = [super init])).

The if statement can be a little confusing to people. There is a possibility that you may not get an object retuned from the super class's init method. If that is the case you don't want to do any further initialization.

Although the scenario just described is possible, it is not common and will not happen in this book (and in general). You might find it in classes that need certain resources to initialize themselves, and if they are not present, the object cannot be created.

There is actually a lot to initialization that I don't cover in this book, but you can find out more in my book *Objective-C For Dummies* (Wiley) as well as in Apple's Objective-C documentation.

Initializing instance variables

Initializing instance variables, including creating the objects you need, is what you probably thought initialization is about. Notice that you're initializing your instance variable after your superclass's initialization, which you can see in Listing 12-3 (shown previously). Waiting until after your superclass does its initialization gives you the opportunity to actually change something your superclass may have done during its initialization, but more important, it allows you to perform initialization knowing that what you have inherited is initialized and ready to be used.

In your initWithDestinationIndex: method, you start by finding the plist that holds the Trip data or location of the data you need:

```
NSString *filePath = [[NSBundle mainBundle]
        pathForResource:@"Destinations" ofType:@"plist"];
```

Next, you create a dictionary to hold the data. You use the method initWithContentsOfFile: which does all the heavy lifting for you. It reads in Destinations plist file and creates a dictionary for you. The plist, as I said previously, is really a dictionary with a single entry with the Key DestinationData. The dictionaryWithContentsOfFile: method creates a dictionary from the plist (and objects and keys for all of its entries) with dictionary Keys that are the Keys you specified in the plist.

This method also allocates and initializes all the elements in the dictionary (including other dictionaries), so when it is done, you are ready to roll:

```
NSDictionary *destinations =
      [NSDictionary dictionaryWithContentsOfFile:filePath];
```

NSDictionary, NSMutableDictionary, NSArray, and NSMutableArray all have the methods initWithContentsOfFile: and writeToFile:: that read themselves in from a file and write themselves out to a file, respectively. This is one of the abilities that make property list objects so useful.

Property list containers — and *only* property list containers (and NSString and NSData) — can read themselves in from a file and write themselves out to a file. The other property list objects can only store themselves, without any effort on your part, as part of a file.

Your next step in initializing instance variables is to offset into the array of dictionaries in the DestinationData entry based on the destination chosen by the user (you'll specify that in the RTAppDelegate in Listing 12-10, later in this chapter, where you will allocate the Trip object):

```
NSArray *destinationsArray =
            [destinations objectForKey:@"DestinationData"];
destinationData =
        [destinationsArray objectAtIndex:destinationIndex];
```

Finally, you allocate and initialize the Destination object:

```
destination = [[Destination alloc]
                initWithDestinationIndex:destinationIndex];
```

Returning self

Earlier in this chapter, I explain that the self = statement ensures that self is set to whatever object you get back from the superclass initializer. No matter what you get back from invoking the superclass initializer, in the initialization method, you need to set self to that value and then return it to the invoking method — the method that wants to instantiate the object or a subclass that invoked the superclass's init method.

After the code block that initializes the variables, you insert the following:

```
return self;
```

The reason the return type is an id is that sometimes what you ask for is not what you get. But don't worry; that becomes transparent to you if you follow the rules for initialization I just explained.

So where do the braces go?

If you look in the code provided by the template, sometimes you see a method implementation look like this

```
(void)viewDidLoad
{
```

and sometimes you'll see one look like this:

```
(IBAction)testDrive(id)sender {
```

I personally prefer the latter and will use it in the methods I have you add.

Quite frankly, it doesn't matter to the compiler but can raise itself to a religious issue among programmers. Do what you'd like.

The reason that you may get back a different class than what you asked for is that under certain circumstances when you allocate a framework object, what you may get back may be a class optimized for you use based on the context.

Initializing the Destination Class

Now it's time to turn to the `Destination` class and its initialization.

Add the bolded code in Listing 12-4 to `Destination.h` to update its interface to add the header files, the properties you'll be using, and the method declarations.

Listing 12-4: **Updating the Destination Interface**

```
#import <Foundation/Foundation.h>
#import <MapKit/MapKit.h>

@interface Destination : NSObject <MKAnnotation>

@property (nonatomic, readwrite)
                        CLLocationCoordinate2D coordinate;
@property (nonatomic, readwrite, copy) NSString *title;
@property (nonatomic, readwrite, copy) NSString *subtitle;
@property (nonatomic, strong) NSString *destinationName;
@property (nonatomic, strong) UIImage *destinationImage;
- (id)initWithDestinationIndex:
                        (NSUInteger)destinationIndex;
@end
```

As you saw in Chapter 4, you'll be displaying the destination on a map with an annotation (that pop up window that displays information about the location when you touch the pin on the map). Doing that requires that the class adopt the MKAnnoation protocol, which requires a coordinate property of type CLLocationCoordinate2d (that's why you need to include the MapKit and CoreLocation frameworks) and optional title and subtitle properties. Although you won't be doing anything with this part of Destination, until Chapter 16, I have you initialize Destination with what is described in the plist but defer the explanation until Chapter 16.

Next you need to add the synthesize statements for the properties to Destination.m by adding the bolded code in Listing 12-5.

Listing 12-5: Updating the Destination Implementation

```
#import "Destination.h"

@implementation Destination

@synthesize coordinate = _coordinate;
@synthesize title = _title;
@synthesize subtitle = _subtitle;
@synthesize destinationName = _destinationName;
@synthesize destinationImage = _destinationImage;
```

When you're done, you can add the initWithDestinationIndex: method in Listing 12-6 to Destination.m.

Listing 12-6: Adding initWithDestinationIndex:

```
- (id)initWithDestinationIndex:
                          (NSUInteger)destinationIndex {

  if (self = [super init]) {

    NSString *filePath = [[NSBundle mainBundle]
         pathForResource:@"Destinations" ofType:@"plist"];
    NSDictionary *destinations = [NSDictionary
                 dictionaryWithContentsOfFile:filePath];
    NSArray *destinationsArray =
         [destinations objectForKey:@"DestinationData"];
    NSDictionary *data =
       [destinationsArray objectAtIndex:destinationIndex];

    self.destinationImage = [UIImage imageNamed:
```

```
                        [data objectForKey:@"DestinationImage"]];
        self.destinationName =
                        [data objectForKey:@"DestinationName"];
        NSDictionary* destinationLocation =
                [data objectForKey:@"DestinationLocation"];
        CLLocationCoordinate2D destinationCoordinate;
        destinationCoordinate.latitude =
          [[destinationLocation
                        objectForKey:@"Latitude"] doubleValue];
        destinationCoordinate.longitude =
          [[destinationLocation
                        objectForKey:@"Longitude"] doubleValue];
        self.coordinate = destinationCoordinate;
        self.title =
                [destinationLocation objectForKey:@"Title"];
        self.subtitle =
                [destinationLocation objectForKey:@"Subtitle"];
    }
    return self;
}
```

`Destination` initializes itself more or less the same way that `Trip` did. It
starts by loading its data:

```
NSString *filePath = [[NSBundle mainBundle]
        pathForResource:@"Destinations" ofType:@"plist"];
NSDictionary *destinations =
    [NSDictionary dictionaryWithContentsOfFile: filePath];
NSArray *destinationsArray =
        [destinations objectForKey:@"DestinationData"];
NSDictionary *data =
      [destinationsArray objectAtIndex:destinationIndex];
```

Then it uses the dictionary data to initialize its properties:

```
self.destinationImage = [UIImage imageNamed:
                [data objectForKey:@"DestinationImage"]];
self.destinationName =
                [data objectForKey:@"DestinationName"];
NSDictionary* destinationLocation =
                [data objectForKey:@"DestinationLocation"];
CLLocationCoordinate2D destinationCoordinate;
destinationCoordinate.latitude =
  [[destinationLocation objectForKey:
                                @"Latitude"] doubleValue];
destinationCoordinate.longitude =
  [[destinationLocation
                objectForKey:@"Longitude"] doubleValue];
```

```
self.coordinate = destinationCoordinate;
self.title = [destinationLocation objectForKey:@"Title"];
self.subtitle =
          [destinationLocation objectForKey:@"Subtitle"];
```

The initialization of the properties is simply done by using the Keys you specified when you created the plist, which turn into dictionary keys when you load the dictionary (and its dictionaries) from the plist file.

Now you can add the Trip methods destinationImage, destination-Name, and destinationCoordinate, which use the Destination object. Add the methods in Listing 12-7 to Trip.m.

Listing 12-7: Adding destinationImage, destinationName, and destinationCoordinate

```
- (UIImage *)destinationImage {

  return  destination.destinationImage;
}

- (NSString *)destinationName {

  return  destination.destinationName;
}

- (CLLocationCoordinate2D)destinationCoordinate {

  return destination.coordinate;
}
```

These Trip methods will be used by the Content controller you created in in Chapter 11 to request the data it needs for its view.

Interestingly, in this case all Trip does is turn around and send the request to the Destination object.

This is, of course, an example of loose coupling, explained earlier.

In this case, there isn't that much for Destination to do, so you could have simply had Trip manage the data. But in a more robust app (like one worth 99 cents), it would likely have more to do. In fact, you could start by having Trip manage all the data and add a Destination object when you felt you needed to. And when you did add the Destination object, doing so would have no impact on the objects needing that data — ah, loose coupling in action.

Creating the Trip object

Finally you have to create the `Trip` object. You need to make it accessible to the view controllers that need to use it, so you'll make it an `RTAppDelegate` property. As you saw earlier, in Chapter 7, any object in your app can find the `RTAppDelegate`, and from it get a pointer to the `Trip` object.

Add the bolded code in Listing 12-8 to `RTAppDelegate.h`.

Listing 12-8:   Updating the `RTAppDelegate` Interface

```
#import <UIKit/UIKit.h>
@class Trip;

@interface RTAppDelegate : UIResponder
            <UIApplicationDelegate>

@property (strong, nonatomic) UIWindow *window;
@property (nonatomic, strong) Trip *trip;

- (void) createDestinationModel:(int)destinationIndex;

@end
```

`createDestinationModel:` is the method that actually creates the `Trip` object.

`@class` is a compiler directive to let the compiler know that `Trip` is a type. You need to import the header to actually use it in your code however, and you'll do that and synthesize the new properties by adding the bolded code in Listing 12-9 to `RTAppDelgate.m`.

Listing 12-9:   Updating the `RTAppDelegate` Implementation

```
#import "RTAppDelegate.h"
#import "Reachability.h"
#import "Trip.h"

@implementation RTAppDelegate

@synthesize window = _window;
@synthesize trip = _trip;
```

Run your application.

When you move your pointer over an object or variable in the Source editor, you can see its contents. In Figure 12-14, I've done that with `destination-Data` (and so should you).

`destinationData` is a pointer to the dictionary that contains the data for the first entry in the Destinations plist's Destination Data array. There are six key/value pairs as there should be, and if you look in the Variables pane in the Debugger, you'll see two objects in the `destinationsArray`, which is also as it should be.

If you move your pointer into the `destinationData` variable display in the Source editor and Control+-click in the up and down arrow, as I have in Figure 12-15, you see a drop-down menu with a Print Description selection.

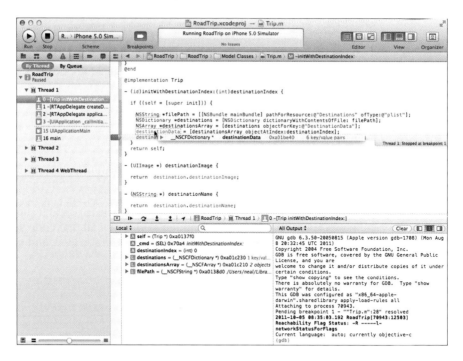

Figure 12-14: Display the contents of a variable in the Source editor.

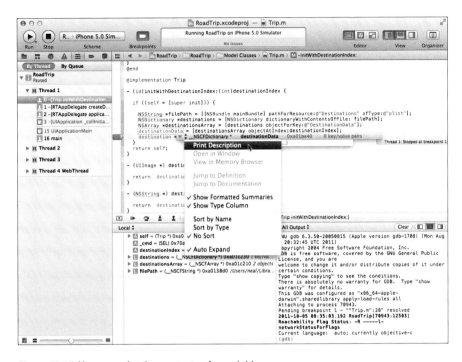

Figure 12-15: You can print the contents of a variable.

If you select Print Description, you will see the values in the destination-Data dictionary "printed" in the Console pane (see Figure 12-16).

You could also have done the same thing by Control+clicking in the Variables pane. One thing you'll notice is that there are no instance variables displayed (at least in this release of Xcode) because you have them in a class extension rather than in the Interface. Oh, well, you can't have everything.

If you select Continue Program Execution in the Debug bar, you can print out variables to be sure that the Destination method initWith DestinationIndex: works as expected.

On I side note, when I was writing this, I found that my code didn't work. I had inadvertently placed a trailing space in the DestinationLocation key, which I found out by printing the contents of the destinationData diction-ary. My discovery of that error was what prompted the trailing space warning in the "Adding a property list to your project" section, earlier in this chapter.

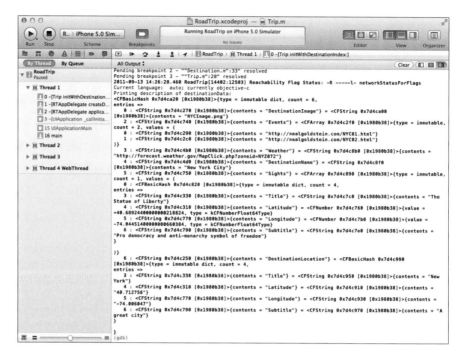

Figure 12-16: "Printing" the contents of a variable to the Console pane.

Chapter 13

Implementing the Content Controller

*W*ith the model in place, you can now return to the Content view controller that you add in Chapter 11 and transform its view into the user interface you fell in love with in Chapter 4. In this chapter, you replace the "generic" `UIViewController` or `UITableViewController` supplied by the storyboard with a custom view controller. By doing so, you add the logic to connect the view to the model.

The way you are about to add the logic to connect the view to the model via the view controller in this chapter is the general formula you will use for the rest of the view controllers in the storyboard. Although you can add the view controllers to the storyboard graphically, as you have done, you need to add some code to have the controller actually do anything, such as get data from the model and send it to the view.

Using Custom View Controllers

The view controller provided by the storyboard is a `UIViewController` and is clueless about what you want to display in a view, much less the model it will need to get the data from. In this section, you create a custom controller that does know about its view and the model. Later in this chapter, you add the logic you need to the custom view controller.

Adding the custom view controller

You start by adding the custom view controller class to your project:

1. **Create a new group to keep your view controller classes in. In the Project navigator, select the RoadTrip group (not the RoadTrip project, which is at the top) and either right-click and choose New Group or choose File⇨New⇨New Group. Name your new group *View Controller Classes*.**

To change a file's group, select the file and drag it to the group you want it to occupy. The same goes for groups as well (after all, they can go into other groups).

2. **In the Project navigator, select the View Controller Classes group and either right-click and then choose New File or choose File➪New➪New File from the main menu (or press ⌘+N) to make the New File dialog appear.**

3. **In the left column of the dialog, select Cocoa Touch under the iOS heading, select the UIViewController subclass template in the top-right pane, and then click Next.**

4. **In the Class field, enter** ContentController **(some people would call this ContentViewController, but that seems like overkill to me; personally the shorter the name you can have without losing any information, the better.). In the Subclass Of drop-down menu, select** UITableViewController. **Make sure that the Target for iPad and With XIB for user interface are deselected. Click Next.**

5. **In the Save sheet, click Create.**

You'll notice some compiler warnings when you add the Content controller. Ignore them for now; you'll fix them shortly.

Setting up the ContentController in the MainStoryboard

Now that you have a custom view controller (it doesn't do anything yet, but it will), you need to tell the storyboard to load your custom view controller rather than a UIViewController.

In the Project navigator, select the MainStoryboard file, and in the Dock, select the Table View Controller in the Table View Controller – Content Scene. I had you enter Content in the Title field, as you recall, so here you are tying up that loose end.

Open the Identify inspector in the Utility area using the Inspector selector bar, and in the Class drop-down menu in the Custom Class section, choose ContentController (replacing UITableViewController) as I have in Figure 13-1. This means that when the Travel button is tapped, your custom controller (the ContentController) will be instantiated and initialized, and will receive events from the user and connect the view to the Trip model.

Notice that in the Dock, the caption changes from a Table View Controller to a Content Controller.

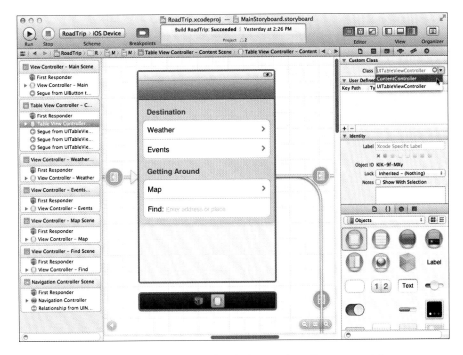

Figure 13-1: Now the Content controller object in the storyboard is connected the `ContentController` class.

When you run this in its current form, you get a serviceable but not very interesting Table view. You are now going to change that.

Open all the Disclosure triangles under Content Controller. The easiest way to do that is Option+click the disclosure triangle in front of the Content Controller (see Figure 13-2) and then follow these steps:

1. **Select the first Table View Cell.**

2. **In the Attribute inspector, choose None in the Accessory pop-up menu in the Table View Cell section, as I have in Figure 13-2.**

3. **In the Attribute inspector, scroll down if you need to and select Clear Color in the Background pop-up menu in the View section, as shown in Figure 13-3.**

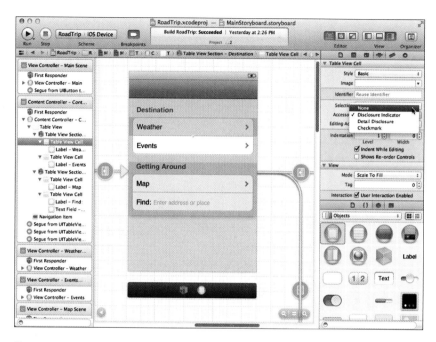

Figure 13-2: Get rid of the disclosure indicator.

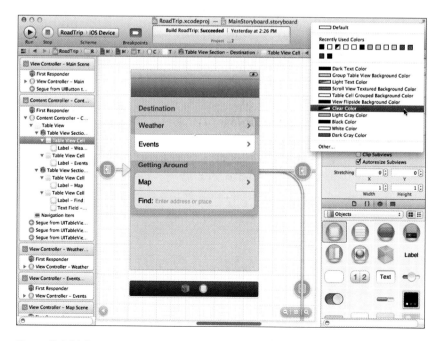

Figure 13-3: Make the Table View Cell Background clear.

4. **Select the Label under that Table View Cell, and in the Attribute inspector, select Clear Color in the Background pop-up menu in the View section, as I have in Figure 13-4.**

5. **Finally, and this is the pièce de résistance, select White in the Text Color pop-up menu in the Label section in the Attribute inspector. Yes, you are barely be able to see the text — but don't worry. You'll fix that soon.**

6. **Do Steps 2-5 for the rest of the Table View Cells and Labels. You also have to select White for the Text Color in the Text Field in the Find: Table View Cell.**

When you are done, your Content Controller should look like that shown in Figure 13-5.

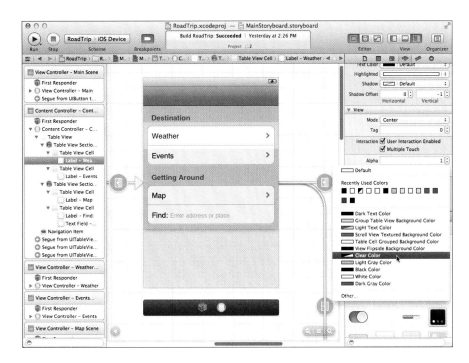

Figure 13-4: Make the Label Background clear.

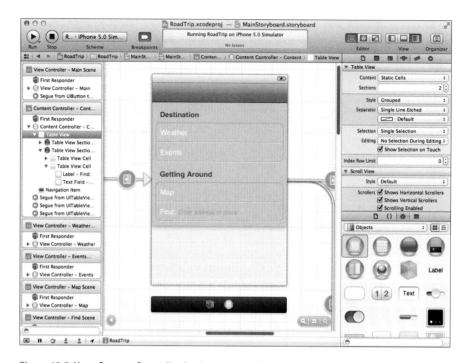

Figure 13-5: Your Content Controller is almost ready for prime time.

Add a Background Image and Title

This type of Table view has static cells, as I mentioned in Chapter 11, and any static cells you set up in Interface Builder. However, in this Table view, two things are not static; instead, they are based upon the destination. Those two things are the background image and the title. You have to set those programmatically.

To begin, because you are using static cells, you need to delete some code that you would need to implement if you weren't using static cells. This code is automatically added whenever you create a UITableViewController subclass.

Hide the Utility areas and show the Project navigator (if you have hidden it) by making the appropriate selections in the toolbar. Then select ContentController.m in the Project navigator.

In the #pragma mark - Table view data source and #pragma mark - Table view delegate sections, you see some methods as well as some commented out methods that you will implement when you use a dynamic Table view in Chapter 17. Note that two of the methods have #warning, which are what is giving you the warnings you see.

```
- (NSInteger)numberOfSectionsInTableView:
                                (UITableView *)tableView
{
#warning Potentially incomplete method implementation.
    // Return the number of sections.
    return 0;
}

- (NSInteger)tableView:(UITableView *)tableView
            numberOfRowsInSection:(NSInteger)section
{
#warning Incomplete method implementation.
    // Return the number of rows in the section.
    return 0;
}
```

I explain what these methods are for in Chapter 17, but for now, delete all of the methods (and commented out methods) in the #pragma mark - Table view data source and #pragma mark - Table view delegate sections in Listing 13-1. Yes, you really do want to delete all of them; the functionality is taken care for you by the storyboard.

Listing 13-1:   Deleting All the Code in the #pragma mark - Table view data source and #pragma mark - Table view delegate sections

```
#pragma mark - Table view data source

- (NSInteger)numberOfSectionsInTableView:(UITableView *)
        tableView
{
#warning Potentially incomplete method implementation.
    // Return the number of sections.
    return 0;
}

- (NSInteger)tableView:(UITableView *)tableView numberOfRowsI
        nSection:(NSInteger)section
{
#warning Incomplete method implementation.
    // Return the number of rows in the section.
    return 0;
}

- (UITableViewCell *)tableView:(UITableView *)tableView cellF
        orRowAtIndexPath:(NSIndexPath *)indexPath
{
    static NSString *CellIdentifier = @"Cell";
```

(continued)

Listing 13-1 *(continued)*

```
    UITableViewCell *cell =
            [tableViewdequeueReusableCellWithIdentifier:
                                        CellIdentifier];
    if (cell == nil) {
        cell = [[UITableViewCell alloc] initWithStyle:UITabl
            eViewCellStyleDefault reuseIdentifier:CellIdentif
            ier];
    }

    // Configure the cell...

    return cell;
}

/*
// Override to support conditional editing of the table view.
- (BOOL)tableView:(UITableView *)tableView canEditRowAtIndexP
        ath:(NSIndexPath *)indexPath
{
    // Return NO if you do not want the specified item to be
        editable.
    return YES;
}
*/

/*
// Override to support editing the table view.
- (void)tableView:(UITableView *)
        tableViewcommitEditingStyle:
                (UITableViewCellEditingStyle)editingStyle
                forRowAtIndexPath:(NSIndexPath *)indexPath
{
    if (editingStyle == UITableViewCellEditingStyleDelete) {
        // Delete the row from the data source
        [tableView deleteRowsAtIndexPaths:[NSArray
            arrayWithObject:indexPath] withRowAnimation:UITabl
            eViewRowAnimationFade];
    }
    else if (editingStyle ==
            UITableViewCellEditingStyleInsert) {
        // Create a new instance of the appropriate class,
            insert it into the array, and add a new row to the
            table view
    }
}
*/
```

```
/*
// Override to support rearranging the table view.
- (void)tableView:(UITableView *)tableView
        moveRowAtIndexPath:(NSIndexPath *)fromIndexPath
        toIndexPath:(NSIndexPath *)toIndexPath
{
}
*/


/*
// Override to support conditional rearranging of the table
        view.
- (BOOL)tableView:(UITableView *)tableView canMoveRowAtIndexP
        ath:(NSIndexPath *)indexPath
{
    // Return NO if you do not want the item to be
        re-orderable.
    return YES;
}
*/


#pragma mark - Table view delegate

- (void)tableView:(UITableView *)tableView
        didSelectRowAtIndexPath:(NSIndexPath *)indexPath
{
    // Navigation logic may go here. Create and push another
        view controller.
    /*
     <#DetailViewController#> *detailViewController
        = [[<#DetailViewController#> alloc]
        initWithNibName:@"<#Nib name#>" bundle:nil];
    // ...
    // Pass the selected object to the new view controller.
    [self.navigationController pushViewController:detailView
        Controller
                                        animated:YES];
    */
}
```

When you are done, the compiler warnings should be gone, and if you run your app, the display should be similar to what you see in Figure 13-5, shown previously.

Now that you have eliminated everything you don't need, you need to add the code to customize elements in the view. You may recall from Chapter 9 that the view controller method to customize a view at launch time is viewDidLoad, which is the method you use here as well.

First, import the headers you need by adding the bolded code in Listing 13-2 to ContentController.m.

Listing 13-2:   Updating the ContentController Implementation

```
#import "ContentController.h"
#import "RTAppDelegate.h"
#import "Trip.h"
@implementation ContentController
```

Now add the bolded code in Listing 13-3 to the viewDidLoad method in ContentController.m.

Listing 13-3:   Updating viewDidLoad

```
- (void)viewDidLoad
{
    [super viewDidLoad];
  RTAppDelegate* appDelegate =
                [[UIApplication sharedApplication] delegate];
  UIImageView* imageView = [[UIImageView alloc]
        initWithImage:[appDelegate.trip destinationImage]];
    self.tableView.backgroundView = imageView;
    self.title = appDelegate.trip.destinationName;
}
```

You want to add to two features to the ContentController's view. The first is to make the title in the Navigation bar the name of the destination, and the second is to add a background image to the view. This data is owned by the Trip model, so you are finally getting to use the model.

To get the information the Content controller needs from the (Trip) model, it needs to know where it is. You may recall that in Chapter 12, when you created and initialized the Trip object in the RTAppDelegate, you assigned the pointer to it to the trip property to make it accessible to the view controllers.

You find the `RTAppDelegate` in the way you have previously: By sending the class message `sharedApplication` to the `UIApplication`, class and then sending the `delegate` message to the UIApplication object.

You use two `Trip` methods. `destinationImage` is a `Trip` method that returns a `UIImage`, pointer; and `destinationName` a `Trip` method that returns an `NSString` pointer that contains the destination name. You added this method in Chapter 12 when you began working with the `Trip` class.

Run the application now and select Travel. Be prepared to be impressed with your work, as shown in Figure 13-6.

Figure 13-6: The destination-based Content controller user interface.

Part V

Adding the Application Content

The 5th Wave
By Rich Tennant

"Okay, the view's just up ahead. Everyone switch to 'America the Beautiful' on your iPhone playlist."

*A*fter the realization dawns that you have to sell a lot of 99-cent applications to afford the gas to drive a '59 Cadillac Eldorado Biarritz to the grocery store, much less across the country on a road trip, you can start thinking about having your application actually do something. In this section, you add the code to create an industrial-strength application that you can charge real money for — something so good that people will actually pay the big bucks for it. In this part, I explain how to do things like display the weather, page through local events like you are reading a book, and even get those events from a server on the Internet. You also display the destination and where you are right now on a map, and (in the Bonus Chapter at www.dummies.com/go/iphoneappdevfd4e) find a location you've always wanted to visit (such as Radio City Music Hall) and display it on a map as well.

You finish off your app by allowing the user to choose from a list of destinations for his or her road trip.

Chapter 14

How's the Weather? Working with Web Views

*G*etting the framework (no pun intended) in place for a new iPhone application is certainly a crucial part of the development process, but in the grand scheme of things, it's only the spadework that prepares the way for the really cool stuff. After all is said and done, you still need to add the content that the users see or interact with. Content is, after all, the reason they bought this application.

Now that you have created the storyboard scenes by specifying the view controller and have spiffed up the Content controller, it's time to make those view controllers earn their keep. As I have explained more than once, view controllers are the key elements here. They're the ones that get the content from the `Trip` model object and send it to the view to display. In this chapter, you create a view controller that lets the Weather view know where to get the weather information.

Setting Up the Weather Controller

If the user selects Weather from the Content view in the RoadTrip application, he comes face-to-face with an Internet site displaying weather information. (You'll start with the URL specified in the `Destination.plist`, but you can use any site that you'd like.)

In this section, you add the `WeatherController` and the logic to it to get the right URL for the weather from the `Trip` object and send it on to the Weather (Web) view to load.

Adding the custom view controller

As you saw in Chapter 13, although you have a view controller defined in the storyboard, it is a generic view controller, and in this case a `UIViewController`. Just as you did for the Content controller, you'll replace the generic controller with a custom one:

1. **In the Project navigator, select the View Controller Classes group, and either right-click and then choose New File or choose File⇨New⇨New File from the main menu (or press ⌘+N) to make the New File dialog appear.**

2. **In the left column of the dialog, select Cocoa Touch under the iOS heading, select the UIViewController subclass template in the top-right pane, and then click Next.**

3. **In the Class field, enter WeatherController. In the Subclass Of field, select UIViewController. Make sure that the Target for iPad and With XIB for User Interface are deselected. Click next.**

4. **In the Save sheet, click Create.**

Setting up the WeatherController in the MainStoryboard File

Now that you have a custom view controller, just as you did in Chapter 13, you need to tell the storyboard to load your custom view controller rather than a `UIViewController`.

In the Project navigator, select the MainStoryboard file, and in the Dock, select View Controller in the View Controller – Weather Scene.

Open the Identify inspector in the Utility area using the Inspector selector bar, and in the Class drop-down menu in the Custom Class section, choose `WeatherController` (replacing UIViewController), as I have in Figure 14-1, so that when Weather is selected in the Content Controller, the `WeatherController`) will be instantiated and initialized and will receive events from the user and connect the view to the Trip model.

For the RoadTrip application, you want to use a `UIWebView` to display the weather information. This makes sense because you will be using a web site to display the weather. As you will see in Chapter 15, it makes sense to display the events as well.

Open the disclosure triangle next to the Weather controller in the Dock (notice that the name changed from View Controller to Weather Controller) and select the view (see Figure 14-2).

Again in the Identify inspector in the Class field, select `UIWebView` (replacing `UIView`). Notice in Figure 14-2 the name of the view in the Dock changes as well.

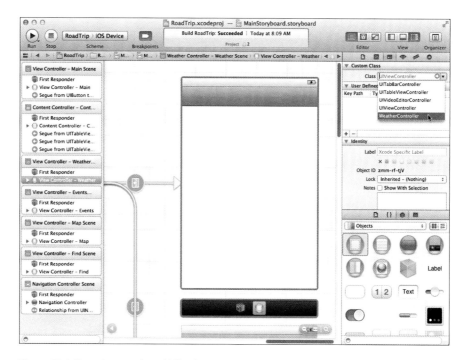

Figure 14-1: Now the storyboard Weather controller is connected to the WeatherController.

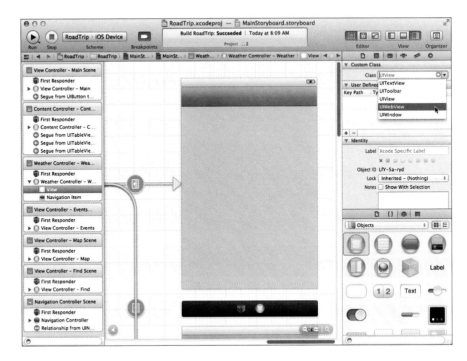

Figure 14-2: Make it a Web view.

As you recall from Chapter 4, the `UIWebView` class provides a way to display HTML content and has the built-in functionality to download HTML content, and web pages, from the web.

Finally, you need to create an outlet so that the `WeatherController` has access to the view so that it can tell it what web site to load.

Close the Utility area and select the Assistant from the Editor selector in the Xcode toolbar. If the `WeatherController.h` file is not the one being displayed, go up to the Assistant's Jump bar and select it, as I have in Figure 14-3.

Now Control+drag from the Web view to the WeatherController interface and create an IBOutlet (just as you do in Chapter 6) named `weatherView`.

Next, Control+drag from the Web view in the Dock to the WeatherController object in the storyboard canvas and then choose Delegate (see Figure 14-4) from the Outlets menu that appears.

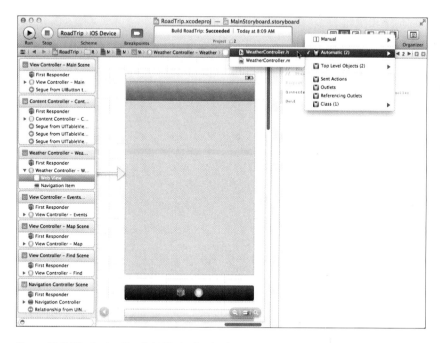

Figure 14-3: Displaying the right file in the Assistant.

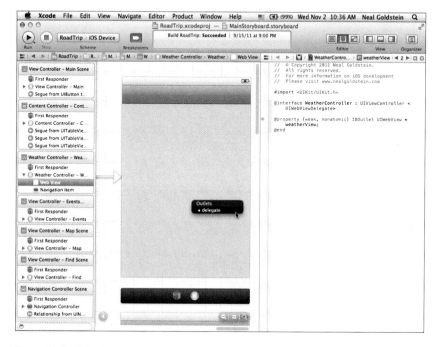

Figure 14-4: Make the `WeatherController` a Web view delegate.

Because you have an outlet set up, you could make the WeatherController a delegate in your code. I prefer to do it that way because it is more visible (it is up to you, though), and you'll do that in the next chapter.

If you think about it, though, is the webView necessary? A pointer to the view object is already safely nestled in the view controller. Here are the two reasons for using webView:

- ✔ **I'm lazy.** If I create a second outlet of type UIWebView, every time I access it, I don't have to cast the UIView into a UIWebView, as you can see in the following line:

    (UIWebView *)[self view] or (UIWebView *)self.view

- ✔ **I'm doing it for you.** It makes the code easier to follow.

At this point, you have the view controller class set up and you've arranged for the storyboard to create a UIWebView object and set all the outlets for you when the user selects Weather for the view he wants to see.

Because the Trip object owns the data, and in this case it is the web site you're using to display the weather information, you add the methods necessary to the Trip model to provide this to the WeatherController.

Close the Assistant in the View selector in the toolbar and select Trip.h in the Project navigator (select it in the View selector if you have closed it or choose View⇨Navigators⇨Show Project Navigator).

Add the declaration for the Weather method (the bolded code) to the Trip interface in Trip.h, as shown in Listing 14-1.

Listing 14-1:   Updating the `Trip.h` Interface

```
#import <Foundation/Foundation.h>
#import <MapKit/MapKit.h>

@interface Trip : NSObject

- (UIImage *)destinationImage;
- (NSString *) destinationName;
- (CLLocationCoordinate2D) destinationCoordinate;

- (id)initWithDestinationIndex:(int)destinationIndex;
- (NSString *)weather;

@end
```

Add the `weather` method in Listing 14-2 to `Trip.m`.

Listing 14-2:   Add the `weather` method.

```
- (NSString *)weather {

    return [destinationData objectForKey:@"Weather"];
}
```

All the `Trip` object does here is return the URL that will be used by the Web view to download the weather HTML page for the site. It got the URL for that site from the dictionary you create in Chapter 12 when you load the Destination plist that provides the data for this destination.

The Weather Controller

Now that you have the Trip set up to deliver the data, the `WeatherController` needs to pass this data on to the view to load the web page.

You need to add some import compiler directives so that the WeatherController can access the `RTAppDelegate` to get the `Trip` reference and request the data it needs.

Add the bolded code in Listing 14-3 to `WeatherController.m`.

Listing 14-3:   Updating the `WeatherController` Implementation

```
#import "WeatherController.h"
#import "RTAppDelegate.h"
#import "Trip.h"

@implementation WeatherController
```

The template provides a commented out `viewDidLoad` method stub when you create the controller file. You may recall from previous chapters that this is where you want to have the Web view (or any other view) load its data. Uncomment `viewDidLoad` in `WeatherController.m` and add the bolded code in Listing 14-4.

Listing 14-4:   Adding to `viewDidLoad`

```
- (void)viewDidLoad
{
  [super viewDidLoad];
  self.title = @"Weather";
  self.weatherView.scalesPageToFit = YES;
  RTAppDelegate *appDelegate =
              [[UIApplication sharedApplication] delegate];
  [self.weatherView loadRequest:
    [NSURLRequest requestWithURL:[NSURL
            URLWithString:[appDelegate.trip weather]]]];
}
```

The first thing you do is set the title to Weather.

Because it is going to be a website, you set `webView.scalesPageToFit` to `YES`.

`scalesPageToFit` is a `UIWebView` property. If it's set to `YES`, the web page is scaled to fit inside your view, and the user can zoom in and out. If it's set to `NO`, the page is displayed in the view and zooming is disabled.

I might set it to `NO` when I'm not displaying a web page and the HTML page I created fits just fine and I don't want it to be scalable. You may want to do something else here, of course; I did it this way to show you how (and where) you have control of web page properties.

You then create `NSURLRequest` object that the Web view needs to load the data. To do that, you create an `NSURL` object (an object that includes the utilities necessary for downloading files or other resources from Web and FTP servers) using the URL you get from the `Trip`. The code uses this `NSURL` and creates an `NSURLRequest` from it. The `NSURLRequest` is what the `WeatherController` needs to send to the Web view in the `loadRequest:` message, which tells it to load the data associated with that particular `NSURL`.

The `NSURLRequest` class encapsulates a URL and any protocol-specific properties, all the time keeping things protocol-independent. It also provides a number of other things which are beyond the scope of this book, but is part of the URL loading system — the set of classes and protocols that provide the underlying capability for an application to access the data specified by a URL. This is the preferred way to access files both locally and on the Internet.

The `loadRequest` message is sent to the Web view, and the Weather website is displayed in the window. This causes the Web view to load the data and display it in the window.

Managing links in a Web view

An interesting thing about the Weather view — or any other view that does or can load real web content into your application instead of using a browser — is that the links are live, and from that view, user cans follow those links *if* you want to let them.

After the user is at the weather website, as you can see in Figure 14-5, the user might want to look at the NWS (National Weather Service) New York, NY link in the upper-left corner. While the link is displayed, there is no way to get back to the originating page. If you click the Back button, it takes you back to Content Controller, not the origination website.

Hmm.

Figure 14-5: You can select a link (left) to get an hourly forecast (right) — but you have no way to get back to the originating view.

When the user makes use of the NWS New York, NY link, the Web view *replaces* the content of the view rather than *creates* a new view controller. Tapping the link doesn't change the controller in any way, so the left button won't change; you won't be able to use it to get back to a previous view — you only go back to the Content view, with the Back button displaying the destination name. To be able to navigate back to the originating view, you need to create another button and label it Back to Weather (or whatever the previous controller is) so that the user knows that she can use it to get back to the previous view. Creating this button is pretty easy to do, as you see in Listing 14-6.

Of course, I don't want to create that button if the user is at the first level of the view controller because, at that point, going back is handled by the Navigation controller's Back button.

So how do you navigate through the links? You are assisted by two Web view delegate methods, `webView:shouldStartLoadWithRequest:navigationType:` and `webViewDidFinishLoad:`.

`webView:shouldStartLoadWithRequest:navigationType:` is a `UIWebView` delegate method. It's called before a Web view begins loading content to see whether the user wants the load to proceed.

First, adopt the `UIWebViewDelegate` protocol by adding the bolded code in Listing 14-5 to `WeatherController.h`.

Listing 14-5: Updating the `WeatherController` Implementation

```
#import <UIKit/UIKit.h>

@interface WeatherController : UIViewController
                                    <UIWebViewDelegate>

@property (weak, nonatomic)
                    IBOutlet UIWebView *weatherView;


@end
```

Remember that when you adopt a delegate protocol, the compiler will then check to make sure that required methods are all there and types are correct — so do it!

Next, add the code in Listing 14-6 to `WeatherController.m`.

Listing 14-6: Implementing the `webView:shouldStartLoadWithRequest:navigationType:` method

```
- (BOOL)webView:(UIWebView *)webView
  shouldStartLoadWithRequest:(NSURLRequest *)request
  navigationType:(UIWebViewNavigationType)navigationType {

  if (navigationType ==
                    UIWebViewNavigationTypeLinkClicked){
    UIBarButtonItem *backButton = [[UIBarButtonItem alloc]
      initWithTitle:[NSString stringWithFormat:
                                @"Back to %@", self.title]
      style:UIBarButtonItemStylePlain target:self
      action:@selector(goBack:)];
    self.navigationItem.rightBarButtonItem = backButton;
    return YES;
  }
  else return YES;
}
```

You check to see whether the user has touched an embedded link. (You have to see whether a link is clicked because this message is sent to the delegate under several different circumstances.)

```
if (navigationType == UIWebViewNavigationTypeLinkClicked){
```

You create the Back to button, using the view controller `title`, and return `YES` to tell the Web view to load from the Internet. The `action:@selector(goBack:)` argument is the standard way to specify Target-Action. It says that when the button is tapped, you need to send the `goBack:` message to the `target:self`, which is the `WeatherController`.

```
UIBarButtonItem *backButton = [[UIBarButtonItem alloc]
  initWithTitle:[NSString stringWithFormat:
                            @"Back to %@", self.title]
  style:UIBarButtonItemStylePlain target:self
  action:@selector(goBack:)];
self.navigationItem.rightBarButtonItem = backButton;
return YES;
```

Next, add the `goBack:` method in Listing 14-7 to the `WebViewController.m` file. This is the message sent when the Back to button is tapped.

Listing 14-7:   Adding the `goBack:` Method

```
- (void)goBack:(id)sender {

    [weatherView goBack];
}
```

Note that you don't need to declare this method in `WeatherContoller.h` because it is used only in the target-action, which is resolved at runtime, not compile time.

The `UIWebView` actually implements much of the behavior you need here. The Web view keeps a backward *and* forward list. When you send the `UIWebView` the message (`goBack:`), it reloads the previous page.

Finally, you want to get rid of the Back button when you're displaying the original page. The code to do that is in Listing 14-8.

Listing 14-8:   Implementing `webViewDidFinishLoad:`

```
- (void)webViewDidFinishLoad:(UIWebView *) webView {

    if ([weatherView canGoBack] == NO ) {
        self.navigationItem.rightBarButtonItem = nil;
    }
}
```

The delegate is sent the `webViewDidFinishLoad:` message after the view has loaded. At this point, you check to see whether there's anything to go back to (the Web view keeps track of those sorts of things). If not, remove the button from the Navigation bar.

That being said, the Apple Human Interface Guidelines say it's best to avoid creating an application that looks and behaves like a mini web web browser. As far as I am concerned, making it possible to select links in a Web view doesn't do that.

But if you really don't want to enable the user to follow links (either because of Apple's suggestion not make your app act as a mini browser or if you'd prefer that your app users stick around for a bit and don't go gallivanting around the Internet), you have to disable the links that are available in the content. You can do that in the `shouldStartLoadWithRequest:` method in the `WeatherController.m` file by coding it as shown in Listing 14-9.

Listing 14-9:   Disabling Links

```
- (BOOL)webView:(UIWebView *)webView
  shouldStartLoadWithRequest:(NSURLRequest *)request
  navigationType:(UIWebViewNavigationType)navigationType {

  if (navigationType ==
      UIWebViewNavigationTypeLinkClicked){
    return NO;
  }
  else return YES;
}
```

You should add an alert to inform the user of the fact that no Internet galli-vanting is to be had here.

More Opportunities to Use the debugger

There are a couple of runtime errors that are easy to get. Two that pop up frequently are `unrecognized selector sent to instance` and `NSUnknownKeyException`. Although the former is pretty easy to track down if you actually read the error message, the latter can be a real mystery (it was to me), especially the first time you encounter it. So I want to explain both of them now.

Unrecognized selector sent to instance . . .

This particular runtime error is probably the most common one I get e-mails about; it (understandably) throws many people for a loop. But if you take time to read the error message, you can make sense of it.

```
2011-09-07 19:34:07.166 RoadTrip[1202:12503] ***
Terminating app due to uncaught exception
'NSInvalidArgumentException', reason: '-[WeatherController
goBack]: unrecognized selector sent to instance 0xb7331f0'
```

This error occurs when you create a selector in your code, and it's not there.

If, in the `webView shouldStartLoadWithRequest:navigationType:` method, you specified `goBack` rather than `goBack:` when you allocated and initialized the `backButton`:

```
UIBarButtonItem *backButton = [[UIBarButtonItem alloc]
    initWithTitle:[NSString stringWithFormat:
    @"Back to %@", self.title]
    style:UIBarButtonItemStylePlain target:self
    action:@selector(goBack)];
```

and then you ran the application, selected Weather, selected a link, and
then tapped the Back to Weather button, what you will see in the Debugger
Console pane is:

```
2011-09-07 19:34:07.166 RoadTrip[1202:12503] ***
Terminating app due to uncaught exception
'NSInvalidArgumentException', reason: '-[WeatherController
goBack]: unrecognized selector sent to instance 0xb7331f0'
```

You see this because the goBack message (not the goBack: message)
is sent to the target — the WeatherController. But although the
WeatherController has a goBack: method implemented, it does not have
a goBack method implemented. (As the debugger so clearly informs you.)

NSUnknownKeyException

As you develop your application, you may decide that you don't like the
outlet name and you want to change it. I don't like weatherView and I want
to call it weatherWebView, for example. Here's what you might do:

```
#import <UIKit/UIKit.h>

@interface WeatherController : UIViewController
                                <UIWebViewDelegate>

//@property (weak, nonatomic)
                        IBOutlet UIWebView *weatherView;
@property (weak, nonatomic)
                    IBOutlet UIWebView *weatherWebView;


@end
```

When you compile your app and then select Weather in the Content view,
you see the following in the Debugger Console:

```
Terminating app due to uncaught exception
'NSUnknownKeyException', reason: '[<WeatherController
0x7c6fe60> setValue:forUndefinedKey:]: this class is not
key value coding-compliant for the key weatherView.'
```

I must admit that the first time I saw this message, I had no clue as to what was going on. This holds true for most of my readers as well. Didn't I just delete the `weatherView` references in the code?

Well, yes and no; go back to your project to find out. There, in the Project navigator, select `MainStoryboard` and right-click WeatherController in the Dock. What do you see in Figure 14-6?

Ack. Even though you changed all the references to the outlet in the code, no one bothered to tell the poor storyboard file. So delete the outlet by clicking the `x` in front of the button in the `Outlets` section, and, oh yes, add the `weatherWebView` outlet by Control+dragging from the Web view to the `weatherWebView` outlet in the WeatherController connections window.

A similar situation arises if you delete an outlet.

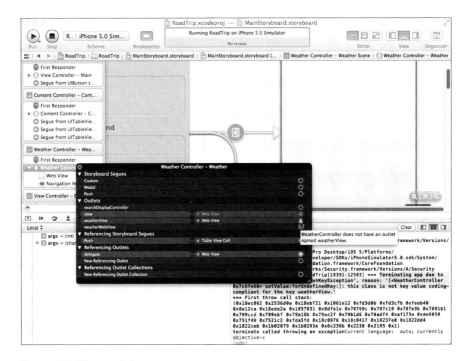

Figure 14-6: What outlet?

Chapter 15

Displaying Events Using a Page View Controller

....

In This Chapter

▷ Displaying HTML pages in a Web view

▷ Creating Page transitions with a `UIPageViewController`

▷ Understanding how Page View controllers work and implementing page turns

....

*I*f the user selects Events from the Content view in the RoadTrip application, he comes face-to-face with a series of pages that update him on the latest activities happening at his destination.

In this chapter, I show you how to use a new feature in iOS 5 that allows you to create a view controller that enables a user to "turn event pages" in the same way as he or she can in an iBook.

You also find out how to use a Web view again to display data, but this time you download an HTML page stored on my website, rather than download a website itself.

The best part of what you discover in this chapter is page-turn transitions. These transitions are implemented by the `UIPageViewController` class — a new container view controller for creating page-turn transitions between view controllers first implemented in iOS 5. Just as a Navigation controller animates the transitions between, say, the Content controller and the Weather controller, the Page View controller does its thing between two view controllers — in this case, two `EventPageControllers`.

You implement this functionality by adding a `UIPageViewController` controller to your view controller — `EventsController` — in your code and then creating a view controller (`EventPageController`) for each page.

Setting Up the Events Controller

In this section, you need to do the same thing as you do in Chapter 14 to create and connect the `EventsController` object to the storyboard. As I explain in Chapter 13, the way you develop using a storyboard is rather formulaic. To review it here (and for the last time):

1. Lay out the view controllers you need for the user experience architecture.

2. Add the custom view controller to your app.

3. Tie the two together in your storyboard.

4. Add the code you need to the custom view controller.

After you get into the routine of how to do it, your life as a developer becomes much easier.

I list the steps here, but if you need a more detailed description, refer to Chapter 14 in the section on adding the controller.

You also add another view controller to the storyboard (the aforementioned EventPageController) that will be used by the UIPageViewController.

Adding the custom view controller

To add the EventsController to the RoadTrip project, follow these steps:

1. **In the Project navigator, select the View Controller Classes group and right-click and then choose New File or choose File⇨New⇨New File from the main menu (or press ⌘+N) to open the New File dialog.**

2. **In the left column of the dialog, select Cocoa Touch under the iOS heading, select the UIViewController subclass template in the top-right pane, and then click Next.**

3. **In the Class field, enter EventsController In the Subclass Of field and then select UIViewController. Make sure that the Target for iPad and With XIB for User Interface are not checked. Click Next.**

4. **In the Save sheet, click Create.**

You will also need to create a controller that manages each event page. I explain that in "The EventPageController," later in this chapter.

To connect the Events view controller in the storyboard to the Events Controller you just created, you need to do the following:

1. **In the Project navigator, select the View Controller Classes group and right-click and then choose New File or choose File⇨New⇨New File from the main menu (or press ⌘+N) to open the New File dialog.**

2. **In the left column of the dialog, select Cocoa Touch under the iOS heading, select the UIViewController subclass template in the top-right pane, and then click Next.**

3. **In the Class field, enter** EventPageController. **In the Subclass Of field, select UIViewController. Make sure that the Target for iPad and With XIB for User Interface are unchecked. Click Next.**

4. **In the Save sheet, click Create.**

Setting up the EventsController in the MainStoryboard

Just as you did in Chapters 13 and 14, you need to tell the storyboard to load your custom view controller rather than a UIViewController.

In the Project navigator, select the MainStoryboard file and then select the View Controller in the View Controller - Events scene.

Open the Identity inspector in the Utility area using the Inspector selector bar, and in the Class drop-down menu in the Custom Class section, choose EventsController (replacing UIViewController) as you did with the WeatherController in Figure 13-1 in Chapter 13.

While in the Weather controller, you changed the view to a Web view, but you won't be doing that here. You also created an outlet, but you don't need that here, either. Instead, you use a Web view and create an outlet in the EventPageController.

The EventPageController is what you'll need to implement a UIPage ViewController. You do that in the next section.

Adding and Setting up the EventPageController in the MainStoryboard

You need a view controller to manage each view within the page view controller. Although you could have added this view controller when you extended the storyboard, I didn't have you do so because I didn't want it to get lost among the discussion about segues.

To add the Event Page Controller to the storyboard, follow these steps:

1. **Add another** *view controller* **— not table view controller — to the storyboard by dragging in a view controller from the Library pane and placing it next to the** EventsController **(you don't have to put it there, but doing so hints that there a relationship exists).**

2. **Open the Identity inspector in the Utility area using the Inspector selector bar, and in the Class drop-down menu in the Custom Class section, choose** EventPageController **(replacing** UIView Controller**).**

3. **In the Attribute inspector, give the controller the Title of EventPage and an Identifier of EventPage.**

4. **Add a Web view to the Event Page controller by dragging in a Web view from the Library pane and into the Event Page Controller, as shown in Figure 15-1.**

   The EventPage view will be a Web view because you'll want it to download and then display an HTML page.

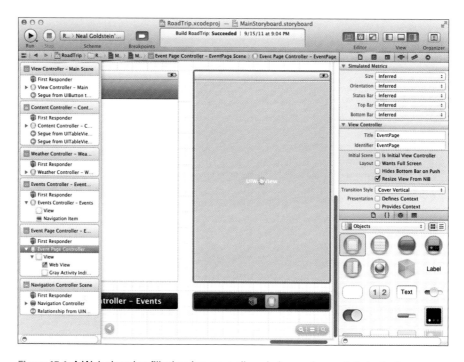

Figure 15-1: A Web view that fills the view controller window and an activity indicator.

   As you may recall from Chapter 13, the UIWebView **class provides a way to display HTML content and has the built-in functionality to download HTML content for the web.**

5. **Drag in an Activity Indicator view from the Library pane and center it in the view, as shown in Figure 15-1.**

   Because these pages can be large and take some amount of time to download, you want to have some kind of Activity Indicator view to let the user know that the application is still running but busy, as opposed to frozen.

As you can see in Figure 15-1, both the Web view and Activity Indicator view are siblings — and subviews of the view. It is important that both are siblings, and that the Activity Indicator view is below the Web view in order for it to display (remember the last-in-is-on top principle from Chapter 4 when it comes to subviews). If that's not the case, rearrange the views in the Dock.

6. **Close the Utility area and select the Assistant from the Editor selector in the toolbar. If the** `EventPageContoller.h` **file is not the one being displayed, go up to the Assistant's Jump bar and select it.**

7. **Control+drag from the Web view to the** `EventPageContoller` **interface and create an IBOutlet (just as you do in Chapter 14) named** `eventDataView`.

8. **Control+drag from the Activity Indicator View to the** `EventPage Contoller` **interface and create an IBOutlet named** `activity Indicator`.

9. **Control+drag from the Web view in the Dock to the Event Page Controller and then select Delegate from the Outlets menu that appears.**

Extending the Trip Model

The Events controller will need two pieces of information from the `Trip` model: the number of events, and the URL for a specific event.

Add the declaration for the two Events methods (bolded) to the Trip interface in `Trip.h` as shown in Listing 15-1.

Listing 15-1: Update the Trip Interface

```
@interface Trip : NSObject

- (UIImage *) destinationImage;
- (NSString *) destinationName;
- (CLLocationCoordinate2D) destinationCoordinate;

- (id)initWithDestinationIndex:(int)destinationIndex;
- (NSString *)weather;
- (int)numberOfEvents;
- (NSString *)getEvent:(int)index;
```

But `Trip` is not going to go at this alone (as it did with `Weather`). It will use an `Event` object (which you will create shortly). To have Trip be able to use the `Event` object add the bolded code in Listing 15-2 to `Trip.m`.

Listing 15-2: Updating the `Trip` Implementation

```
#import "Trip.h"
#import "Destination.h"
#import "Events.h"

@interface Trip () {
  NSDictionary *destinationData;
  NSMutableArray *sights;
  Destination* destination;
  Events *events;
}
@end
```

Add the implementation of methods you need in Listings 15-3 and 15-4 to `Trip.m`.

Listing 15-3: The Number of Events

```
- (int)numberOfEvents {

  return [events numberOfEvents];
}
```

Listing 15-4: Get an Event

```
- (NSString *)getEvent:(int)index {

  return [events getEvent:index];
}
```

As you can see, `Trip` is not going to do this alone. It is using an `Events` object, and `Trip` will have to create it. Add the bolded code in Listing 15-5 to `initWithDestination:` in `Trip.m`.

Listing 15-5: Updating `initWithDestination:`

```
- (id)initWithDestinationIndex:(int)destinationIndex {

  if ((self = [super init])) {

    NSString *filePath = [[NSBundle mainBundle]
        pathForResource:@"Destinations" ofType:@"plist"];
```

```
    NSDictionary *destinations = [NSDictionary
            dictionaryWithContentsOfFile: filePath];
    NSArray *destinationsArray =
            [destinations objectForKey:@"DestinationData"];
    destinationData = [destinationsArray
                        objectAtIndex:destinationIndex];
    destination = [[Destination alloc] initWithDestinationInd
            ex:destinationIndex];
    events = [[Events alloc]
                initWithDestinationIndex:destinationIndex];
  }
  return self;
}
```

As I mention in Chapter 12, `Trip` is a composite object that uses other objects to carry out its responsibilities. Whereas you put the `Weather` logic in the `Trip` object itself, in this case you create a new model object to handle the events responsibilities. That's because handling the events is a bit more complex and deserving of its own model object to encapsulate the logic. Hiding the `Events` object behind the `Trip` makes things more loosely coupled — a very good thing, which you'll find as you extend and enhance your app. (See Chapter 12 for an explanation of loose coupling.)

Adding the Events Class

If `Trip` is to use an Events object, you had better create the class:

1. **In the Project navigator, select the Model Classes group and right-click and then choose New File or choose File⇨New⇨New File from the main menu (or press ⌘N) to open the New File dialog.**

2. **In the left column of the dialog, select Cocoa Touch under the iOS heading, select the Objective-C Class template in the top-right pane, and then click Next.**

3. **Enter Events in the Class field.**

4. **In the `Subclass of` field, select NSObject and then click Next.**

5. **Click Create (make sure the Target field has the RoadTrip text box checked).**

The `Events` class is the model object that manages the events. Earlier, I said that I am creating this model object to encapsulate the event logic, and although doing so may seem to be an overreaction here given that the logic is not that complex, I mainly want to show you how to do that. And in reality, you can imagine that the `Events` class could be expanded to do a lot more — such as return the location, process events from multiple sources, or even allow a user to add her own events.

To start adding the `Events` class, add the bolded code in Listing 15-6 to `Event.h`.

Listing 15-6: Updating the `Events` Interface

```
@interface Events : NSObject

- (id)initWithDestinationIndex:
                                (NSUInteger)destinationIndex;
- (int)numberOfEvents;
- (NSString *)getEvent:(int)index;

@end
```

This code has three methods: an initialization method and two methods to process the `Trip` requests.

Next, you need to add an instance variable. Add the code in Listing 15-7 to `Events.m`.

Listing 15-7: Updating the Events Implementation

```
#import "Events.h"

@interface Events() {
  NSMutableArray *events;
}
@end

@implementation Events
```

As you can see, in Listing 15-6 you declare an initialization method (which is used by `Trip` when it creates the `Events` object). Add the code in Listing 15-8 to `Events.m` to implement the `initWithDestinationIndex:` initialization method.

Listing 15-8: Initializing the `Events` Object

```
- (id)initWithDestinationIndex:
                                (NSUInteger)destinationIndex {

  if (self = [super init]) {

    NSString *filePath = [[NSBundle mainBundle]
        pathForResource:@"Destinations" ofType:@"plist"];
    NSDictionary *destinations = [NSDictionary
```

```
                dictionaryWithContentsOfFile: filePath];
    NSArray *destinationsArray =
        [destinations objectForKey:@"DestinationData"];
    NSDictionary *data =
      [destinationsArray objectAtIndex:destinationIndex];
    events = [NSMutableArray arrayWithArray:
                           [data objectForKey:@"Events"]];
    }
    return self;
}
```

All this method does at this point is get the array of URLs for the HTML pages I created and you entered in the Destination plist. It puts these URLS in an array that you create — for more efficient retrieval later. I make this a mutable array because in the future you may want to allow a user to add his own events.

The EventsController, as you will see, will need to know the number of events. Add the code in Listing 15-9 to the Trip class to implement that method.

Listing 15-9:   The Number of Events

```
- (int)numberOfEvents {

  return [events count];
}
```

To get the number of events, you return the count of the array.

The EventsController, as you will see, will also need to have a list of the event URLs. Add the code in Listing 15-10 to the Trip class to implement that method.

Listing 15-10:   Getting an Event

```
- (NSString *)getEvent:(int)index {

  return [events objectAtIndex:index];
}
```

To return an Event, you return the URL based on the index into the array. This will make more sense when go through the EventsController and EventPageController code, which you do next.

The EventsController and Its PageViewController

At the start of this chapter, I promised to show you how to enable users to turn the page between one view controller and another. To implement this cool page-turning stuff, you need a `UIPagebiewController`. You create that in the `EventsController` in its `viewDidLoad` method.

To start, though, you need to make the `EventsController` a page view data source and delegate. (Actually, in this implementation you won't need to use any of the delegate methods, but it's good for you to know about them). Add the bolded code in Listing 15-11 (and add the declaration of another method that you'll use shortly) to `EventsController.h`.

Listing 15-11: Updating the `EventsController` Interface

```
#import <UIKit/UIKit.h>
@class EventPageController;

@interface EventsController : UIViewController
                <UIPageViewControllerDelegate,
                        UIPageViewControllerDataSource>

- (EventPageController *)viewControllerAtIndex:
  (NSUInteger)index storyboard:(UIStoryboard *)storyboard;

@end
```

Now read on to learn about the data source and delegate.

Data sources and delegates

You've used delegates a few times already, such as when you add the code to the app delegate in Chapter 9. A data source is really just another kind of delegate that supplies the data a framework object needs. In Chapter 18, when you implement a dynamic table view, you do that as well, and data sources are also used in many other places in the framework — in picker views, for example, when you select a time or date in the Calendar application.

Data source

The `UIPageViewController` is a new container view controller for creating page-turn transitions between view controllers first implemented in iOS 5. This means that for every page, you create a new view controller.

The UIPageViewControllerDataSource protocol is adopted by an object that provides view controllers (you'll be using the PageDataController) to the Page View controller as they are needed, in response to navigation gestures.

UIPageViewControllerDataSource has two required methods:

- ✔ pageViewController:viewControllerAfterViewController:
  Returns the view controller after the current view controller.

- ✔ pageViewController:viewControllerBeforeViewController:
  Returns the view controller before the current view controller.

Delegate

The delegate of a page view controller must adopt the UIPageView ControllerDelegate protocol. The methods in this protocol allow you to receive a notification when the device orientation changes or when the user navigates to a new page. In the implementation in this book, you don't need to be concerned with either of those two situations.

The EventsController

Before you add any code, update the EventsController.m with the bolded code in Listing 15-12.

Listing 15-12: Updating The EventsController Implementation

```
#import "EventsController.h"
#import "RTAppDelegate.h"
#import "Trip.h"
#import "EventPageController.h"

@interface EventsController () {

  NSUInteger pageCount;
  UIPageViewController *pageViewController;
}
@end

@implementation EventsController
```

The viewDidLoad method is where most of the work gets done. Uncomment out the viewDidLoad stub and add the bolded code in Listing 15-13 to viewDidLoad in EventsController.m.

Listing 15-13: Updating `viewDidLoad`

```
- (void)viewDidLoad
{
    [super viewDidLoad];
    RTAppDelegate *delegate =
                [[UIApplication sharedApplication] delegate];
    pageCount = [delegate.trip numberOfEvents];
    pageViewController = [[UIPageViewController alloc]
        initWithTransitionStyle:
                    UIPageViewControllerTransitionStylePageCurl
        navigationOrientation:
          UIPageViewControllerNavigationOrientationHorizontal
        options:nil];
    pageViewController.dataSource = self;
//pageViewController.delegate = self;
    EventPageController *startingViewController =
        [self viewControllerAtIndex:0
                                    storyboard:self.storyboard];
    NSArray *viewControllers =
            [NSArray arrayWithObject:startingViewController];
    [pageViewController setViewControllers:viewControllers
        direction:
                UIPageViewControllerNavigationDirectionForward
        animated:NO completion:NULL];
    [self addChildViewController:pageViewController];
    [self.view addSubview:pageViewController.view];
    self.view.gestureRecognizers =
                    pageViewController.gestureRecognizers;
}
```

First, you get the number of events from the `Trip` model so that you know how many pages you'll have:

```
RTAppDelegate *delegate = [[UIApplication
                            sharedApplication] delegate];
pageCount = [delegate.trip numberOfEvents];
```

Then you allocate and initialize the `PageViewController` and make yourself the data source. I have commented out the delegate assignment because you are not implementing any of the delegate methods, but here is where you would do it:

```
pageViewController = [[UIPageViewController alloc]
    initWithTransitionStyle:
                UIPageViewControllerTransitionStylePageCurl
    navigationOrientation:
        UIPageViewControllerNavigationOrientationHorizontal
        options:nil];
    pageViewController.dataSource = self;
//pageViewController.delegate = self
```

You are using a `UIPageViewControllerTransitionStylePageCurl` (which gives the appearance of turning a page), and you use a navigation orientation of horizontal, which gives you left-to-right page turn (`UIPageViewControllerNavigationOrientationVertical` gives you pages turning up and down).

You then request the first view controller (I show this method in Listing 15-14 and explain it there), create an array and add it to the array, and pass that array to the `pageViewController`:

```
EventPageController *startingViewController = [self
      viewControllerAtIndex:0 storyboard:self.storyboard];
NSArray *viewControllers =
         [NSArray arrayWithObject:startingViewController];
[pageViewController setViewControllers:viewControllers
   direction:UIPageViewControllerNavigationDirectionForward
   animated:NO completion:NULL];
```

This array will hold the view controllers that the `UIPageController` manages. You specify the direction as forward. You set animated to `NO` for this transition (setting the view controller array, not the page turning) and you specify no completion block.

Although this approach is pretty simple, you can get way more sophisticated and include features such as double pages and even two-sided pages and so on. You won't be doing that here.

Next, you add the `pageViewController` as the view controller and make its view a subview so that it is displayed:

```
[self addChildViewController:pageViewController];
[self.view addSubview:pageViewController.view];
```

Finally, add the Page View controller's gesture recognizers to the `Events Controller` view controller's view so that the gestures are started more easily. (I explain gesture recognizers in Chapter 11.)

```
self.view.gestureRecognizers =
                  pageViewController.gestureRecognizers;
```

As a supplier of view controllers, you will be responsible for creating, managing, and returning the right view controller for a page. You'll do that in the `viewControllerAtIndex:storyboard:` method.

Add the `viewControllerAtIndex:storyboard:` method in Listing 15-14 to `EventsController.m`.

Listing 15-14: Adding the `viewControllerAtIndex:storyboard:` Method

```
- (EventPageController *)viewControllerAtIndex:
    (NSUInteger)index
                    storyboard:(UIStoryboard *)storyboard {

  if ((pageCount == 0) || (index >= pageCount)) {
    return nil;
  }
  EventPageController *eventPageController = [storyboard
    instantiateViewControllerWithIdentifier:@"EventPage"];
  eventPageController.page = index;
  return eventPageController;
}
```

Here you simply do some error checking to make sure that both pages are available and that the page for the view controller you are supposed to return is available:

```
  if ((pageCount == 0) || (index >= pageCount)) {
    return nil;
  }
```

You then allocate and initialize the view controller for that page, setting its page (relative number of the URL to display) so that it knows which event URL to load:

```
  EventPageController *eventPageController = [storyboard
    instantiateViewControllerWithIdentifier:@"EventPage"];
  eventPageController.page = index;
```

There are more efficient ways to do this. You could create a cache of controllers that you have created and reuse them as needed. (As you see in Chapter 18, that's how I do it with table view cells.) I'll leave you to explore that topic on your own.

You also need to add the required data source methods in Listing 15-15 to `EventsController.m`.

Listing 15-15: Implementing `pageViewController:viewController AfterViewController:` and `pageViewController:viewController BeforeViewController:`

```
- (UIViewController *)pageViewController:
              (UIPageViewController *)pageViewController
                 viewControllerBeforeViewController:
                    (UIViewController *)viewController {

    NSUInteger index =
```

```
                ((EventPageController *)viewController).page;
    if (index == 0)
      return nil;
    index--;
    return [self viewControllerAtIndex:index
                  storyboard:viewController.storyboard];
  }

- (UIViewController *)pageViewController:
              (UIPageViewController *)pageViewController
                viewControllerAfterViewController:
                    (UIViewController *)viewController {
  NSUInteger index =
              ((EventPageController *)viewController).page;
  index++;
  if (index == pageCount)
    return nil;
  return [self viewControllerAtIndex:index
                    storyboard:viewController.storyboard];
  }
```

Both of these methods return an `EventDisplayController` initialized with the right page (relative event number) to display. They use the `viewContro llerAtIndex:storyboard:` method that you add in Listing 15-14 and indicate which view controller is required by taking the current view controller's page number and then either incrementing or decrementing it appropriately. It then does some error checking to be sure that the page requested is within bounds. If it's not, the method returns `nil` and the `UIPageViewController` inhibits the page turn.

These data source methods are used by the UIPageViewController to get the view controllers that can display the next or previous page, depending on the way the user is turning the page. As mentioned previously, the `UIPageViewController` just manages controllers and the transitions between them. The view controllers that you return operate like the run-of-the-mill view controller you have been using, such as the Weather controller that display s a website.

The next section gives you a look at how these controllers work.

The EventPageController

The `EventPageController` is almost identical to the `WeatherController` that you implemented in Chapter 14.

To follow along in this section, you need to close the Assistant, display the Project navigator, and select `EventPageController.m`.

I have you add the same functionality to this controller as you did to the `WeatherController` so that you can select a link and navigate back from it. You could have created an abstract class — a `WebViewController`, for example — that both `WeatherController` and `EventPageController` were derived from, but because the `EventPageController` is contained by the `UIPageViewController`, having an abstract class gets to be a bit more complex.

The `EventPageController` is what actually displays the event and works exactly the same as the `Weather` controller.

First, add the `page` property, which is set by the `viewControllerAtIndex :storyboard:` method, by adding the code to the interface in Listing 15-16.

Listing 15-16: Updating the `EventPageController` Interface

```
#import <UIKit/UIKit.h>

@interface EventPageController : UIViewController
                                <UIWebViewDelegate>

@property (weak, nonatomic) IBOutlet UIWebView
        *eventDataView;
@property (weak, nonatomic)
    IBOutlet UIActivityIndicatorView *activityIndicator;
@property (readwrite, nonatomic) int page;
@end
```

Here is where you make the `page` a property to enable you to determine which URL to load. You also have the `EvenPageController` adopt the `UIWebViewDelegate` protocol.

You also have to add a synthesize statement for the property you just added and import the headers you'll need, which you do by adding the bolded code in Listing 15-17.

Listing 15-17: Updating the `EventPageController` Implementation

```
#import "EventPageController.h"
#import "RTAppDelegate.h"
#import "Trip.h"

@implementation EventPageController
@synthesize eventDataView;
@synthesize activityIndicator;
@synthesize page = _page;
```

All the work gets done in `viewDidLoad` and other methods you add. These methods are the same as the code and methods you added to create the `WeatherController`. If you are hazy on what each does, please refer to Chapter 14.

Start by uncommenting out the `viewDidLoad` method in `EventPage Controller.m` and add the bolded code in Listing 15-18.

Listing 15-18:   Updating `viewDidLoad`

```
- (void)viewDidLoad
{
  [super viewDidLoad];
  self.eventDataView.delegate = self;
  [self.activityIndicator startAnimating];
  self.activityIndicator.hidesWhenStopped = YES;
  [self.eventDataView setScalesPageToFit:YES];
  RTAppDelegate *appDelegate =
              [[UIApplication sharedApplication] delegate];
  [self.eventDataView loadRequest:
    [NSURLRequest requestWithURL:
        [NSURL URLWithString:
                [appDelegate.trip getEvent:self.page]]]];
}
```

Next, add the rest of the Web view delegate methods in Listing 15-19, just as I have you do in Chapter 14.

Listing 15-19:   Implementing `webView:shouldStartLoadWithRequest: navigationType:`, and `webViewDidFinishLoad:`, and add `goBack`

```
- (BOOL)webView:(UIWebView *)webView
    shouldStartLoadWithRequest:(NSURLRequest *)request
  navigationType:(UIWebViewNavigationType)navigationType {

  if (navigationType ==
                    UIWebViewNavigationTypeLinkClicked){
    UIBarButtonItem *backButton = [[UIBarButtonItem alloc]
      initWithTitle:[NSString stringWithFormat:
        @"Back to %@", self.parentViewController.
                              parentViewController.title]
      style:UIBarButtonItemStylePlain target:self
                          action:@selector(goBack:)];
    self.parentViewController.parentViewController.
          navigationItem.rightBarButtonItem = backButton;

  return YES;
  }
  else return YES;
```

(continued)

Listing 15-19 *(continued)*

```
}

- (void)goBack:(id)sender {

  [self.eventDataView goBack];
}

- (void)webViewDidFinishLoad:(UIWebView *)webView {

  [self.activityIndicator stopAnimating];
  if ([self.eventDataView canGoBack] == NO ) {
    self.parentViewController.parentViewController.
                navigationItem.rightBarButtonItem = nil;
  }
}
```

This code enables you to click a link in an event and then return to the original event page.

Finally, if you would like to enable the user to view events either in Portrait or Landscape mode, delete the commented-out line in Listing 15-20 and add the line in bold to it.

Listing 15-20:   Updating `shouldAutorotateToInterfaceOrientation`:

```
- (BOOL)shouldAutorotateToInterfaceOrientation:
            (UIInterfaceOrientation)interfaceOrientation
{
 //return (interfaceOrientation ==
                        UIInterfaceOrientationPortrait);
   return (interfaceOrientation !=
            UIInterfaceOrientationPortraitUpsideDown);
}
```

`shouldAutorotateToInterfaceOrientation`: is a view controller method that returns a Boolean value if the view controller supports the specified orientation. In the code supplied by the template (the code you delete), the only time YES is returned is if the device is in Portrait model. In this case, you support any orientation except upside down.

`shouldAutorotateToInterfaceOrientation`: is implemented in the view controller according to the view controller's fashion. That is, you can have some views that are portrait only and others that are any combination of portrait, upside down, landscape left, and landscape right.

Chapter 16

Finding Your Way

In This Chapter

▷ Using the `MapKit` framework

▷ Specifying and changing the type, location, and zoom level of a map

▷ Identifying the iPhone's current location

▷ Annotating significant locations on the map

*O*ne of the things that makes iPhone applications compelling is the ability you have as a developer to incorporate the user's location into the application functionality. One of the more compelling ways to do that is through the use of maps.

Including the ability to display a map in an application became important as people began to realize the kinds of solutions that can be delivered on the iPhone. To many travelers, nothing brands you as a tourist like unfolding a large paper map (except, of course, looking through a thick guidebook). In this chapter, I show you how to take advantage of the iPhone's built-in capability to display a map of virtually anywhere in the world, as well as to determine the iPhone's location and then indicate it on the map. As I mention way back in Chapter 1, the iPhone's awareness of your location is one of the things that enables you to develop a totally new kind of application.

In this chapter, I show you how to center your map on an area you want to display (New York, for example), add annotations (those cute pins in the map that display a callout to describe that location when you touch them), and even show the user's current location.

Setting Up the Map Controller

Here you go again!

Adding the custom view controller

To add the `MapController` to the RoadTrip project, follow these steps:

1. **In the Project navigator, select the View Controller Classes group and right-click and then choose New File or choose File⇨New⇨New New File from the main menu (or press ⌘+N) to get the New File dialog.**

2. **In the left column of the dialog, select Cocoa Touch under the iOS heading, select the UIViewController Subclass template in the top-right pane, and then click Next.**

3. **In the Class field, enter** MapController. **In the Subclass Of field, select** UIViewController. **Make sure that the Target for iPad and With XIB from user interface are deselected.**

4. **In the Save sheet, click Create.**

Setting up the MapController in the MainStoryboard

To connect the Map view controller in the storyboard to the MapController you just created, you need to do the following:

1. **In the Project navigator, select the MainStoryboard and select the view controller in the View Controller - Map scene.**

2. **Open the Identity inspector in the Utility area using the Inspector selector bar, and in the Class drop-down menu in the Custom Class section, choose** MapController **(replacing** UIViewController**).**

3. **Scroll down in the Library pane until you find the toolbar and then drag in a toolbar (make sure that you choose a toolbar and not a Tab bar) from the library to the bottom of the view, as shown in Figure 16-1.**

Because the Google brand must display on the map, you must ensure that the toolbar does not cover the Google logo. Although you may discover other ways to add a toolbar, doing it the following way ensures the Google branding remains in full view.

4. **In the Inspector selector bar, click the Attributes inspector, and set the style in the Style drop-down menu in the Toolbar section to Black Opaque.**

5. **In the Library pane, scroll back up and drag in a Map View above the toolbar.**

The MKMapView class provides a way to display maps and has a lot of functionality that I describe in this chapter.

When you're done, the storyboard looks like Figure 16-2.

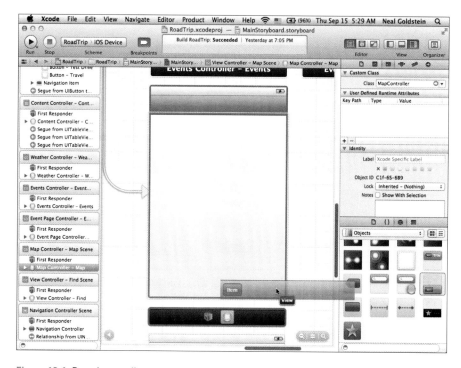

Figure 16-1: Drag in a toolbar.

Next, to set up the toolbar, follow these steps:

1. **Select the Bar button in the toolbar (the one that says Item) and delete it by pressing Delete.**

2. **Drag in a Segmented Control from the Library into the toolbar.**

3. **Select the Segmented Control in the Dock, and in the Attributes inspector, in the Segmented Control section, change the number of Segments to 3.**

4. **In the Segment menu in the Segmented Control section, make sure that Segment – 0 is selected, change the title to Standard, and press Return.**

   The Segment menu should change to Segment – 0 Standard.

5. **In the Segment menu, select Segment – 1 and change the title to Satellite; then select Segment 2 and change its title to Hybrid.**

   Be sure to press return after each change.

6. **In the Tint pop-up menu in the Segmented Control section, select Black Color.**

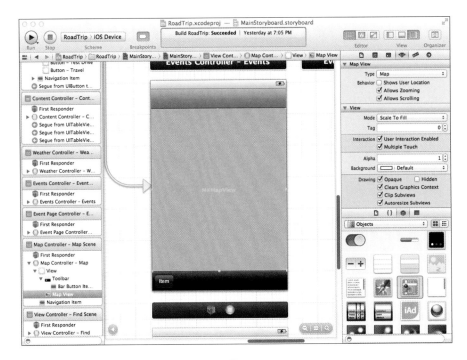

Figure 16-2: Putting a Map view above the toolbar.

Finally, you need to create an outlet so that the `MapController` has access to the Map view; to center the map and have the annotations display. Follow these steps:

1. **Close the Utility area and select the Assistant from the Editor selector in the toolbar. If the `MapController.h` file is not the one being displayed, go up to the Assistant's Jump bar and select it.**

2. **Control+drag from the Map view to the `MapController` interface and create an Outlet (just as you do in Chapter 6) named `mapView`.**

   Notice a compiler error (see Figure 16-3) — Unknown type name MKMapView.

3. **Because you are using the `MapKit` framework that you add in Chapter 12, and have a property of type `MKMapView`, you need to update the `MapController` interface with the bolded code in Listing 16-1. Because you already have the Interface open in the Assistant, you can do that right here.**

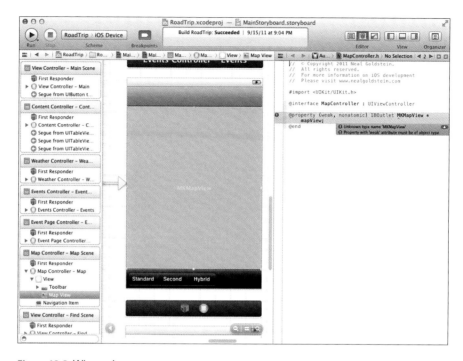

Figure 16-3: Whoops!

Listing 16-1: Updating the `MapController` Interface

```
#import <UIKit/UIKit.h>
#import <MapKit/MapKit.h>

@interface MapController : UIViewController
                                    <MKMapViewDelegate>

@property (weak, nonatomic) IBOutlet MKMapView *mapView;

@end
```

 4. **Select and then Control+drag from the segmented control to the**
    `MapController` **interface and create an Action (just as you did in**
    Chapter 6) named `mapType`**.**

    The Event should be Value Changed. (See Figure 16-4.) I explain more
    about Value Changed when you implement the `mapType` method.

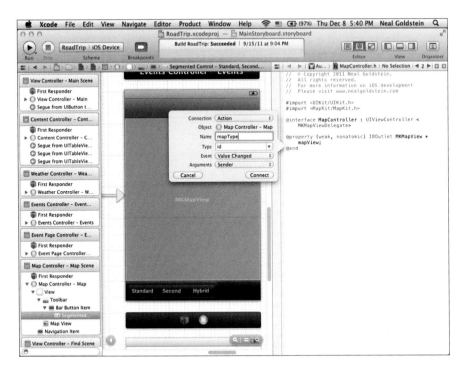

Figure 16-4: Connecting the segmented control.

5. Control+drag from the Map view to the `MapController` in the Dock and then select Delegate from the Outlets menu that appears.

Alternatively, because you have an outlet set up, you can make the `MapController` a delegate in your code. As I mention in Chapter 15, I prefer this approach because it is more visible (but it's up to you), and I show you how to do that shortly in `viewDidLoad`.

Go ahead and run the project.

Presto change-o! If you select the Map entry in the Content controller, you see, as shown in Figure 16-5, a map centered in the United States (at least you will if you are in the United States). It's as easy as that.

Cute — and impressive, given how little work you've done (the segmented control doesn't count because you still have to implement it). You need to do some more work to make the map really useful, though.

This is the general approach that you follow when you add more functionality to your application — add the new controller classes, update the storyboard, and so on.

Figure 16-5: Your first map.

But you — and your users — want and deserve more than a map centered on the United States. Figure 16-6 shows what you'd like to see on your road trip, rather than the standard Map view you get right out of the box.

Figure 16-6: New York and some sights to see.

Putting MapKit through Its Paces

You prepared the ground for some great map functionality, and now it's time to put the code in place get that done. Undergirding all this effort is the `MapKit.framework`. `MapKit` enables you to bring up a simple map and also do things with your map without having to do much work at all.

The map looks like the maps in the built-in applications and creates a seamless mapping experience across multiple applications.

MKMapView

The essence of mapping on the iPhone is the `MKMapView`. It's a `UIView` subclass, and as you saw in the previous section, you can use it out of the box to create a map. You use this class as-is to display map information and to manipulate the map contents from your application. It enables you to center the map on a given coordinate, specify the size of the area you want to display, and annotate the map with custom information (by becoming a Map view delegate).

When you initialize a Map view, you can specify the initial region for that map to display. You do this by setting the *region* property of the map. A region is defined by a center point and a horizontal and vertical distance, referred to as the *span*. The span defines how much of the map will be visible and also determines the zoom level. The smaller the span, the greater the zoom.

The Map view supports the standard map gestures:

- Scroll
- Pinch zoom
- Double-tap zoom in
- Two-finger-tap zoom out (you may not even have known about that one)

You can also specify the map type — regular, satellite, or hybrid — by changing a single property.

Because `MapKit.framework` was written from scratch, it was developed with the limitations of the iPhone in mind. As a result, it optimizes performance on the iPhone by caching data as well as managing memory and seamlessly handling connectivity changes (such as moving from 3G to Wi-Fi, for example).

The map data itself is Google-hosted map data, and network connectivity is required. And because `MapKit.framework` uses Google services to provide map data, using it binds you to the Google Maps/Google Earth API terms of service.

Although you shouldn't subclass the `MKMapView` class itself, you can tailor a Map view's behavior by providing a delegate object. The delegate object can be any object in your application, as long as it conforms to the `MKMapViewDelegate` protocol.

Enhancing the map

Having this nice global map centered on the United States is kind of interesting but not very useful if you're planning to go to New York. The following sections show you what you would have to do to make the map more useful.

You need to close the Assistant, show the Project navigator, and select `MapController.m`.

Landscape mode and the current location

To start with, the ability to see any map in landscape mode would be very useful.

As I explain in Chapter 15, the permitted orientations are determined in the view controller method `shouldAutorotateToInterfaceOrientation`. Right now, the default is

```
return (interfaceOrientation ==
                        UIInterfaceOrientationPortrait);
```

The only time `YES` is returned is if the device in portrait mode. In Listing 16-2, I have commented that out (you can delete it) and replaced the statement with the bolded code. You should do likewise in the `shouldAutorotate ToInterfaceOrientation:` method in `MapController.m`. That will allow your device to rotate to any orientation except upside down.

Listing 16-2:   Updating `shouldAutorotateToInterfaceOrientation:`

```
- (BOOL)shouldAutorotateToInterfaceOrientation:
                (UIInterfaceOrientation)interfaceOrientation
{
//return (interfaceOrientation ==
                        UIInterfaceOrientationPortrait);
   return (interfaceOrientation !=
                UIInterfaceOrientationPortraitUpsideDown);
}
```

That's all you have to do to view the map in landscape mode. You can move back and forth between landscape and portrait modes and `MapKit.frame-work` takes care of it for you!

What about showing your location on the map? That's just as easy!

In the `MapController.m` file, uncomment out `viewDidLoad` method and add the code in bold, as shown in Listing 16-3.

Listing 16-3: Updating `viewDidLoad`

```
- (void)viewDidLoad
{
    [super viewDidLoad];
    mapView.delegate = self;
    mapView.showsUserLocation = YES;
}
```

You start by making the `MapController` the Map view delegate (I know you have already done that in the storyboard previously in this chapter, but as I said, I want to you to know how to do it in your code as well).

`showsUserLocation` is a `MKMapView` property that tells the Map view whether to show the user location. If `YES`, you get that same blue pulsing dot displayed in the built-in Map application.

If you were to compile and run the application as it stands, on your phone, you'd get what you see in Figure 16-7 — a U.S. map in landscape mode with a blue dot that represents the phone's current location. (You may have to pan the map to see it. A lag may occur while the iPhone determines that location, but you should see it eventually.) Of course, to see it in landscape mode, you have to turn the iPhone, or choose Hardware⇨Rotate Right (or Rotate Left) from the Simulator menu.

Figure 16-7: Displaying a map in landscape mode with a user location.

If you don't see the current location, you might want to check and make sure that you've created the `mapView` outlet to the Map view in the storyboard.

You get your current location if you are running your app *on the iPhone.* If you're running it on the Simulator, you get to choose a simulated location.

After launching the application in the Simulator (see Figure 16-8), I've chosen San Francisco by showing the Debug area in the View selector in the tool-bar, and then selecting Simulate Location (the standard location icon) in the Debug bar in the Workspace window and selecting San Francisco. I did not choose New York because later you add some code to shift your map back and forth from the current location to your destination. You can also add more locations (but you don't in this book).

Figure 16-8: Simulating a location

Touching the blue dot also displays what's called an *annotation,* and I tell you how to customize the text to display whatever you cleverly devise — including, as you discover in Chapter 17, the address of the current location.

It's about the region

Okay, now you've got a blue dot on a map. Cute, but still not that useful for the purposes of the app.

As I mention at the beginning of this chapter, ideally, when you get to New York (or wherever), you should see a map that centers on New York as opposed to the entire United States. To get there from here, however, is also pretty easy. First, you need to look at how you center the map.

You add the method declaration to `setInitialRegion` to `MapController.h`.

First, update the Interface by adding the bolded code in Listing 16-4 to `Map Controller.h`.

Listing 16-4:   Updating the `MapController` Interface

```
#import <UIKit/UIKit.h>
#import <MapKit/MapKit.h>

@interface MapController : UIViewController
        <MKMapViewDelegate>

@property (weak, nonatomic) IBOutlet MKMapView *mapView;
- (IBAction)mapType:(id)sender;
- (void)setInitialRegion;
@end
```

Because the map controller will be getting its data from the `Trip` object, as it should, you have to update the Implementation to import the `Trip` class as well. Add the bolded code in Listing 16-5 to `MapController.m`.

Listing 16-5:   Updating the `MapController` Implementation

```
#import "MapController.h"
#import "RTAppDelegate.h"
#import "Trip.h"
```

Finally, add the `setInitialRegion` method in Listing 16-6 to `MapController.m`.

Listing 16-6:   Add `setInitialRegion`

```
- (void) setInitialRegion {

   RTAppDelegate* appDelegate =
                [[UIApplication sharedApplication] delegate];
   MKCoordinateRegion region;
   CLLocationCoordinate2D  initialCoordinate =
                    [appDelegate.trip destinationCoordinate];
```

```
    region.center.latitude = initialCoordinate.latitude;
    region.center.longitude = initialCoordinate.longitude;
    region.span.latitudeDelta = .05;
    region.span.longitudeDelta = .05;
    [mapView setRegion:region animated:NO];
}
```

You then need to update `viewDidLoad` to use this method. Add the code in bold in Listing 16-7 to `viewDidLoad` in `MapController.m` to send this message.

Listing 16-7:   Updating `viewDidLoad`

```
- (void)viewDidLoad
{
  [super viewDidLoad];
  mapView.delegate = self;
  mapView.showsUserLocation = YES;
  [self setInitialRegion];
}
```

If you run this now, you see what appears in Figure 16-9.

Setting the *region* is how you center the map and set the zoom level. You accomplish all this with the following statement:

```
[mapView setRegion:region animated:NO];
```

A region is a Map view property that specifies four pieces of information (as illustrated in Figure 16-8):

✔ `region.center.latitude` specifies the latitude of the center of the map.

✔ `region.center.longitude` specifies the longitude of the center of the map.

For example, if I were to set those values as

```
region.center.latitude = 40.714756;
region.center.longitude = -74.006047;
```

the center of the map would be New York.

✔ `region.span.latitudeDelta` specifies the north-to-south distance (in latitudinal degrees) to display on the map. One degree of latitude is approximately 111 kilometers (69 miles). A `region.span.latitude`

`Delta` of 0.0036 would specify a north-to-south distance on the map of about a quarter of a mile. Latitudes north of the equator have positive values, whereas latitudes south of the equator have negative values.

✔ `region.span.longitudeDelta` specifies the east-to-west distance (in longitudinal degrees) to display on the map. Unfortunately, the number of miles in one degree of longitude varies based on the latitude. For example, one degree of longitude is approximately 69 miles at the equator, but shrinks to 0 miles at the poles. Longitudes east of the zero meridian (by international convention, the zero or Prime Meridian passes through the Royal Observatory, Greenwich, in east London) have positive values, and longitudes west of the zero meridian have negative values.

Although the span values provide an implicit zoom value for the map, the actual region you see displayed may not equal the span you specify because the map will go to the zoom level that best fits the region that is set. This also means that even if you just change the center coordinate in the map, the zoom level may change because distances represented by a particular span may change at different latitudes and longitudes. To account for that, those smart developers at Apple included a property you can set that changes the center coordinate without changing the zoom level:

```
@property (nonatomic)
                  CLLocationCoordinate2D centerCoordinate
```

When you change the value of this property with a new `CLLocation Coordinate2D`, the map is centered on the new coordinate, and the span values are updated to maintain the current zoom level.

That `CLLocationCoordinate2D` type is something you will use a lot, so I explain that before I take you any further.

`CLLocationCoordinate2D` type is a structure that contains a geographical coordinate using the WGS 84 reference frame (the reference coordinate system used by the Global Positioning System):

```
typedef struct {
CLLocationDegrees latitude;
CLLocationDegrees longitude;
} CLLocationCoordinate2D;
```

Here's a little explanation:

✔ `latitude` is the latitude in degrees. This is the value you set in the code you just entered (`region.center.latitude = latitude;`). Positive values indicate latitudes north of the equator. Negative values indicate latitudes south of the equator.

✔ longitude is the longitude in degrees. This is the value you set in the code you just entered (region.center.longitude = longitude;). Measurements are relative to the zero meridian, with positive values extending east of the meridian and negative values extending west of the meridian.

CLLocationDegrees represents a latitude of longitude value specified in degrees and is a double.

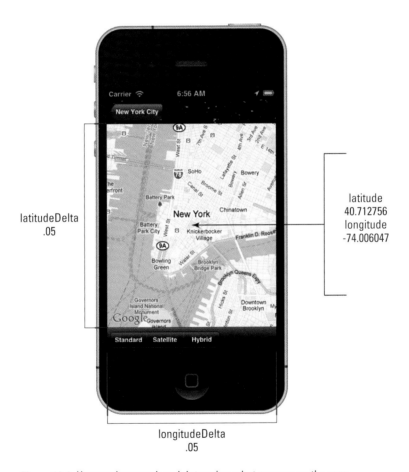

latitudeDelta
.05

latitude
40.712756
longitude
-74.006047

longitudeDelta
.05

Figure 16-9: How regions work and determine what you see on the map.

To center the map display on New York, you send the setInitialRegion message (the code you just entered) when the view is loaded in the view DidLoad: method.

Tracking location changes

You can also track changes in user location by using key-value observing, which enables you to move the map as the user changes location. I don't go into detail on key-value observing here, other than to show you the code.

First, you implement the method `viewWIllAppear:` in `MapController.m` to add an observer that's to be called when a certain value is changed — in this case, `userLocation`:

```
- (void) viewWillAppear:(BOOL)animated {

   [super viewWillAppear:animated];
   [mapView.userLocation addObserver:self forKeyPath:@"location"
                               options:0 context:NULL];
}
```

Adding that code causes the `observeValueForKeyPath:` message to be sent to the observer (`self` or the `Trip`). To implement the method in `Trip.m`, enter this method:

```
- (void)observeValueForKeyPath:(NSString *)keyPath
     ofObject:(id)object change:(NSDictionary *)change
                              context:(void *)context
   {

   NSLog (@"Location changed");
}
```

You need to add the following to remove yourself as a delegate as well:

```
- (void) viewWillDisappear:(BOOL)animated {

   [mapView.userLocation  removeObserver:self
                              forKeyPath:@"location"];
   [super viewWillDisappear:animated];
}
```

In the `observeValueForKeyPath:` message, the `change` field returns an `NSDictionary`, which you can use to get the value for the current location. In this example, I'm simply displaying a message on the Debugger Console, but as I said, after the user moves a certain amount, you may want to recenter the map. I also remove the observer when the view disappears.

Note: This isn't exactly the same location you'd get from `CLLocationManager` — it's optimized for the map, whereas `CLLocationManager` provides the raw user location.

Of course, you have to run this on the iPhone for the location to change.

Dealing with network failure

But what if the Internet isn't available? The Apple Human Interface Guidelines (and common sense) say that you should keep the user informed of what's going on. By virtue of the fact that you've made the MapController a MKMapView delegate, your app is in the position to send a message in the event of a load failure because if there is a failure, you are notified if you implement the mapViewDidFailLoadingMap: method. You can respond to a load failure by adding the code in Listing 16-8 toMapController.m.

Listing 16-8:   Implementing mapViewDidFailLoadingMap:

```
- (void)mapViewDidFailLoadingMap:(MKMapView *)mapView
                    withError:(NSError *)error {

  NSLog(@"Unresolved error %@, %@", error,
                                 [error userInfo]);

  UIAlertView *alert = [[UIAlertView alloc]
     initWithTitle:@"Unable to load the map"
     message:@"Check to see if you have internet access"
     delegate:self cancelButtonTitle: @"Thanks"
     otherButtonTitles:nil];
  [alert show];
}
```

Testing this failure business on the Simulator doesn't always work because it does some caching. You're better off testing it on the device itself by turning on Airplane mode.

Changing the Map Type

mapKit supports the three map types you see on Google maps — Standard, Satellite, and Hybrid.

The map type is a Map view property and is represented as an enumerated type, which I have cleverly made the segment numbers in the segmented control correspond to:

```
enum {
  MKMapTypeStandard,
  MKMapTypeSatellite,
  MKMapTypeHybrid
};
```

Avoiding the cast

Because I know that the sender in the `map-Type:` method is a `UISementedControl`, I could have been clever and instead changed the sender type in the method declaration:

```
- (IBAction)mapType:
    (UISegmentedControl *)sender
    {

    mapView.mapType = sender.
        selectedSegmentIndex;
}
```

I could have changed the sender type because you have the option to specify the sender type when you create the action (just be sure you are right). In fact, I could have changed it when I created the action by changing the type in the dialog in Step 4 in the "Setting up the MapController in the MainStoryboard," section earlier in this chapter.

Add the code in bold in Listing 16-9 to the `mapType:` method stub that was created when you added the action in Interface Builder.

Listing 16-9: Updating `mapType`:

```
- (IBAction)mapType:(id)sender {

    mapView.mapType =
        ((UISegmentedControl *)sender).selectedSegmentIndex;
}
```

When the user selects a segment in segmented control, a value-changed event is generated. This is the event that you specified when you created the action in Step 4 in the "Setting up the MapController in the MainStoryboard" section, earlier in this chapter.

The segmented control has a `selectedSegmentIndex` property, which contains the value of the selected segment.

I had to do a cast here because the sender is of type `id`, a pointer to an object, which doesn't have a `selectedSegmentIndex` property.

Adding Annotations

The `MKMapView` class supports the ability to annotate the map with custom information. The annotation has two parts: the annotation itself, which contains the data for the annotation; and the Annotation view, which displays the data.

Creating the annotation

Any object that conforms to the MKAnnotation protocol is an annotation object; typically, annotation objects are existing classes in your application's model. The job of an Annotation object is to know its location (coordinate) on the map along with the text to be displayed in the callout. The MKAnnotation protocol requires a class that adopts that protocol to implement the coordinate property. It can also optionally implement title and subtitle properties. In that case, that text is displayed in the annotation callout when the user taps the annotation.

Actually, you already have one class that meets that criteria — Destination.

And that is why, when you create the Destination class in Chapter 12 (I told you I would explain this), I have you add the property with the attributes in the way I do. They are required by the protocol to have the attributes I have bolded in the following code:

```
@property (nonatomic, readwrite)
                          CLLocationCoordinate2D coordinate;
@property (nonatomic, readwrite, copy) NSString *title;
@property (nonatomic, readwrite, copy) NSString *subtitle;
```

That's it. You already have the properties in place and initialized (see Chapter 12 if you need to review why that's the case).

Also in Chapter 12, you include some sight data in your plist. Although in this example, there is only one sight (annotation), you can imagine that in a complete RoadTrip app you'd have quite a few. You want your sights to be annotations as well.

Go back to the Trip object to create the annotations, but first you have to add an Annotation class to the Model Classes group by following these steps:

1. **In the Project navigator, select the Model Classes group, and right-click and then choose New File or choose File⇨New⇨New File from the main menu (or press ⌘+N) to open the New File dialog.**

2. **In the left column of the dialog, select Cocoa Touch under the iOS heading, select the Objective-C Class template in the top-right pane, and then click Next.**

3. **Enter** Annotation **in the Class field.**

4. **In the** Subclass of **field, select** NSObject **and then click Next.**

5. **Click Create (make sure that the Target field has the RoadTrip text box selected).**

Next, you need to add the code necessary for an annotation.

Add the code in bold in Listing 16-10 to Annotation.h.

Listing 16-10:   Updating the `Annotation` Interface

```
#import <Foundation/Foundation.h>
#import <MapKit/MapKit.h>

@interface Annotation: NSObject   <MKAnnotation>

@property (nonatomic, readwrite)
                         CLLocationCoordinate2D coordinate;
@property (nonatomic, readwrite, copy) NSString *title;
@property (nonatomic, readwrite, copy) NSString *subtitle;

@end
```

Now all the code you need to add is shown in Listing 16-11. Add the bolded code to `Annotation.m`.

Listing 16-11:   Update the `Annotation` Implementation

```
#import "Annotation.h"

@implementation Annotation

@synthesize coordinate;
@synthesize title;
@synthesize subtitle;
@end
```

I'm using a generic annotation class to display the sights. As you build out the app, you could also include more information about the sight and other information, and create a `Sight` class. Then you could make it and `Destination` subclasses of `Annotation`. In an annotation, you can also have a right and left Callout Accessory view, which displays on the right and left side of the standard callout bubble, respectively.

The callout view is typically used to link to more detailed information about the annotation. Also, you could link to something such as the `EventController` to display information about a `Sight`. Just food for thought.

You need to update the `Trip` initialization method to create the annotation, but first you have to import the headers you need. Add the bolded code in Listing 16-12 to `Trip.m`.

Listing 16-12:   Updating the `Trip` Implementation

```
#import "Trip.h"
#import "RTAppDelegate.h"
#import "Destination.h"
#import "Events.h"
#import "Annotation.h"
```

Now you can add the bolded code in Listing 16-13 to `initWithDestination Index:` in `Trip.m`.

Listing 16-13: Updating initWithDestinationIndex:

```
- (id)initWithDestinationIndex:(int)destinationIndex {

  if ((self = [super init])) {

    NSString *filePath = [[NSBundle mainBundle]
       pathForResource:@"Destinations"    ofType:@"plist"];
    NSDictionary *destinations =
     [NSDictionary dictionaryWithContentsOfFile:filePath];
    NSArray *destinationsArray =
         [destinations objectForKey:@"DestinationData"];
    destinationData =
       [destinationsArray objectAtIndex:destinationIndex];
    destination = [[Destination alloc]
             initWithDestinationIndex:destinationIndex];
    events = [[Events alloc] initWithDestinationIndex:
          destinationIndex];

    NSArray *sightsData =
                [destinationData objectForKey:@"Sights"];
    sights = [[NSMutableArray alloc]
                 initWithCapacity:[sightsData count]+1];
    [sights addObject:destination];

    for (NSDictionary *aSight in sightsData) {
      Annotation *annotation = [[Annotation alloc] init];
      CLLocationCoordinate2D coordinate;
      coordinate.latitude =
         [[aSight objectForKey:@"Latitude"] doubleValue];
      coordinate.longitude =
         [[aSight objectForKey:@"Longitude"] doubleValue];

      annotation.coordinate = coordinate;
      annotation.title = [aSight objectForKey:@"Title"];
      annotation.subtitle =
                        [aSight objectForKey:@"Subtitle"];
      [sights addObject:annotation];
    }
  }
  return self;
}
```

As you can see, you are creating an `Annotation` for each sight in the `sightsData` array, which you get from `destinationData` (which was created from the `Destination.plist`). But instead of adding an initialization method to `Annotation`, you are simply assigning the properties directly rather than sending them as parameters in an initialization method.

As you can see, I am adding `Destination` to the `sights` array as well. That way, it, too, will display on the map.

You have to add some new methods to the interface so that `Trip` can return the annotations (and a map title).

You also need to update the `Trip` interface. Add the bolded code in Listing 16-14 to `Trip.h`.

Listing 16-14: Updating the `Trip` Interface

```
@interface Trip : NSObject

- (UIImage *) destinationImage;
- (NSString *) destinationName;
- (CLLocationCoordinate2D) destinationCoordinate;

- (id)initWithDestinationIndex:(int)destinationIndex;
- (NSString *)weather;
- (int)numberOfEvents;
- (NSString *)getEvent:(int)index;
- (NSArray *)createAnnotations;
- (NSString *)mapTitle;

@end
```

Now you can add the `Trip` methods that will be used by the `MapController`. Add the `createAnnotations` method in Listing 16-15 to `Trip.m`.

Listing 16-15: Adding `createAnnotations`

```
- (NSArray *)createAnnotations {

    return sights;
}
```

Even though `sights` is a mutable array, I return it as a basic array because that is all that is needed. `MapController` won't be adding any annotations to it.

You also need to add a method to return the map title. Add the `mapTitle` method in Listing 16-16. to `Trip.m`.

Listing 16-16:   Adding `mapTitle`

```
- (NSString *)mapTitle {

  return destination.destinationName;
}
```

All that's really left at this point is to add the code to MapController to get the annotations and send them to the Map view.

Displaying the annotations

Displaying the title is easy. All you have to do is add the line of code in bold to the viewDidLoad method in MapController.m. You also display the annotations by sending yourself the addAnnotations message in view DidLoad as well.

Start by adding the bolded code in Listing 16-17 to update the interface in MapController.h.

Listing 16-17:   Updating the `MapController` Interface

```
@interface MapController : UIViewController
            <MKMapViewDelegate>

@property (weak, nonatomic) IBOutlet MKMapView *mapView;
- (IBAction)mapType:(id)sender;
- (void) setInitialRegion;
- (void) addAnnotations;
@end
```

Then you can update viewDidLoad by adding the bolded code in Listing 16-18 to viewDidLoad in MapController.m.

Listing 16-18:   Update `viewDidLoad`

```
- (void)viewDidLoad
{
  [super viewDidLoad];
  mapView.delegate = self;
  mapView.showsUserLocation = YES;
  RTAppDelegate* appDelegate =
              [[UIApplication sharedApplication] delegate];
  self.title = [appDelegate.trip mapTitle];
  [self addAnnotations];

  [self setInitialRegion];

}
```

`viewDidLoad` now sets the map title by after sending the `mapTitle` message to the `Trip` object — adding another model responsibility. (This gives you a chance to title the map based on whatever criteria you would like, such as the current location.)

Add the `addAnnotations` method in Listing 16-19 to `MapController.m` to add the annotations.

Listing 16-19:   Add `addAnnotations`

```
- (void) addAnnotations {

  RTAppDelegate* appDelegate =
              [[UIApplication sharedApplication] delegate];
  [mapView addAnnotations:
                    [appDelegate.trip createAnnotations]];

}
```

I make this a separate method because I want to be able to add additional annotations after the view is loaded. Although you won't be doing that here, you take advantage of this method when you implement the `FindController` in Chapter 18 to display locations the user wants to see on a map.

To add annotation to a Map view, just send the `addAnnotations` message with an array of annotations that have adopted the `MKAnnotation` protocol; that is, each one has a `coordinate` property and an optional `title` (and `subtitle`) method if you want to actually display something in the annotation callout.

The Map view places annotations on the screen by sending its delegate the `mapView:viewForAnnotation:` message. This message is sent for each annotation object in the array. Here you can create a custom view or return `nil` to use the default view. (If you don't implement this delegate method — which you won't, in this case — the default view is also used.)

Creating your own Annotation views is beyond the scope of this book (although I can tell you that the most efficient way to provide the content for an Annotation view is to set its image property). Fortunately, the default Annotation view is fine for your purposes. It displays a pin in the location specified in the coordinate property of the Annotation delegate. When the user touches the pin, the optional title and subtitle text displays if the `title` and `subtitle` methods are implemented in the annotation delegate.

You can also add callouts to the Annotation callout, such as a Detail Disclosure button (the one that looks like a white chevron in a blue button in a Table view cell) or the Info button (like the one you see in many of the utility apps), without creating your own Annotation view by using the built-in `MKPinAnnotationView`.

If you compile and build your project, you can check out the annotation you just added in Figure 16-10.

Figure 16-10: Displaying an annotation and its callout.

Going to the Current Location

Although you require the user to pan to the user location on the map if he or she wants to see it, in this case, it's kind of annoying unless you're actually coding this in or around New York. To remove at least that annoyance from your life, I show you how easy it is to add a button to the Navigation bar to zoom in to the current location and then back to the map region and span you're currently displaying.

Add the bolded code in Listing 16-20 to add the button in the MapController method viewDidLoad.

Listing 16-20: Updating `viewDidLoad`

```
- (void)viewDidLoad
{

  [super viewDidLoad];
  mapView.delegate = self;
  mapView.showsUserLocation = YES;
  RTAppDelegate* appDelegate = [[UIApplication
          sharedApplication] delegate];
  self.title = [appDelegate.trip mapTitle];
  [self addAnnotations];
  [self setInitialRegion];

  UIBarButtonItem *locateButton =
    [[UIBarButtonItem alloc] initWithTitle: @"Locate"
     style:UIBarButtonItemStylePlain target:self
     action:@selector(goToLocation:)];
  self.navigationItem.rightBarButtonItem = locateButton;
}
```

This may look familiar because it's what you did to add the Back button in Chapter 14. When the user taps the Locate button you create here, you've specified that the `goToLocation:` message is to be sent (`action:@ selector(goToLocation:)`) to the `MapController` (`target:self`).

```
UIBarButtonItem *locateButton =
    [[UIBarButtonItem alloc] initWithTitle: @"Locate"
     style:UIBarButtonItemStylePlain target:self
     action:@selector(goToLocation:)];
self.navigationItem.rightBarButtonItem = locateButton;
```

Next, add the `goToLocation:` method in Listing 16-21 to `MapController.m`.

Listing 16-21: Adding `goToLocation:`

```
- (void)goToLocation:(id)sender {

  MKUserLocation *annotation = mapView.userLocation;
  CLLocation *location = annotation.location;
  if (nil == location)
    return;
  CLLocationDistance distance =
                  MAX(4*location.horizontalAccuracy,500);
  MKCoordinateRegion region =
    MKCoordinateRegionMakeWithDistance
                (location.coordinate, distance, distance);
  [mapView setRegion:region animated:NO];
  self.navigationItem.rightBarButtonItem.action =
                              @selector(goToDestination:);
  self.navigationItem.rightBarButtonItem.title =
                                      @"Destination";
}
```

When the user presses the Locate button, your app first checks to see whether the location is available (it may take a few seconds after the application starts for the location to become available). If not, you simply return. (You could, of course, show an alert informing the user what's happening and to try again in 10 seconds or so — I leave that up to you.)

If location is available, your app computes the span for the region the user is moving to. In this case, the following code:

```
CLLocationDistance distance =
            MAX(4*location.horizontalAccuracy,500);
```

computes the span to be four times the horizontalAccuracy of the device (but no less than 1,000 meters). horizontalAccuracy is a radius of uncertainty given the accuracy of the device; that is, the user is somewhere within that circle.

You then call the MKCoordinateRegionMakeWithDistance function that creates a new MKCoordinateRegion from the specified coordinate and distance values. distance and distance correspond to latitudinalMeters and longitudinalMeters, respectively. (I'm using the same value for both arguments here.)

If you didn't want to change the span, you could have simply set the Map view's centerCoordinate property to userLocation, and, as I said earlier in the "It's about the region" section, that would have centered the region at the userLocation coordinate without changing the span.

When the user taps the Location button, you change the title on the button to the map title and change the @selector to (goToDestination:), which means that the next time the user touches the button, the goToDestination: message will be sent, so you'd better add the code in Listing 16-22 to MapController.m. This sets the region back to the Destination region and toggles the button title back.

Listing 16-22:   Adding goToDestination:

```
- (void)goToDestination:(id)sender {

  [self setInitialRegion];
  self.navigationItem.rightBarButtonItem.title =
                                          @"Locate";
  self.navigationItem.rightBarButtonItem.action =
                                @selector(goToLocation:);
}
```

Now run your app (and if you are running on the Simulator, choose your default location as explained in "Enhancing the map," earlier in this chapter.

By the way, look at the button style. Because you use an appearance proxy in Chapter 9, all your buttons will be customized in the way you specified.

You can see the result of touching the Locate button in Figure 16-11.

Figure 16-11: Go to the current location.

Because you have the user location, you might be tempted to use that to center the map, and that would work fine, as long as you start the location-finding mechanism stuff as soon as the program launches. The problem is that the hardware may take a while to find the current location, and if you don't wait long enough, you get an error. You can add the code to center the map to a method that executes later, such as

```
- (void)observeValueForKeyPath:(NSString *)keyPath
    ofObject:(id)object change:(NSDictionary *)change
                            context:(void *)context {
```

This message gets sent as soon as the map starts getting location information. But you will see an initial view and then a redisplay of the centered view. For aesthetic reasons, you really need to initialize the `MapController` and `MapView` at program start — an exercise for the reader.

Chapter 17

Geocoding

In This Chapter
- Understanding geocoding
- Getting a feel for reverse geocoding
- Displaying the address of the user's current location

*B*eing able to see where I am on an iPhone map has visual appeal — that dot is a real nice shade of blue — but I'm an exacting kind of guy who'd like to know *exactly* where I am in the scheme of things. I'd like to know the street address of where I'm standing, in other words. Geocoding makes that possible. (If I have the address, I can also write some code to turn the iPhone's current address into an Address Book contact.)

In this chapter, I explain geocoding and have you write the code that will take the user's current location and turn it into an address that you display in the current location annotation. In the bonus chapter, at `www.dummies.com/go/iphoneappdevfd4e`, I show you how to take an address or point of interest and forward geocode it so you can display it as an annotation on a map.

Understanding Geocoding on the iPhone

Being able to go from a coordinate on a map to an address is called *reverse geocoding,* and `MapKit` is used to supply the ability to do that. But whereas `MapKit` implements reverse geocoding, *forward geocoding,* the kind of geocoding that converts an address to a coordinate, just became available with iOS 5. Both forward and reverse geocoding have been moved into a new class — the `CLGeocoder` class — and moved to the core location framework. So, now all's right with the world. (Previously you had to use one of the free or commercial services available to do forward geocoding.)

The `CLGeocoder` class (which is part of the `CoreLocation` framework that I show you how to add in Chapter 12) provides services for converting between a coordinate (specified as a latitude and longitude) and the user-friendly representation of that coordinate. A user-friendly representation of the coordinate is the technical term for the street, city, state, and country information of a given location, but it may also be a relevant point of interest, landmark, or other identifying information. It also provides services for the reverse: returning the coordinate value for a text string that is the user-friendly representation of that coordinate.

To use a `CLGeocoder` object, create it, and send it a forward- or reverse-geocoding message. Reverse-geocoding requests take a latitude and longitude value and find a user-readable address. Forward-geocoding requests take a user-readable address and find the corresponding latitude and longitude value. Forward-geocoding requests may also return additional information about the specified location, such as a point of interest or building at that location. For both types of request, the results are returned as an array of `CLPlacemark` objects to a completion handler block. In the case of forward-geocoding requests, multiple `placemark` objects may be returned if the provided information yielded multiple possible locations.

A `CLPlacemark` object, contains, among other things, the following properties:

- `location`: Very useful for forward geocoding, which I explain in Chapter 18
- `name`: The name of the placemark
- `addressDictionary`: A dictionary containing the Address Book keys and values for the placemark
- `ISOcountryCode`: The abbreviated country name
- `country`: The name of the country
- `postalCode`: The postal code
- `administrativeArea`: The state or province
- `subAdministrativeArea`: Additional administrative area information (such as county)
- `locality`: The city
- `subLocality`: Additional city-level information such as neighborhood or a common name for the location
- `thoroughfare`: The street
- `subThoroughfare`: Additional street-level information, such as the street number
- `region`: The `CLRegion`

There may also be landmark and geographic information available in the `CLPlacemark` object in the following properties:

✔ `areasOfInterest`: The relevant areas of interest associated with the placemark

✔ `inlandWater`: The name of the inland water body associated with the placemark

✔ `ocean`: The name of the ocean associated with the placemark

To make smart decisions about what types of information to return, the geocoder server uses all the information provided to it when processing the request. For example, if the user is moving quickly along a highway, the geocoder might return the name of the overall region rather than the name of a small park that the user is passing through.

Here are some rather loose rules (Apple's) for using the `CLGeocoder` object:

✔ Send at most one geocoding request for any single user action. That is, don't start another request until the first one has completed.

✔ If the app needs the geocoded location in more than one place, save and then reuse the results from the initial geocoding request instead of doing another one.

✔ When you want to update the user's current location automatically (such as when the user is moving), issue new geocoding requests only when the user has moved a significant distance, or a reasonable amount of time has passed, or both. For example, in a typical situation, you should not send more than one geocoding request per minute.

✔ Do not start a geocoding request if your application is inactive or in the background.

✔ An iOS-based device must have access to the network in order for the `CLGeocoder` object to return detailed placemark information. Although the iOS stores enough information locally to report the localized country name and ISO country code for many locations, if country information is not available for a specific location, the `CLGeocoder` object may still report an error to your completion block.

You can use `CLGeocoder` object either in conjunction with, or independent of, the classes of the `MapKit` framework.

In this chapter, I show you how to add the code to do a reverse geocode. In the bonus chapter, at `www.dummies.com/go/iphoneappdevfd4e`, you essentially do the same thing to do a forward geocode, although you send a different message and process the placemark differently.

You are going to update the `goToLocation:` method to use reverse geocoding to display the address of the current location in the annotation.

Reverse Geocoding

You begin the process of implementing reverse geocoding by adding the bolded code in Listing 17-1 to add a new instance variable to Map Controller.m to store a reference to the CLGeocoder object. As you see later, you need that reference to cancel a request.

Listing 17-1: Updating the MapController Implementation

```
#import "MapController.h"
#import "RTAppDelegate.h"
#import "Trip.h"

@interface MapController () {
  CLGeocoder* geocoder;
}
@end
```

Next, you allocate and initialize the CLGeocoder and send it a message to return the information for the current location. Add the bolded code in Listing 17-2 to goToLocation in MapController.m.

Listing 17-2: Updating goToLocation

```
- (void)goToLocation:(id)sender {

void (^clGeocodeCompletionHandler)(NSArray *, NSError *) =
  ^(NSArray *placemarks, NSError *error){
    CLPlacemark *placemark = [placemarks objectAtIndex:0];
    if (error!= nil || placemark == nil) {
      NSLog(@"Geocoder failure! Error code: %u,
        description: %@, and reason: %@", error.code [error
          localizedDescription],
                          [error localizedFailureReason]);
    }
    else {
    mapView.userLocation.subtitle =
        [NSString stringWithFormat: @" lat:%f lon:%f",
          placemark.location.coordinate.latitude,
                    placemark.location.coordinate.longitude];
      if ([placemark.areasOfInterest objectAtIndex:0]) {
        mapView.userLocation.title =
              [placemark.areasOfInterest objectAtIndex:0];
      }
      else {
        if (placemark.thoroughfare) {
          if (placemark.subThoroughfare)
```

```
                mapView.userLocation.title =
                  [NSString stringWithFormat:@"%@ %@",
                            placemark.subThoroughfare,
                              placemark.thoroughfare];
            else
               mapView.userLocation.title =
                 [NSString stringWithFormat:@"%@",
                              placemark.thoroughfare];
        }
        else {
          if (placemark.locality) {
            mapView.userLocation.title =
                                  placemark.locality;
          }
          else
            mapView.userLocation.title = @"Your location";
        }
      }
    }
  };


    MKUserLocation *annotation = mapView.userLocation;
    CLLocation *location = annotation.location;
    if (nil == location)
      return;
    CLLocationDistance distance = MAX(4*location.
          horizontalAccuracy,500);
    MKCoordinateRegion region = MKCoordinateRegionMakeWithDista
          nce(location.coordinate, distance, distance);
    [mapView setRegion:region animated:NO];
    self.navigationItem.rightBarButtonItem.action = @
          selector(goToDestination:);
    self.navigationItem.rightBarButtonItem.title =
          @"Destination";

    geocoder = [[CLGeocoder alloc]init];
    [geocoder reverseGeocodeLocation:locationcompletionHandler:
          clGeocodeCompletionHandler];
}
```

The code you have added allocates and initializes the CLGeocoder, sends it
the message to reverse geocode, and provides it with a completion handler
block.

```
geocoder = [[CLGeocoder alloc]init];
[geocoder reverseGeocodeLocation:location completionHandler
      :clGeocodeCompletionHandler];
```

Sending the `reverseGeocodeLocation:completionHandler:` message is how you make a reverse-geocoding request for the specified location.

This method submits the location data to the geocoding server asynchronously and returns. Your completion handler block will be executed on the main thread. After initiating a reverse-geocoding request, you should not make another reverse- or forward-geocoding request until the first request is completed.

For both types of requests, the results are returned to the completion block in a `CLPlacemark` object. In the case of forward-geocoding requests, multiple placemark objects may be returned if what you submitted resulted in more than one possible location.

Note that the block is called *whether the request is successful or unsuccessful.* It is invoked when the `CLGeocoder` either finds placemark information for its coordinate or receives an error. The `CLPlacemark` object, as you previously saw in section "Understanding Geocoding on the iPhone" in this chapter, contains placemark data for a given latitude and longitude, which I explain later in this section. Placemark data includes the properties that hold the country, state, city and so on.

The completion handler is a block that appears in the following form:

```
void (^CLGeocodeCompletionHandler)
                        (NSArray *placemark, NSError *error);
```

As you can see, `placemark` contains an array of `CLPlacemark` objects. For most geocoding requests, this array should contain only one entry. However, forward-geocoding requests may return multiple placemark objects in situations in which the specified address could not be resolved to a single location.

If the request was canceled or an error in obtaining the placemark information occurred, `placemark` is `nil`.

`error` contains a pointer to an error object (if any) indicating why the placemark data was not returned.

```
if (error!= nil || placemark == nil) {
  NSLog(@"Geocoder failure! Error code:%u, description:
     %@, and reason: %@", error.code,
        [error localizedDescription],
                     [error localizedFailureReason]);
  }
```

The CLGeocoder can fail for a variety of reasons, such as the service is down or it can't find an address for the coordinate. If the CLGeocoder fails, you get back an error object that can have some useful information. I'll leave it you to explore the details of the error information on your own.

If the request is canceled, the placemark is nil.

Although I simply log a message here, you may want to expand the user inter-face to inform the user what is happening. Doing so isn't important in this case because you can always just leave the annotation as Current Location, but when you start dragging annotations (which you can do, but won't in this book), you might want to develop a plan for what to display in the annotation if the CLGeocoder fails.

If the CLGeocoder is successful, in the completion handler, you update the userLocation annotation, which is provided by the map view. user Location, as I explain in Chapter 16, is a map view property representing the user's current location.

As I explain earlier, the CLPlacemark object returned when the block is invoked stores placemark data for a given latitude and longitude. To update what is displayed in the annotation using the information you get back from the geocoder, you start by setting the subtitle using the coordinate in the placemark location property:

```
mapView.userLocation.subtitle =
  [NSString stringWithFormat: @" lat:%f lon:%f",
     placemark.location.coordinate.latitude,
                 placemark.location.coordinate.longitude];
```

If there is an areasOfInterest in the placemark, you set the title to that:

```
if ([placemark.areasOfInterest objectAtIndex:0]) {
  mapView.userLocation.title =
              [placemark.areasOfInterest objectAtIndex:0];
}
```

Otherwise, you see whether there is a thoroughfare and use that for the title (along with a subthoroughfare; together they provide the "street address"). Occasionally however, you may find that there is a thoroughfare (street), but no sub thoroughfare (street number). When that is the case you just display the thoroughfare

```
if (placemark.thoroughfare) {
  if (placemark.subThoroughfare)
    mapView.userLocation.title =
        [NSString stringWithFormat:@"%@ %@",
          placemark.subThoroughfare, placemark.thoroughfare];
  else
    mapView.userLocation.title =
              [NSString stringWithFormat:@"%@",
                                    placemark.thoroughfare];
}
```

If there is no `thoroughfare`, you try for a `locality`, and if all else fails, you use a general-purpose location string.

```
if (placemark.locality ) {
  mapView.userLocation.title = placemark.locality;
}
else
  mapView.userLocation.title = @"Your location";
```

Because the `CLGeocoder` operates asynchronously, the user might tap the button to return to the destination map before the `CLGeocoder` has completed the request. If that is the case, you'll want to cancel the `CLGeocoder` request. To do so, add the bolded code in Listing 17-3 to `goToDestination` in MapController.m.

Listing 17-3:   Updating `goToDestination:`

```
- (void)goToDestination:(id)sender {

  [geocoder cancelGeocode];
  geocoder = nil;
  [self setInitialRegion];
  self.navigationItem.rightBarButtonItem.title =
  @"Locate";
  self.navigationItem.rightBarButtonItem.action =
  @selector(goToLocation:);
}
```

The `cancelGeocode` message cancels a pending geocoding request. Canceling a pending request causes the completion handler block to be called.

You cancel the `CLGeocoder` request in this method because although you start the `CLGeocoder` in the `goToLocation:` method, it actually doesn't return the information in that method. It operates asynchronously when it constructs the placemark, gives up, or sends an error. You also set the instance variable to `nil` so that ARC will release the `CLGeocoder`.

But not only might the user return to the destination map before the geocoder request completes, he or she might also leave the map view entirely and return to the Content controller.

This means that you'll want to cancel the request when the view disappears as well, and the logical place to do that is in `viewWillDisappear:`.

`viewWillDisappear:` notifies the view controller that its view is about to be dismissed, covered, or otherwise hidden from view. In the Map controller that will happen only if the user taps the back button to return to the main view.

Add the overridden `viewWillDisappear:`.method code in Listing 17-4 to MapController.m.

Listing 17-4:   Overriding `viewWillDisappear:`

```
- (void) viewWillDisappear:(BOOL)animated {

  [geocoder cancelGeocode];
  geocoder = nil;
  [super viewWillDisappear:animated];
}
```

After initiating a forward-geocoding request, do not make another forward- or reverse-geocoding request until the first one completes, or you cancel it.

Figure 17-1 shows the result of your adventures in reverse geocoding.

Figure 17-1: Reverse geocoding the current location.

Chapter 18

Selecting a Destination

In This Chapter

▹ Finding an address for a map coordinate and displaying it on the map

▹ Finding the map coordinate from an address and displaying it on the map

*I*n this chapter, you are down to the final parts needed for the RoadTrip app to be complete. In Chapter 12, you add multiple destinations to the `Destinations.plist`, and now it would be nice if the user could select any of them.

Providing the user with the ability to select a destination is what you implement in this chapter. You also discover more about table views along the way. I also show you how to work with modal controllers (which present views that require the user to do something) by creating your own protocol.

Adding the DestinationController

If you've followed along throughout this book, by now you should know the drill. As you might expect, you need a view controller to implement the Selecting a Destination interface.

Adding the custom view controller

1. **In the Project navigator, select the View Controller Classes group and right-click and then choose New File or choose File⇨New⇨New File from the main menu (or press** cmd+N**) to open the New File dialog.**

2. **In the left column of the dialog, select Cocoa Touch under the iOS heading, select the UIViewController Subclass template in the top-right pane, and then click Next.**

3. **In the Class field, enter** DestinationController**. In the Subclass Of field, select** UIViewController **(be careful not to ignore this step and leave** MapController **in the Subclass Of field). Make sure that the Target for iPad and With XIB for User Interface are deselected.**

4. In the Save sheet, click Create.

The Destination controller will be using a table view, but it won't be a table view controller class. That's because I show you how to use a table view, with dynamically generated cells, and cell selection handled by the controller, as only one element in the view. This is a handy thing to know if you want to take advantage of the power of a Table view without letting a Table view take over the entire screen.

Adding and Setting up the DestinationController in the MainStoryboard

As I said earlier, you need a view controller to manage destination selection. Although you could have added this view controller when you extended the storyboard in Chapter 12, I didn't have you do that because I didn't want it to get lost among all the content discussion. To add a view controller to manage destination selection, follow these steps:

1. **Add another *view controller* — not table view controller — to the storyboard by dragging in a view controller from the Library pane and placing it below the Main View controller. (You don't have to put it there, but that location at least hints that there is some relationship.)**

2. **Open the Identity inspector in the Utility area using the Inspector selector bar, and in the Class drop-down menu in the Custom Class section, choose** `DestinationController` **(replacing** `UIViewController`**).**

3. **In the Attribute inspector, fill in Title with** Destination **and Identifier with** Destination**.**

   Your screen should look like Figure 18-1 when you are done.

The Destination controller will have a Table view, Label view, and very spiffy image as well after you follow these steps:

1. **Drag a Navigation bar from the Library in the Utility area and place it at the top of the view.**

   Because this is to be modal controller, you have to add the Navigation bar yourself.

2. **In the Navigation bar section in the Attributes inspector, select Black Opaque in the Style pop-up menu.**

3. **Click the Title and change the title to Destinations.**

4. **Drag a Bar Button Item from the Library and place it on the left side of the Navigation bar. In the Bar Button section in the Attribute inspector, select Cancel in the Identifier pop-up menu (you use this button to cancel selecting a new destination).**

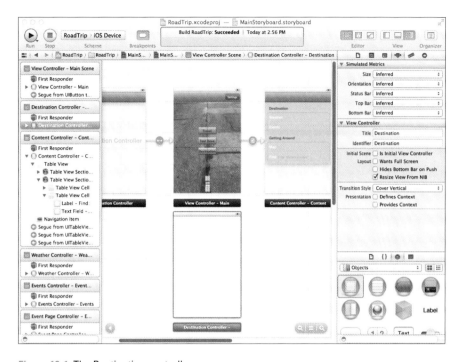

Figure 18-1: The Destination controller.

5. **In the Bar Button Tint section in the Attribute inspector, you don't have to select a tint for the button. When you selected Black Opaque, you gave all the Bar Button items the right tint as well. You will, by the way, get yellow text because of how you set the Bar Button appearance in Chapter 9.**

6. **Drag an Image View from the Library in the Utility area so that it takes up the rest of the view.**

7. **In the Image View section of the Attributes inspector select** `DestinationImage.png` **in the Image drop-down menu.**

8. **Drag a Label from the Library and add it to the view.**

9. **Enter** Pick a place, any place **in the Text field in the Label section of the Attribute inspector.**

10. **Change the Font size to System 24 by selecting the Text icon in the Font field or using the stepper control.**

11. **Choose Editor⁚Size Fit to Content.**

12. **Position the Label as shown in Figure 18-2.**

13. **Change the Text Color to White Color.**

14. **Drag a Table view (not Table View Controller) from the Library and position it.**

    Although I've made it the width of the view behind it, you can make it any width you'd like, and you can drag it as I have so that it ends just above the bottom of the view. This is the area in which the table view will display. If there are more selections than can fit in the visible area, the user will be able to scroll the Table view.

15. **In the Attributes inspector, make the Style Grouped and then scroll down and in the View section, select Clear Color from the Background pop-up menus.**

    Leave these as Prototype cells because you'll be providing the content for the cells programmatically.

16. **Select the Prototype cell and enter DestinationCell in the Identifier field. You will need to have a reuse identifier (which I explain in "Displaying the cell," later in this chapter). Then scroll down and in the View section, select Clear Color from the Background pop-up menus.**

17. **Control+drag from the Destination button in the main view to the Destination controller.**

18. **Select Modal in the Storyboard Segues pop-up menu.**

    As I explain in Chapter 4, a *modal dialog* requires the user to do something (tap a table view cell or the Cancel button, for example) before returning to the application.

19. **Select the segue and enter Destination as the Identifier.**

    I selected Flip Horizontal in the Transition pop-up menus. You can select whatever transition you'd like.

20. **Close the Utility area and select the Assistant in the Editor selector.**

21. **If the `DestinationController.h` file does not appear, select it in the Jump bar.**

22. **Control+drag from the Navigation bar to the `Destination.h` Interface and create an outlet named `navigationBar`.**

23. **Control+drag from the Table view to the `DestinationController.h` Interface and create an outlet named `destinationTableView`.**

24. **Control+drag from the Cancel button to the `DestinationController.h` Interface, create an action item, and name it `cancel`.**

When all is said and done, you should see a screen that looks like Figure 18-2.

Figure 18-2: Ready to code.

Adding a Modal View

In this section, I explain modal views.

You use a modal view when you want the user (or the user wants) to do something out side the application flow. Rather than use a navigation controller with a Back button, you display a model view with controls that allow the user to select an action or cancel.

You can see that when you added the Destination controller to the story-board, you enabled the user to select a destination in the Table view or to press Cancel to leave things as they are.

The usual way to manage modal views is by creating a protocol that is adopted by the controller presenting the modal view. The modal view, when the user has selected an action or cancel, calls the presenting controller's delegate method. The requesting controller then dismisses the modal controller. Using this approach means that before it dismisses the model controller, the presenting controller can get any data it needs.

You start implementing the Modal view by declaring the protocol and a few other properties you'll need, as well as the protocols the DestinationController needs to adopt.

Add the bolded code in Listing 18-1 to `DestinationController.h`.

Listing 18-1: Updating the `Destination` Interface

```
#import <UIKit/UIKit.h>
@protocol DestinationControllerDelegate;

@interface DestinationController : UIViewController
             <UITableViewDelegate, UITableViewDataSource>

@property (weak, nonatomic) IBOutlet UINavigationBar
             *navigationBar;
@property (weak, nonatomic) IBOutlet UITableView
             *destinationTableView;
@property (strong, nonatomic) id
                   <DestinationControllerDelegate> delegate;
@property (nonatomic, readonly)
                         NSUInteger selectedDestination;

- (IBAction)cancel:(id)sender;
@end

@protocol DestinationControllerDelegate
- (void)destinationController:
    (DestinationController *)controller
                         didFinishWithSave:(BOOL)save;
@end
```

The Objective-C language provides a way to formally declare a list of methods (including declared properties) as a protocol. You use framework supplied protocols extensively in this book, and now you define your own protocol.

You declare formal protocols with the `@protocol` directive. Here you have declared a `DestinationControllerDelegate` protocol with one method, `destinationController:didFinishWithSave:`, which is *required*. Required is the default; if you wanted to declare optional methods, you would use the keyword `@optional`, and all methods following that keyword would be optional. For example:

```
@protocol SimpleDelegate
@optional
- (void)doNothing;
@end
```

The `@protocol DestinationControllerDelegate;` statement (at the top) tells the compiler that a protocol is on the way. Like the `@class` statement, it says, "Trust me, you'll find the protocol." You need this here only because you added:

```
@property (strong, nonatomic) id
             <DestinationControllerDelegate> delegate;
```

This statement tells the compiler to type check whatever it is you assign to `delegate` to make sure that it implements the `DestinationController Delegate` protocol.

You also added the `selectedDestination` property, which you use in the `ViewController` to determine which destination the user selected. Notice that you have made it read-only because there is no reason for any other object to be able to set it.

You also adopted two protocols, `UITableViewDelegate` and `UITableViewDataSource`, which you'll use to manage the table view.

Next, update the `DestinationController` implementation in Listing 18-2 with the bolded code to synthesize the getters and setters for the new properties.

Listing 18-2:   Updating the `DestinationController` Implementation

```
#import "DestinationController.h"

@implementation DestinationController
@synthesize navigationBar;
@synthesize destinationTableView;
@synthesize delegate = _delegate;
@synthesize selectedDestination = _selectedDestination;
```

Now that you have the plumbing in, you can look at what will go on in the `DestinationController`.

Table views

The action in the `DestinationController` is in the Table view. You've worked with table views before, but those used static cells, and all the work was done for you by the storyboard. Now it's time to branch out on your own and understand what the storyboard was doing.

It's a good thing to know how table views work, because table views are front and center in several applications that come with the iPhone out of the box; they play a major role in many of the more complex applications that you can download from the App Store. (Obvious examples: Almost all the views in the Mail, Music, and Contacts applications are Table views.) Table views take on such a significant role because, in addition to displaying data, they can also serve as a way to navigate a hierarchy.

If you take a look at an application such as Mail or Music, you find that Table views present a scrollable list of *items* (or *rows* or *entries* — I use all three terms interchangeably) that may be divided into *sections.* A row can display text or images. So, when you select a row, you may be presented with another Table view or with some other view that may display a web page or even controls such as buttons and text fields. You can see an illustration of this diversity in Chapter Figure 4-6. Selecting Map leads to a Map view displaying a map of New York, which is very handy when you roll into town.

Table views are used a lot in iPhone applications to do two things:

- **Display hierarchal data:** For an example, think of the Music application, which gives you a list of albums and, if you select one, a list of songs.

- **Act as a table of contents:** Now, think of the Settings application, which gives you a list of applications that you can set preferences for. When you select one of those applications from the list, it takes you to a view that lists what preferences you're able to set as well as a way to set them.

To kick off the process, you first need to decide what you want to have happen when the user selects a particular row in the table view of your app. As you saw with static cells, you can have virtually anything happen. You can display a web view as you do in Weather or even display another Table view.

In this case, however, the Destination view controller will be dismissed, and the user will find herself in the Main view, ready to make another selection.

A Table view is an instance of the class `UITableView`, whereas each visible row of the table uses a `UITableViewCell` to draw its contents. Think of a *Table view* as the object that creates and manages the table structure, and the *Table view cell* as being responsible for displaying the content of a single row of the table.

Creating the Table View

Although powerful, Table views are surprisingly easy to work with. To create a table, there are only four — count 'em, four — steps, in the following order:

1. **Create and format the view itself.**

   This includes specifying the table style and a few other parameters, most of which you do in Interface Builder.

2. **Specify the table view configuration.**

   Not too complicated, actually. You let `UITableView` know how many sections you want, how many rows you want in each section, and what you want to call your section headers. You do that with the help of the `numberOfSectionsInTableView:` method, the `tableView:number OfRowsInSection:` method, and the `tableView:titleForHeader InSection:` method, respectively.

3. **Supply the text (or graphic) for each row.**

   You return that from the implementation of the `tableView:cellFor RowAtIndexPath:` method. This message is sent for each visible row in the Table view, and you return a Table view cell to display the text or graphic.

4. **Respond to a user selection of the row.**

   You use the `tableView:didSelectRowAtIndexPath:` method to take care of this task. In this method, you can create a view controller and push it on to the stack (as the storyboard does in a segue), or you can even send a message to the controller that presented a modal view controller (or any other object).

A `UITableView` object must have a *data source* and a *delegate:*

✔ The data source supplies the content for the Table view.

✔ The delegate manages the appearance and behavior of the Table view.

The data source adopts the `UITableViewDataSource` protocol, and the delegate adopts the `UITableViewDelegate` protocol — no surprises there. Of the preceding methods, only `tableView:didSelectRowAtIndexPath:` is included in the `UITableViewDelegate` protocol. All the other methods that I list earlier are included in the `UITableViewDataSource` protocol.

The data source and the delegate are often (but not necessarily) implemented in the same object, which is often a subclass of `UITableViewController`. `UITableViewController` adopts the necessary protocols and even furnishes some method stubs for you. In this case, the table view is just another object in the `DestinationController` view. I had you do that so I could explains the real guts of table views and because I wanted you to be able to display that Pick a Destination label, which you couldn't have done if you had made this `UITableView` subclass.

Implementing these five (count 'em, five) methods (in the four steps earlier) is all you need to do to implement a Table view.

Not bad.

I already had you adopt the table view delegate and data source protocols in Listing 18-1, so you are already part way there.

Uncomment out the `viewDidLoad` method in `destinationController.m` and add the bolded code in Listing 18-3 to `DestinationController.m`.

Listing 18-3: Updating `viewDidLoad`

```
- (void)viewDidLoad
{
    [super viewDidLoad];
    self.destinationTableView.delegate = self;
    self.destinationTableView.dataSource = self;
    [self.navigationBar setTitleTextAttributes:
    [NSDictionary dictionaryWithObject:
    [UIColor yellowColor]forKey:UITextAttributeTextColor]];

}
```

As you might surmise, this makes the `DestinationController` the delegate and data source. You also set the title color to yellow. Remember that in Chapter 9, you don't set the appearance of all navigation bars, just the one in the Navigation controller.

Adding sections

In a grouped Table view, each group is referred to as a *section*.

In an indexed table, each indexed grouping of data is also called a section. For example, in the iPod application, all the albums beginning with *A* would be one section, those beginning with *B* another section, and so on. Although the indexed grouping has the same name, this is not the same thing as sections in a grouped table (which doesn't have an index).

The two methods you need on hand to start things off are as follows:

```
numberOfSectionsInTableView:(UITableView *)tableView

tableView:(UITableView *)tableView
          numberOfRowsInSection:(NSInteger)section
```

Each of these methods returns an integer, and that integer tells the Table view something — the number of sections and the number of rows in a given section, respectively.

Add the methods in Listing 18-4 to `DestinationController.m` to create a Table view that has one section with the number of rows equal to the number of destinations you have in your `Destinations.plist`.

Listing 18-4:   Implementing `numberOfSectionsInTableView:` and `tableView:numberOfRowsInSection:`

```
- (NSInteger)numberOfSectionsInTableView:
                            (UITableView *)tableView {

   return 1;
}

- (NSInteger)tableView:(UITableView *)tableView
            numberOfRowsInSection:(NSInteger)section {

   NSString *filePath = [[NSBundle mainBundle]
         pathForResource:@"Destinations" ofType:@"plist"];
   NSDictionary *destinations =
     [NSDictionary dictionaryWithContentsOfFile: filePath];
   destinationsArray =
            [destinations objectForKey:@"DestinationData"];

   return [destinationsArray count];
}
```

`numberOfSectionsInTableView:` method is obvious.

In the `tableView:numberOfRowsInSection:` method, you do what you did in both the `Trip` and `Events` classes — you access the `Destination. plist` to extract what you need. In this case it's the `DestinationData` array, which, to refresh your memory, is an array of dictionaries that have the data for each destination and return back the count.

Keep in mind that the first section is zero, as is the first row. This means, of course, that whenever you want to use an index to get to the first row or section, you need to use 0, not 1 — and an index of 1 for the second row and so on.

You also need to add the new `destinationsArray` instance variable because you need to use this same array later in `tableView:cellForRowAtIndexP ath:`. Add the bolded code in Listing 18-5 to `DestinationController.m`.

Listing 18-5: Updating the DestinationController Implementation

```
#import "DestinationController.h"

@interface DestinationController () {
  NSArray *destinationsArray;
}
@end

@implementation DestinationController
```

Displaying the cell

To display the cell content, your delegate is sent the `tableView:cell ForRowAtIndexPath:` message. Add this method in Listing 18-6 to `DestinatsionController.m`.

Listing 18-6: Implementing tableView:cellForRowAtIndexPath:

```
- (UITableViewCell *)tableView:(UITableView *)tableView
        cellForRowAtIndexPath:(NSIndexPath *)indexPath {

  static NSString *CellIdentifier = @"DestinationCell";
  UITableViewCell *cell = [tableView
      dequeueReusableCellWithIdentifier:CellIdentifier];
  if (cell == nil) {
    cell = [[UITableViewCell alloc] initWithStyle:UITableView
        CellStyleDefault
                            reuseIdentifier:CellIdentifier];
  }

  NSDictionary * destinationData =
      [destinationsArray objectAtIndex:indexPath.row];
  cell.textLabel.text =
      [destinationData objectForKey:@"DestinationName"];
  cell.textLabel.textColor = [UIColor whiteColor];

  return cell;
}
```

First you determine whether any cells that you can use are lying around.

Although a Table view can display only a few rows at a time on the iPhone's small screen, the table itself can conceivably hold a lot more. A large table chews up a lot of memory if you create cells for every row. Fortunately, Table views are designed to *reuse* cells. As a Table view's cells scroll off the screen, they're placed in a queue of cells available to be reused.

If the system runs low on memory, the Table view gets rid of the cells in the queue, but as long as it has some available memory for them, it holds on to them in case you want to use them again.

You create a string to use as a *cell identifier* to indicate what cell type you're using:

```
static NSString *CellIdentifier = @"DestinationCell";
```

You recall that this is what you entered in the Identifier field of the prototype cell in Step 16 in the earlier section "Setting up the DestinationController in the MainStoryboard."

Table views support multiple cell types, which makes the identifier necessary. In this case, you need only one cell type, but sometimes you may want more than one.

You ask the Table view for a specific reusable cell object by sending it a `dequeueReusableCellWithIdentifier:` message:

```
UITableViewCell *cell = [tableView
        dequeueReusableCellWithIdentifier:CellIdentifier];
```

This determines whether any cells of the type you want are available.

If no cells are lying around, you have to create a cell by using the cell identifier you just created:

```
cell = [[UITableViewCell alloc]
                initWithStyle:UITableViewCellStyleDefault
                    reuseIdentifier:CellIdentifier];
```

You now have a Table view cell that you can return to the Table view.

You have several choices on how to format the Table view cell. Although you are going to use `UITableViewCellStyleDefault,`, there are several styles, as follows:

- ✔ `UITableViewCellStyleDefault` gives you a simple cell with a text label (black and left-aligned) and an optional Image view.

- ✔ `UITableViewCellStyleValue1` gives you a cell with a left-aligned black text label on the left side of the cell and a right-aligned label with smaller blue text on the right side. (The Settings application uses this style of cell.)

✔ `UITableViewCellStyleValue2` gives you a cell with a right-aligned blue text label on the left side of the cell and a left-aligned black label on the right side of the cell.

✔ `UITableViewCellStyleSubtitle` gives you a cell with a left-aligned label across the top and a left-aligned label below it in smaller gray text. (The iPod application uses cells in this style.)

You then set the label properties that you're interested in.

You get out the name of each destination by accessing the `DestinationName` in each destination dictionary. You do that by accessing the dictionary in the (saved) `destinationsArray` corresponding to the sections and row you are passed in. `indexPath`, contains the section and row information in a single object. To get the row or the section out of an `NSIndexPath`, you just have to invoke its section method (`indexPath.section`) or its row method (`indexPath.row`), either of which returns an int:

```
NSDictionary * destinationData =
        [destinationsArray objectAtIndex:indexPath.row];
```

Next, assign the label text to the `DestinationName` and set the text color to white:

```
cell.textLabel.text =
        [destinationData objectForKey:@"DestinationName"];
cell.textLabel.textColor = [UIColor whiteColor];
```

Finally, return the formatted cell with the text it needs to display in that row:

```
return cell;
```

Working with user selections

Now you can look at what happens when the user selects a row with a destination displayed.

When the user taps a Table view entry, what happens next depends on what you want your Table view to do for you.

If you're using the Table view to display data (as the Albums view in the iPod application does, for example), you want a user's tap to show the next level in the hierarchy, such as a list of songs or a detail view of an item (such as information about a song).

In the case of the RoadTrip app, you want a user's taps to take you back to the Main view and, behind the covers, create the right model so that when you tap the Travel button, the right data is there.

To do that, add the final delegate method you need to implement, `tableView:didSelectRowAtIndexPath:`. Add the code in Listing 18-7 to `DestinationController.m`.

Listing 18-7:   Implementing `tableView:didSelectRowAtIndexPath:`

```
- (void)tableView:(UITableView *)tableView
        didSelectRowAtIndexPath:(NSIndexPath *)indexPath
{
  [tableView deselectRowAtIndexPath:
                             indexPath animated:YES];
  _selectedDestination = indexPath.row;
  [self.delegate destinationController:
                            self didFinishWithSave:YES];

}
```

You set the `selectedDestination` property to the selected row. Notice that you access the instance variable here instead of using the setter because you made the *property* `readonly`.

Then you send the delegate the `destinationController:didFinish WithSave:` message with a value of `YES`.

Before I explain the `destinationController:didFinishWithSave:` method, implement the last part of the `DestinationController`. Add the bolded code in Listing 18-8 to the `cancel` method (generated when you created the action) in `DestinationController.m`.

Listing 18-8:   Adding `cancel:`

```
- (IBAction)cancel:(id)sender {

  [self.delegate destinationController:self
                                didFinishWithSave:NO];

}
```

When the user taps Cancel, the `DestinationController` sends the `destinationController:didFinishWithSave:` message with a value of `NO` to its delegate — which will be the `RTViewController`. Now go back to the `RTViewController` and implement the `destinationController: didFinishWithSave:` message.

Import the headers you need into `RTViewController.m` by adding the bolded code in Listing 18-9 to `RTViewController.m`.

Listing 18-9:   Updating the `RTViewController` Implementation

```
#import "RTViewController.h"
#import <AVFoundation/AVFoundation.h>
#import <AudioToolbox/AudioToolbox.h>
#import "RTAppDelegate.h"
#import "Trip.h"
```

You also have to have the RTViewController adopt the Destination ControllerDelegate protocol and declare the destinationController: didFinishWithSave: method. Add the bolded code in Listing 18-10 to RTViewController.m.

Listing 18-10:   Updating the `RTViewController` Interface

```
#import <UIKit/UIKit.h>
#import "DestinationController.h"

@interface RTViewController : UIViewController
                           <DestinationControllerDelegate>

@property (weak, nonatomic) IBOutlet UIImageView *car;
@property (weak, nonatomic) IBOutlet UIButton
          *testDriveButton;
@property (weak, nonatomic) IBOutlet UIImageView
          *backgroundImage;

- (IBAction)testDrive:(id)sender;
- (void)rotate;
- (void)returnCar;
- (void)continueRotation;
- (void)destinationController:(DestinationController *)
                 controller didFinishWithSave:(BOOL)save;

@end
```

Next, add the destinationController:didFinishWithSave: method in Listing 18-11 to RTViewController.m.

Listing 18-11:   Adding `destinationController:didFinishWithSave:`

```
- (void)destinationController:
            (DestinationController *)controller
                              didFinishWithSave:(BOOL)save {

  RTAppDelegate *appDelegate =
              [[UIApplication sharedApplication] delegate];

  if (save) {
    [appDelegate createDestinationModel:
                            controller.selectedDestination];
  }

  if (appDelegate.trip == nil)
    [appDelegate createDestinationModel:0];

  [self dismissModalViewControllerAnimated:YES];

}
```

If the user has chosen a new destination, you send the app delegate a message to create that model:

```
[appDelegate
    createDestinationModel:controller.selectedDestination];
```

It determines the selection the user made by accessing the `selected Destination` property you set in the `tableView:didSelectRowAtIndex Path:` method.

As you may recall, `createDestinationModel:` is an already existing method in the app delegate. As I say in Chapter 12, the `create DestinationModel:` method will actually be creating the model, and I made this a separate method because you will need to be able to send the `RTAppDelegate` a message to create a new `Trip` when the user chooses a new destination in Chapter 18. Well, here you are.

If the user hasn't chosen a new destination but there is no model yet (when the user first launches the program, there is no model yet, and you see how that works in a second), you'll have the app delegate create a model using a default destination. I have arbitrarily chosen the first one.

You then send the `dismissModalViewControllerAnimated:` message, which, as you might expect, dismisses the view controller using the transition you specified in "Setting up the DestinationController in the MainStoryboard," earlier in this chapter.

If the user has canceled, you simply send the `dismissModalView ControllerAnimated:` message, and the user finds herself back in the Main view.

But you still have some more work to do.

Previously, you added a `delegate` property to the `DestinationController`, which it uses when it sends the `destination Controller:didFinishWithSave:` message when the user selects a cell or taps cancel.

The problem is, how do you set that property? Because you use a segue to take care of creating and initializing the controller, how do you assign the delegate property? As you may recall from Chapter 11, you don't use a segue, so you could assign any property you wanted after you created but before you launched the FindController in `textFieldShouldReturn:` I've bolded where you do that in the code:

```
- (BOOL)textFieldShouldReturn:(UITextField *)textField {

    [textField resignFirstResponder];
    FindController *findController =
        [[UIStoryboard storyboardWithName:@"MainStoryboard"
                                                   bundle:nil]
            instantiateViewControllerWithIdentifier:@"Find"];
    findController.findLocation = textField.text;
    [self.navigationController
            pushViewController:findController animated:YES];

    return YES;
}
```

Fortunately, there is a way to use a segue and still be able to pass some data on to the view controller that's being instituted by the segue.

`prepareForSegue:sender:` is a view controller method used to notify the view controller that a segue is about to be performed. `segue` is the `UIStoryboardSegue` object that contains information about the view controllers involved in the segue.

The default implementation of this method does nothing. Subclasses override it and use it to pass data to the view controller that is about to be displayed. The segue object contains pointers to both source view controller and the destination view controller (among other information).

`sender` is the object that initiated the segue, and you might use this parameter to perform different actions based on which control (or other object) initiated the segue.

You use the `prepareForSegue:sender:` method to assign the delegate property in the `DestinationController`. So add the `prepareForSegue:sender:` method in Listing 18-12 to `RTViewController.m`.

Listing 18-12: Overriding `prepareForSegue:sender:`

```
- (void)prepareForSegue:(UIStoryboardSegue *)segue
                                    sender:(id)sender {

  UIStoryboardSegue *destinationSegue = segue;

  if ([destinationSegue.identifier
                    isEqualToString:@"Destination"]) {
    DestinationController *destinationController =
             destinationSegue.destinationViewController;
    destinationController.delegate = self;
  }
}
```

You first check to see whether the segue is the `Destination` segue (see those identifiers are really useful):

```
if ([destinationSegue.identifier
                    isEqualToString:@"Destination"])
```

If it is, set the `destinationController`'s `delegate` property to `self` and you're on your way. You let the segue do the rest of the work for you:

```
DestinationController *destinationController =
            destinationSegue.destinationViewController;
destinationController.delegate = self;
```

If it is not the `Destination` segue you ignore it.

Handling the Destination the First Time RoadTrip is Launched

At this point, if you were to run your project, you would be able to tap the Destination button, choose a destination, and see the data for either New York or San Francisco.

But you're not done yet.

First, if the application is terminated (and I mean terminated, not running in the background and re-launched), the user will find that the destination she selected has reverted back to being the default one. You would like to see

RoadTrip able to save, and then restore, the user's destination preference. (In Chapter 12, you see how to default to the first destination in the plist. I mention in that chapter that I show you how to fix that situation in Chapter 18, and here you are.)

In addition, when the application is launched for the first time, it would be nice if the user started up in the Destination view, rather than have to figure out for themselves that they need to tap the Destination button to decide where to go.

Both of these features are actually pretty easy to implement, and as you will see, they revolve around including RTAppDelegate property — destinationPreference.

Start by adding the destinationPreference property to RTAppDelegate by adding the bolded code in Listing 18-13 to RTAppDelegate.h.

Listing 18-13: Updating the RTAppDelegate Interface

```
#import <UIKit/UIKit.h>
#import "Reachability.h"
@class Trip;

@interface AppDelegate : UIResponder
                                <UIApplicationDelegate>

@property (strong, nonatomic) UIWindow *window;
@property (nonatomic, strong) Trip *trip;
@property (nonatomic, strong) NSString *
                                destinationPreference;

- (void) createDestinationModel:(int)destinationIndex;

@end
```

Now create the accessors for this property and the name of the key you'll use in NSUserDefaults for the destination preference by adding the bolded code in Listing 18-14 to RTAppDelegate.m.

Listing 18-14: Updating the RTAppDelegate Implementation

```
#import "RTAppDelegate.h"
#import "Reachability.h"
#import "Trip.h"


static NSString *DestinationPreferenceKey =
                        @"DestinationPreferenceKey";
```

```
@implementation RTAppDelegate

@synthesize window = _window;
@synthesize trip = _trip;
@synthesize destinationPreference  =
                                    _destinationPreference;
```

In addition to the `@synthesize` statement, you're adding a key (string) that you'll need to use when you save the preference.

You can also have the Destination view pop up whenever the application is launched for the first time on a device. To do so, add the code bolded code in Listing 18-15 to `viewDidLoad` in `RTViewController.m`.

Listing 18-15:   Adding to `viewDidLoad`

```
- (void)viewDidLoad
{
  [super viewDidLoad];
  self.title = @"Road Trip";

  NSURL* backgroundURL = [NSURL fileURLWithPath:
    [[NSBundle mainBundle] pathForResource:
                            @"CarRunning" ofType:@"aif"]];
  backgroundAudioPlayer = [[AVAudioPlayer alloc]
          initWithContentsOfURL:backgroundURL error:nil];
  backgroundAudioPlayer.numberOfLoops = -1;
                  [backgroundAudioPlayer prepareToPlay];

  NSURL* burnRubberURL = [NSURL fileURLWithPath:
    [[NSBundle mainBundle] pathForResource:@"BurnRubber"
                                    ofType:@"aif"]];
  AudioServicesCreateSystemSoundID((__bridge CFURLRef)
                    burnRubberURL, &burnRubberSoundID);
    [testDriveButton setBackgroundImage:
      [UIImage animatedImageNamed:@"Button" duration:1.0 ]
                            forState:UIControlStateNormal];

  UISwipeGestureRecognizer *swipeGesture =
    [[UISwipeGestureRecognizer alloc] initWithTarget:self
                action:@selector(handleSwipeGesture:)];
  swipeGesture.direction =
          UISwipeGestureRecognizerDirectionLeft;
  [self.view addGestureRecognizer:swipeGesture];

  RTAppDelegate * appDelegate =
            [[UIApplication sharedApplication] delegate];
```

(continued)

Listing 18-15 *(continued)*

```
    if(appDelegate.destinationPreference == nil) {
      DestinationController *destinationController =
        [[UIStoryboard storyboardWithName:
                            @"MainStoryboard" bundle:nil]
        instantiateViewControllerWithIdentifier:
                                       @"Destination"];
      destinationController.delegate = self;
      [self.navigationController
          presentModalViewController:destinationController
                                    animated:YES];
    }
  }
```

As you can see, if the `appDelegate.destinationPreference` property is
`nil`, youl get the Destination controller from the storyboard and launch it.

Now, every time you compile and run your app, you see the Destination view
because there is never anything other than `nil` in the `appDelegate.`
`destinationPreference` property.

In Listing 18-16, you fix that problem. At application launch check to see
whether a user preference is saved. If one is, assign it to `destination-`
`Preference`. If no preference is saved, leave that preference as `nil`, and the
Destination view is launched by the `RTViewController`.

Add the bolded code in Listing 18-16 to `application:didFinish`
`LaunchingWithOptions:` in `RTAppDelegate.m` and delete the code that
has been commented out.

Listing 18-16: Updating `application:didFinishLaunchingWithOptions:`

```
- (BOOL)application:(UIApplication *)application
    didFinishLaunchingWithOptions:
                        (NSDictionary *)launchOptions
  {
    ...
    self.destinationPreference = [[NSUserDefaults
            standardUserDefaults] objectForKey:Destination
            PreferenceKey];
    if (self.destinationPreference == nil) {
      NSDictionary *currentDestinationDict = [NSDictionary
            dictionaryWithObject:@"0" forKey:Destination
            PreferenceKey];
      [[NSUserDefaults standardUserDefaults] registerDefaults:
            currentDestinationDict];
    }
```

```
    else
      [self createDestinationModel:
                    [self.destinationPreference intValue]];
    //[self createDestinationModel:0];

    return YES;
  }
```

At application launch, you check an `NSUserDefaults` object to see whether there is entry with a key of `DestinationPreferenceKey` (you added this in Listing 18-14):

```
self.destinationPreference =
    [[NSUserDefaults standardUserDefaults]
                objectForKey:DestinationPreferenceKey];
```

You use `NSUserDefaults` to read and store preference data to a defaults data base, using a key value, just as you access keyed data from an `NSDictionary`. In this case, the preference is the destination.

`NSUserDefaults` is implemented as a *singleton,* meaning that only one instance of `NSUserDefaults` is running in your application. To get access to that one instance, I invoke the class method `standardUserDefaults`:

```
[NSUserDefaults  standardUserDefaults]
```

`standardUserDefaults` returns the `NSUserDefaults` object. As soon as you have access to the standard user defaults, you can store data there and then get it back when you need it.

`objectForKey:` is an `NSUserDefaults` method that returns the object associated with the specified key, or `nil` if the key was not found.

Obviously, the first time the app is launched, no data is there, so you create a dictionary with the default value:

```
NSDictionary *currentDestinationDict =
  [NSDictionary dictionaryWithObject:@"0"
                        forKey:DestinationPreferenceKey];
```

Note that you save the value as an `NSString`. That's because the `NSUserDefaults` requires a property list object.

You then send the NSUserDefaults object the registerDefaults message. This creates a new entry in the NSUserDefaults database that you can later access and update using the key you provided in the dictionary.

Because destinationPreference is still nil, when viewDidLoad executes, it launches the Destination controller.

If there is a value in NSUserDefaults, you create the destination model by sending the createDestinationModel: message with the value you had stored — which will be, as you will see, the index of the destination in the Destinations plist:

```
[self createDestinationModel:
[self.destinationPreference intValue]];
```

Note that you use an NSString method intValue. This method returns the value in a string as an int, which is handy because that is what the createDestinatsionModel: method expects.

You also could have made the currentDestinationIndex an NSNumber. It is an object wrapper for any C scalar (numeric) type. It defines a set of methods that allow you to set and access the value in many different ways, including as a signed or unsigned int, double, float, BOOL, and others. Also, NSNumber defines a compare: method to determine the ordering of two NSNumber objects.

The last piece of saving the destination preference is actually storing the destinationPreference, and you do that in createDestination-Model:. Add the bolded code in Listing 18-17 to createDestination-Model: in RTAppDelegate.m.

Listing 18-17: Updating createDestinationModel:

```
- (void) createDestinationModel:(int)destinationIndex {

    NSString *selectedDestinationIndex =
        [NSString stringWithFormat: @"%i",destinationIndex];
    if(![
        selectedDestinationIndex]
            isEqualToString:self.destinationPreference]) {
      self.destinationPreference =
        selectedDestinationIndex];
      [[NSUserDefaults standardUserDefaults]
          setObject:self.destinationPreference
                          forKey:DestinationPreferenceKey];
    }
    self.trip = [[Trip alloc] initWithDestinationIndex:
            destinationIndex];
}
```

You start by converting the destinationIndex parameter to a string and comparing it to see whether the destination preference is the same as the one just selected by the user (the user may have chosen the same destination again in the Destination controller):

```
NSString *selectedDestinationIndex =
    [NSString stringWithFormat: @"%i",destinationIndex];
if(![[NSString
    stringWithFormat:@"%i",selectedDestinationIndex]
        isEqualToString:self.destinationPreference])
```

If the destination is not the same, you assign the new value to the destinationPreference:

```
self.destinationPreference =
[NSString stringWithFormat: @"%i",destinationIndex];
```

and then you save the new value in NSUserDefaults:

```
[[NSUserDefaults standardUserDefaults]
   setObject:self.destinationPreference
                    forKey:DestinationPreferenceKey];
```

To store data, you use the setObject;forKey: method. The first argument, setObject:, is the object I want NSUserDefaults to save. This object must be NSData, NSString, NSNumber, NSDate, NSArray, or NSDictionary. In this case, savedData is an NSString, so you're in good shape.

The second argument is forKey:. To get the data back (and for NSUserDefaults to know where to save it), you have to be able to identify it to NSUserDefaults. You can, after all, have a number of preferences stored in the NSUserDefaults database, and the key tells NSUserDefaults which one you're interested in.

Next, you create the model passing in the destination index:

```
self.trip = [[Trip alloc]
            initWithDestinationIndex:destinationIndex];
```

You're done. Run your app and test your work.

To test this part of your app, you need to first stop it in the Simulator (or device) by clicking the Stop button in the Xcode toolbar. Then remove RoadTrip from the background by following these steps:

1. **Double-click the Home button to display the applications running in the background.**

2. **Select the RoadTrip icon and hold down the mouse button until the icon starts to wiggle.**

3. **Click the Remove button, the red circle with the *X* that appears in the upper-left corner of the icon.**

4. **Run your app.**

A Word about Adding Settings

Although space does not allow me to show you how to implement settings — for example, letting the user choose whether she wants to hear the car sound when she taps the Test Drive button, or to change the speed of the car — you implement such settings in exactly in the same way that you just implemented the destination preference. You add a setting to NSUserDefaults and create an RTAppDelegate property that you check in the car animation messages, for example, before you play the sound. To get even more sophisticated, you could create a Preferences class, in the same way you create a Trip class, that manages all preferences and uses that rather than the RTAppDelegate to provide preference data to the rest of your app.

What's Next?

Although this point marks the end of your guided tour of iPhone software development, it should also be the start — if you haven't started already — of your own development work.

Developing for the iPhone is one of the most exciting opportunities I've come across in a long time. I'm hoping that it ends up being as exciting for you.

Do keep in touch, though. Check out my website, www.nealgoldstein. com, on a regular basis. There you can find the completed RoadTrip Xcode project.

Finally, keep having fun. I hope I have the opportunity to download one of your applications from the App Store someday.

Part VI
The Part of Tens

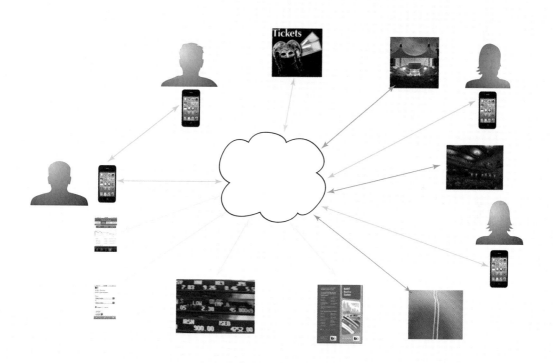

1 once had a boss who liked to hire smart-but-lazy people. He figured that if he gave them a hard job, they'd find an easy way to do it.

In this part, I show you some ways to (first) avoid doing more work than you have to, and (second) avoid redoing things because you outsmarted yourself. I also explain how to take the RoadTrip app further and create an app that you can really sell (and people will want to buy) in the App Store.

Chapter 19

Ten Ways to Extend the RoadTrip App

In This Chapter

▷ Discovering some additional features for the RoadTrip app

▷ Making structural improvements to the app

▷ Creating an application ecosystem

*A*lthough the example app developed in this book, the RoadTrip app, has the basic structure and features that you would include in a commercial app of this type, you would have some additional tasks to take care of if you intended to make it a commercial application.

Of course, you would have to add more content to the app. But you would also need to add more features, as well as strengthen the basic structure a bit.

In this chapter, I suggest some of the additions you would need to give RoadTrip to make it a commercial success.

Add Preferences

If you go international, roaming charges could make your app prohibitively expensive to use, and the user may want to turn off those features in your app. There are also some features in an app (see "Monitor the Current Location's Distance from the Destination") that the user may want to use only under certain circumstances. To make for happy users, you want to make these (and other optional-able features) preferences, and enable setting preferences both through the Settings application as well as in the RoadTrip app.

Cache Data

If you allow users to turn off Internet access, or if the user is someplace where Internet service is not available, you need to add the logic to RoadTrip to cache data (such as events). Then, when the Internet is not available or the user doesn't want to use it, RoadTrip would use the cached data.

Monitor the Current Location's Distance from the Destination

In other books and in my classes, I show developers how to add a feature to the RoadTrip application that is kind of fun. When the user shakes the device, a semitransparent window drops down from the top of the screen and displays the distance for either a found location or the final destination. You add this feature by using the accelerometer and core location frameworks. But because this can be annoying and can chew up the battery, you want to enable the user to selectively turn it on and off (see "Add Preferences," a couple of sections earlier).

Post to Facebook and Twitter

Unless you are living under a rock, you know that social networking apps are all the rage. Twitter support is built into the SDK, but you are on your own when it comes to Facebook.

Send Postcards from the Road

In some of my applications, I have a postcard feature. It would be nice in RoadTrip to allow the user to take a photo and attach it to an e-mail to make all their friends jealous.

Add Hotels and Reservations

A great feature to include in the RoadTrip app is to allow the user to add hotel reservations. You keep track of them in the app by enabling the user to add a reservation to her calendar, a hotel to the address book, and so on.

Create an Itinerary

You can build in a feature in the app that helps the user plan his trip. Have the user be able to add his own points of interest and create an itinerary. You should be able to see the itinerary both as a list view and plotted on the map.

Make the App Part of an Application Ecosystem

As I mention in Chapter 1, you want to do the right task on the right device. Although the iPhone is great to use when you are traveling, the iPad or even a Mac is better suited to planning for a trip. Add an iPad (or Mac) version of RoadTrip that does planning, and refine the iPhone version to focus on execution. To do that, you need to implement a web services infrastructure of the kind I refer to in Chapter 1.

In my *iPad Application Development For Dummies,* for example, I add a planning function and change the UI to take advantage of the iPad's capabilities.

It's Never Early Enough to Start Speaking a Foreign Language

With the world growing even flatter and the iPhone available worldwide, the potential market for your app is considerably larger than just among people who speak English. Localizing an application isn't difficult, just tedious. You can postpone some of the tasks involved until late in the project, but when it comes to the strings you use in your application, you had better build them right — and build them in from the start. The painless way: Use the `NSLocalizedString` macro from the very start, and you'll still be a happy camper at the end.

Some Implementation Enhancements

You could definitely tighten up some of the implementation code in the RoadTrip app. Some of the things I did (or didn't do) in the book were intentional to make the initial app building easier for you to follow. To remedy the less-than-stellar structure that came about as a result, there are a few things you could add on your own.

Because both the Event Page controller and the Weather controller use a Web view, you could create a Web view superclass that implements all the Web view functionality.

Because `Trip` is designed to be a singleton, you could add a class method to `Trip` that returns a reference to itself so that you don't have to go through the App Delegate every time.

I also recommend putting all your constants into a single file and replacing all hard-coded values with constants as well. As you change, or experiment with, those values during the development process, having *one* place to find constants makes life much easier.

Chapter 20

Ten Ways to Be a Happy Developer

In This Chapter

▷ Finding out how not to paint yourself into a corner

▷ Avoiding "There's no way to get there from here"

There are lots of things you know you're supposed to do but don't because you think they'll never catch up with you. (After all, not flossing won't cause you problems until your teeth fall out years from now, right?)

But in iPhone application development, those things catch up with you early and often, so I want to tell you about what I've learned to pay attention to from the very start in app development, as well as a few tips and tricks that lead to happy and healthy users.

Keep Things Loosely Coupled

A loosely coupled system is one in which each of its components has little or no knowledge (or makes no use of the knowledge it may have) of other components.

Loose coupling refers to the degree of direct knowledge that one class has of another — not about encapsulation, or to one class's knowledge of another class's attributes or implementation, but rather knowledge of that other class itself.

Remember Memory

The iOS does not store "changeable" memory (such as object data) on the disk to free space and then read it back in later when needed.

This fact means that running out of memory is easy, and you should use Automatic Reference Counting (ARC) to make the most of the memory available to you. All you have to do is follow the rules:

- **Rule 1:** Do not send `retain`, `release`, or `autorelease` messages.
- **Rule 2:** Do not store object pointers in C structures.
- **Rule 3:** Inform the compiler about ownership when using Core Foundation-style objects.
- **Rule 4:** Use the `@autoreleasepool` keyword to mark the start of an autorelease block.
- **Rule 5:** Follow the naming conventions.

If you follow the rules, all you have to worry about is the retain cycle. This cycle occurs when one object has a back pointer to the object that creates it (either directly or through a chain of other objects, each with a strong reference to the next leading back to the first). Use the `__weak` lifetime qualifiers for objects and the `weak` property attribute.

But even if you have done everything correctly, in a large application, you may simply run out of memory and will need to implement the methods that `UIKit` provides to respond to low-memory conditions, as follows:

- Override the `viewDidUnload` and `didReceiveMemoryWarning` methods in your custom `UIViewController` subclass.
- Implement the `applicationDidReceiveMemoryWarning:` method of your application delegate.
- Register to receive the `UIApplicationDidReceiveMemoryWarningNotification:` notification.

Don't Reinvent the Wheel

The iPhone is cutting-edge enough that opportunities to expand its capabilities are plentiful — and many of them are (relatively) easy to implement. You're also working with a very mature framework. So if you think that something you want your app to do is going to be really difficult, check the framework; somewhere in there you may find an easy way to do what you have in mind.

For example, I once needed to compute the distance between two points on a map. So I got out my trusty trig books, only to find out later that the `distanceFromLocation:` method did exactly what I needed.

Understand State Transitions

The `UIApplication` object provides the application-wide control and coordination for an iOS application. It is responsible for handling the initial routing of incoming user events (touches, for example) as well as dispatching action messages from control objects (such as buttons) to the appropriate target objects. The application object sends messages to its Application Delegate to allow you to respond, in an application-unique way when your application is executing, to things such as application launch, low-memory warnings, and state transitions such as moving into background and back into foreground.

You should implement the following `UIAppDelegate` methods in your application:

Method	*What You Do with It*
`application:didFinish LaunchingWithOptions:`	In this method, do what you need to do to initialize your application after it has been launched.
`applicationWill ResignActive:`	This message is sent when the application is about to move from active to inactive state. Use this method to do things such as pause ongoing tasks and anything that is based on a timer (such as a game). Using this method does not mean that you will be entering background, but it does mean your application will not be executing.
`applicationDid EnterBackground:`	This message is sent when your application is going to be entering background. At this point, you need to assume that your application may eventually be terminated without warning, so save user data, invalidate timers, and store enough application state information.
`applicationWill EnterForeground:`	This message is sent when your application has been rescued from background. In this method, reverse what you did in `applicationDidEnterBackground:`.
`applicationDid BecomeActive:`	Your application is now active. You should reverse whatever you did in `application WillResignActive:`. You also might want to refresh the user interface.

Do the Right Thing at the Right Time

When it comes to the view controller, you need to be aware of two methods, and it is important that you know what to do in each method.

The `viewDidLoad` message is sent to a view controller when the view has been loaded and initialized by the system. It is sent only when the view is created and not, for example, when your app returns from background or when a view controller is returned to after another view controller has been "dismissed."

The `viewWillAppear:` message, on the other hand, is sent whenever the view appears, including when the view reappears after another view controller is "dismissed."

Do view initialization in `viewDidLoad`, but make sure that anything you do to refresh a view whenever it appears is done in `viewDidAppear:`.

Avoid Mistakes in Error Handling

A lot of opportunities for errors are out there; use common sense in figuring out which ones you should spend work time on. For example, don't panic over handling a missing bundle resource in your code. If you included it in your project, it's supposed to be there; if it's not, look for a bug in your program. If it's *really* not there, the user has big problems, and you probably won't be able to do anything to avert the oncoming catastrophe.

There are, however, some potential pitfalls you do have to pay attention to, such as these two big ones:

- ✐ Your app goes out to load something off the Internet, and (for a variety of reasons) the item isn't there or the app can't get to it. You especially need to pay attention to Internet availability and what you're going to do when the Internet isn't available.

- ✐ You are working with geocoding, so be aware that the geocoder may fail for any number of reasons. For example, the service may be down, there may not be a street address at a certain GPS coordinate, or the user may access the data before the geocoder has returned.

Use Storyboards

Storyboards are a great way to examine the flow of the application as a whole. In addition, they require you to use less code. They are one of my favorite parts of Xcode 4.2 and iOS 5.0, and I use them in all my apps.

Remember the User

I've been singing this song since Chapter 1, and I'm still singing it now: Keep your app simple and easy to use. Don't build long pages that take lots of scrolling to get through, and don't create really deep hierarchies. Focus on what the user wants to accomplish, and be mindful of the device limitations, especially battery life. And don't forget international roaming charges.

In other words, try to follow the Apple's iPhone Human Interface Guidelines, found with all the other documentation in the iPhone Dev Center website at `http://developer.apple.com/iphone` under the iPhone Reference Library section — Required Reading. Don't even *think* about bending those rules until you really, *really* understand them.

Keep in Mind that the Software Isn't Finished Until the Last User Is Dead

If there's one thing I can guarantee about app development, it's that nobody gets it right the first time. The design for RoadTrip evolved over time, as I learned the capabilities and intricacies of the platform and the impact of my design changes. Object orientation makes extending your application (not to mention fixing bugs) easier, so pay attention to the principles.

Keep It Fun

When I started programming the iPhone, it was the most fun I'd had in years. Keep things in perspective: Except for a few tedious tasks (such as provisioning and getting your application into the Apple Store), expect that developing iPhone apps will be fun for you, too. So don't take it *too* seriously.

Especially remember the *fun* part at 4 a.m., when you've spent the last five hours looking for a bug.

Index

• S •